GOVERNANCE INNOVATIONS IN THE ASIA-PACIFIC REGION

Governance Innovations in the Asia-Pacific Region

Trends, cases and issues

Edited by

GAMBHIR BHATTA, Ph.D.
Department of Political Science
National University of Singapore

and

JOAQUIN L. GONZALEZ III, Ph.D.
Department of Political Science
National University of Singapore

LONDON AND NEW YORK

First published 1998 by Ashgate Publishing

Reissued 2018 by Routledge
2 Park Square, Milton Park, Abingdon, Oxon OX14 4RN
711 Third Avenue, New York, NY 10017, USA

Routledge is an imprint of the Taylor & Francis Group, an informa business

Copyright © Gambhir Bhatta and Joaquin L. Gonzalez III 1998

All rights reserved. No part of this book may be reprinted or reproduced or utilised in any form or by any electronic, mechanical, or other means, now known or hereafter invented, including photocopying and recording, or in any information storage or retrieval system, without permission in writing from the publishers.

Notice:
Product or corporate names may be trademarks or registered trademarks, and are used only for identification and explanation without intent to infringe.

Publisher's Note
The publisher has gone to great lengths to ensure the quality of this reprint but points out that some imperfections in the original copies may be apparent.

Disclaimer
The publisher has made every effort to trace copyright holders and welcomes correspondence from those they have been unable to contact.

A Library of Congress record exists under LC control number : 97078327

ISBN 13: 978-1-138-31929-5 (hbk)
ISBN 13: 978-1-138-31935-6 (pbk)
ISBN 13: 978-0-429-45397-7 (ebk)

Contents

List of Figures   viii
List of Tables   ix
List of Contributors   x
Acknowledgements   xiii

PART I: INTRODUCTION

1. Evolving Context of Governance in the Asia-Pacific Region
   Joaquin L. Gonzalez III and Gambhir Bhatta   3

2. Does Governance Matter?
   John M. Page   23

PART II: BUREAUCRACY AND LEADERSHIP

3. Bureaucratic Rationality in an Evolving Developmentalist State: The Case of Singapore
   Gillian Koh   49

4. Public Service Leadership and Political Adaptation of the Hong Kong Civil Servants
   Jermain T.M. Lam   75

PART III: CITIZEN, BUSINESS, AND GOVERNMENT

5. Total Quality Governance (TQG): A New Model for Government-Citizen Relations
   Emil P. Bolongaita, Jr.   103

6	Small Business Policy Reform: A New Approach to Old Problems *William Cole and Stephen Parker*	113
7	Building a Government-Citizen-Business Partnership: Linking Business with Government in Laos *Sirisamphanh Vorachith*	127

PART IV: ACCOUNTABILITY, CORRUPTION, AND ENFORCEMENT

8	A Strategic Approach for Donor-Assisted Counter Corruption Programs *James R. Klein*	143
9	Methodology for Evaluating Dimensions, Characteristics and Costs of Corruption *Pasuk Phongpaichit*	155
10	Combat Training: Using Seminars to Fight Corruption *Denis Osborne*	163
11	Strengthening Legislative Audit Institutions: A Catalyst to Enhance Governance and Combat Corruption *Vinod Sahgal and John Burns*	183

PART V: REGULATION AND INFORMATION

12	Regulation in the Information Age: Indonesian Public Information Program for Environmental Management *Shakeb Afsah, Benoit Laplante and David Wheeler*	205
13	Building Information "City Streets": The Internet as a Tool for Effective Governance *Bhavya Lal*	219

PART VI: CAPACITY BUILDING AND LOCAL GOVERNANCE

14 Decentralised Governance: Empowerment Without
    Capacity Enhancement is Meaningless   231
    Gambhir Bhatta

15 Capacity Building and Administrative Innovations in the
    Philippines: The Integrated Capability Building Program 245
    Alex B. Brillantes, Jr.

16 Choice of Community Forestry by Voice of Local
    Participation in Northeastern Villages of Thailand   257
    Tipaporn Phimphisut

PART VII: CONCLUSIONS

17 Moving Beyond 20th Century Myths to an Appreciation
    of State-Society Synergy   269
    Peter Evans

18 The Future of Governance in the Asia-Pacific and
    Areas for Further Research   285
    Joaquin L. Gonzalez III and Gambhir Bhatta

Index   *299*

List of Figures

2.1	GDP Per Capita (as Share of US GDP) and Institutional Capability Index	26
2.2	GDP Per Capita and Institutional Capability Index	27
2.3	Investment Rate Regressed on Institutional Capability Index	28
2.4	Total Factor Productivity Growth, 1960-89, and GDP Per Capita Relative to US, 1960	30
2.5	TFP Growth Regressed on Institutional Capability Index	31
2.6	TFP Growth Rate and the Share of Manufactured Exports in Total Exports	39
12.1	Setting Optimal Standards and Prices	207
12.2	Process and Reliability of Information	213

List of Tables

2.1	Institutional Capability and Investment	29
2.2	Institutional Capability and Total Factor Productivity (TFP) Growth	32
2.3	Summary Statistics of World Bank Project Performance (1974-1993)	34
2.4	Participation and Project Performance	35
2.5	An Evaluation of Export Promotion Programs	40
3.1	Officers' Perception of Their Role vis-à-vis the Political Leadership in the NEXT LAP of Singapore's Development	59
3.2	Areas of Training Which Can be Improved	61
3.3	Officers' Perception of Their Role vis-à-vis the Political Leadership in the NEXT LAP of Singapore's Development by Rank	64
3.4a	Nature of First Degree of all Administrative Officers (1991)	66
3.4b	Percentage of Specialist and Non-Specialist Personnel in the Administrative Service (1983)	66
3.5	Intra-Ministry Interaction among Administrative Officers	67
3.6	Inter-Ministry Interaction among Administrative Officers	68
4.1	Modes of Adaptation to Changes	80
4.2	Structure and Establishment of Administrative Officers	81
12.1	PROPER PROKASIH's Five Colour Scheme	212
12.2	Impact of PROPER PROKASIH	214
16.1	Attitudes of Villagers toward the Effectiveness of Community Forestry Management in Bung Phra Village	261
16.2	Attitudes of Villagers toward the Formulation of Community Forestry Policy by the State in Bung Phra Village	261
16.3	Attitudes of Villagers toward the Effectiveness of Community Forestry Management in Tha Wang Sai	264
16.4	Attitudes of Villagers toward the Formulation of Community Forestry Policy by the State in Tha Wang Sai	265
16.5	Strength of Internal and External Factors and Effectiveness of Community Forestry Management	266

List of Contributors

Editors

Gambhir Bhatta is a Lecturer, Public Policy and Administration, at the Department of Political Science, National University of Singapore (NUS). He also teaches at the Singapore Institute of Management. Dr. Bhatta received his Ph.D. in Public and International Affairs from the University of Pittsburgh, USA. Prior to NUS, he was with the United Nations Development Programme (UNDP) in Uganda as UNV Programme Officer, and he has also served as a consultant to the UN as well as the private sector in various countries. He is a specialist on planning, management, and evaluation of development projects/programmes, and on management training. His research work has appeared in the *Policy Studies Journal* (US), the *American Asian Review* (US), *Asian Profile* (Hong Kong), and *Regional Development Dialogue* (Japan), among others.

Joaquin L. Gonzalez III is a Lecturer, Public Policy and Administration, Department of Political Science, National University of Singapore (NUS). He received his Ph.D. in Political Science from the University of Utah, USA. Before joining NUS, he was previously associated with the Policy Research and Operations Policy Departments of the World Bank in Washington, DC, the Philippine Presidential Commission on Government Reorganization (PCGR), and the Congress of the Philippines. Aside from his University position, Dr. Gonzalez is concurrently the Research Coordinator of the Canada-ASEAN Governance Innovations Network Program (CAGIN), and the Principal Adviser of the Philippine Overseas Workers Welfare Administration (OWWA)-Filipino Overseas Workers in Singapore (FOWS) Skills Training Program. Dr. Gonzalez is the author of three forthcoming books - *Philippine Labour Migration: Critical Dimensions of Public Policy* (Singapore: Institute of Southeast Asian Studies), *Development Sustainability Through Community Participation: Mixed Results from the Philippine Health Sector* (Aldershot, UK: Ashgate Publishing), and *Succeed in Business: Philippines* (Singapore: Times Editions) (with Luis Ma. Calingo).

Contributors

Shakeb Afsah is a Consultant at the Environment, Infrastructure and Agriculture Division, Policy Research Department, The World Bank, Washington, DC (USA).

Emil P. Bolongaita, Jr. is Professor and Director of the Politics and Governance Desk of the Washington Sycip Policy Forum, the policy arm of the Asian Institute of Management (AIM) in Manila, Philippines.

Alex B. Brillantes, Jr. is Associate Professor at the College of Public Administration of the University of the Philippines, and was on secondment to the Local Government Academy, Philippine Department of the Interior and Local Government, as its Executive Director.

John Burns is one of the partners at the Centre for Public Management in Ottawa, Canada.

William Cole is Program Manager, Participation and Policy for Microenterprise Project, with the Asia Foundation, Jakarta, Indonesia.

Peter Evans is a Professor in the Department of Sociology, University of California at Berkeley (USA).

James R. Klein is the Asia Foundation's Representative for Thailand, Laos and Vietnam, and has previously served as the Foundation's Representative for Cambodia (1993-1995), and for Malaysia, Singapore and Brunei (1991-1993).

Gillian Koh is a Research Fellow at the Institute of Policy Studies, Singapore. She received her doctoral degree from the University of Sheffield, UK, for her thesis based on an analysis of the Singapore Administrative elite.

Bhavya Lal is Senior Policy Analyst with the International Development Unit of Abt Associates in Cambridge, Massachusetts (USA).

Jermain T. M. Lam is Associate Professor with the Department of Public and Social Administration, City University of Hong Kong.

Benoit Laplante is a Consultant at the Environment, Infrastructure and Agriculture Division, Policy Research Department, The World Bank, Washington, DC (USA).

Denis Osborne is a UK-based independent advisor and consultant on development and governance, and was previously the British High Commissioner in Malawi.

John M. Page is Chief Economist for the Middle East and North Africa Region at The World Bank, Washington, DC (USA), and was one of the principal authors of the highly-acclaimed *The East Asian Miracle: Public Policy and Economic Growth*.

Stephen Parker is Chief Economist at the Asia Foundation Headquarters in San Francisco, California (USA).

Tipaporn Phimphisut is the Director of the Research Centre for Policy and Development, Faculty of Political Science at Ramkhamhaeng University, Bangkok, Thailand.

Pasuk Phongpaichit is an Associate Professor at the Political Economy Centre, Faculty of Economics, Chulalongkorn University, Bangkok, Thailand.

Vinod Sahgal is a Principal at the Office of the Auditor General of Canada, and is presently responsible for the audit of the Canadian International Development Agency (CIDA).

Sirisamphanh Vorachith is the Head of Personnel and Administration at the Department of the Societe Lao d'Import-Export, Vientiane, Lao People's Democratic Republic.

David Wheeler is Principal Economist at the Environment, Infrastructure and Agriculture Division, Policy Research Department, The World Bank, Washington, DC (USA).

Acknowledgements

This book emerged out of the International Conference on Governance Innovations held on October 20-23, 1996 in Manila, Philippines. Hence, we would like to express our gratitude to the Institute On Governance (IOG) for organising the conference and providing us with the opportunity to oversee this exciting project. Special thanks goes to Kathleen Lauder, Brenda Melles, and Jose Edgardo L. Campos.

We are grateful to all the contributors from around the world for their patience and support: John Page, Gillian Koh, Jermain T.M. Lam, Emil P. Bolongaita, Jr., William Cole, Stephen Parker, Sirisamphanh Vorachith, James R. Klein, Pasuk Phongpaichit, Denis Osborne, Vinod Sahgal, John Burns, Shakeb Afsah, Benoit Laplante, David Wheeler, Bhavya Lal, Alex B. Brillantes, Tipaporn Phimphisut, and Peter Evans. Our sincere appreciation also goes to the many conference participants who provided useful comments and suggestions towards the revision of the book materials.

We would like to make special mention of Dr. Gillian Koh of the Institute of Policy Studies (Singapore) for her useful comments and suggestions, especially in the early stages of the manuscript preparation. We are also indebted to our families and friends for bearing with our absence during the many months it took to complete this project.

Gambhir Bhatta
Joaquin L. Gonzalez III
Singapore
January 1998

PART I

INTRODUCTION

1 Evolving Context of Governance in the Asia-Pacific Region

Joaquin L. Gonzalez III and Gambhir Bhatta

The issue of governance - and particularly that of good governance - has for some time now dominated the research and practice agenda in contemporary development management. With the rise in the 1980s of market-orientation in public policy in the developed economies on the one hand, and a sharper focus on the role of governments in explaining the rise of the newly developing economies of East Asia on the other, there has now been a great deal of rethinking about the roles of the State, the Market and the Community or Civil Society in engendering social and economic development. The momentum for rethinking the traditional mores of civil administration and public policy mechanisms has thrown up 'governance' as a conceptual as well as an analytical tool in viewing how governments go about managing their economies, societies and polities. More importantly, it has sought to explore the potential that is to be harnessed when government involves an active partnership between the three key elements of the State, Citizens and Business. Much has been discussed and written on this issue and much more will be forthcoming in the years ahead.

Meaning and Origins of Governance

What is governance? Governance - as envisioned by international development agencies and others - is the power, influence, and relationship between governments and citizens that is utilised to implement social and economic programs. Public policy and administration specialists all over the world argue that without good governance, sustainable economic performance is not possible. Conceptually, it is one of the 1990s' buzzwords in development assistance currently being underscored by multilateral and bilateral donors like the World Bank, the United Nations Development Programme (UNDP), Asian Development Bank (ADB), the United States Agency for International Development (USAID), and the Canadian International Development Agency (CIDA).[1]

Reforming the governmental machinery of developing countries to effectively achieve planned economic and social development activities is not a new undertaking in development assistance. Under colonial rule, the indigenous administrative systems of developing countries were reorganised to successfully pursue their colonisers' political and economic agenda. After independence, developing countries turned to public administration specialists from western countries, mostly their former colonial masters, to assist them in restructuring their postcolonial public bureaucracies for the effective implementation of their bilaterally and multilaterally funded economic and social projects and programs. Some of the early governance strategies prescribed by these public administration experts were basically public sector management reforms that dealt with the civil service, personnel pay and promotion, tax administration, budget, and finance. However, interest in governance declined after funding agencies shifted their emphasis to issues of technical efficiency and economic soundness of development projects and programs. Moreover, there was a shift in concern to substantive policy areas such as women in development (WID), energy and infrastructure, health and education, human resources and labour markets, and the environment.[2]

A resurgence of interest in governance re-surfaced in the 1990s after a series of studies conducted by the World Bank found that a country's capacity to implement carefully planned projects was a critical determining component of project success and sustainability.[3] These World Bank findings, based on its 50-year experience of funding development projects, were also reinforced by a 1994 ADB study, "Report of the Task Force on Improving Project Quality," which similarly pointed out that the quality of a recipient country's public administration system was a strong determinant of a project's success or failure.[4] In the 1996 ADB Annual Meeting in Manila, Bank of Japan Governor, Yasuo Matsushita, further stressed its importance when he said: "Good governance and sound development management in developing member countries must accompany development assistance from the Bank in order to ensure its impact."[5]

In addition to the World Bank and ADB, some bilateral aid agencies like the UK's Overseas Development Agency (ODA), USAID, as well as other multilateral development organisations like UNDP, and non-governmental organisations like the Institute on Governance (IOG) of Canada, and Asia Foundation and Ford Foundation in the US, also echoed the same views as the World Bank and ADB about the importance of governance to their clients and beneficiaries as part of the overall institutional reform needed by their public sectors to increase the rates of success in their policy formulation and implementation.[6] For example, Canada's IOG states that with "effective governance, business, government, and citizens act as partners in building a stronger economy and a better society."[7]

According to World Bank publications, there are essentially three dimensions of governance that need to be examined: (1) political regime character; (2) organisational process by which authority and control are exercised; and (3) institutional capacity to plan and implement policies and carry out functions. However, the focus of its governance assistance is on the last two dimensions since reforms pertaining to the political regime character of a developing country are beyond the limited economic and social development mandate of the World Bank and other international aid agencies. In the governance work at the World Bank and the Development Assistance Committee (DAC) of the Organisation for Economic Co-operation and Development (OECD), seven specific areas of the developing countries' public sectors are targeted for improvement as embodied in their business operations: (1) public sector management; (2) accountability; (3) legal and regulatory framework; (4) transparency and information; (5) human rights; (6) participatory approaches; and (7) military expenditure. The ADB and European Bank for Reconstruction and Development (EBRD) subscribe to the first four areas in much the same way. Some variations in interpretation though are evident in their operations and prescribed applications. Moreover, the United Nations, the Inter-American Development Bank (IADB), the African Development Bank (AFDB), the ODA, and CIDA all concur with this renewed concern in development governance but place a greater emphasis on basic public sector management in the personnel pay and promotion, tax administration, budget, and finance areas.[8]

At the ODA, serious developing country attempts towards improving the quality of public administration (or in their terms "good government") is a key determining factor for development assistance, and certain cases of non-compliance with the ODA's good government guidelines, have resulted in the suspension or reduction of aid to a recipient country.[9] This runs parallel to the U.S. government's strong view about the seriousness by which aid beneficiaries should take this matter. For instance, in last year's ADB Annual meeting, US Treasury Department Under Secretary, Jeffrey Shafer, opposed Myanmar's access to ADB loans unless the government there undertook serious reforms.

Across the Pacific in the United States, implementing governance changes is interpreted to mean simply the restructuring and reorganisation of government,[10] but new ways of managing the people's business has expanded beyond the context of American government or the U.S. public sector.[11] Mounting domestic pressure and a changing global environment have persuaded the Reagan, Bush, and Clinton administrations to implement policies that encourage: (1) privatisation of public services; (2) use of non-governmental organisations; and (3) development of more public-private partnerships. Thus, a new era of governance concern was born in the U.S.[12]

The Clinton Administration's "reinvention exercises" are clear manifestations of the United States' commitment to a new type of governance even in a developed country setting. At the federal government level, it is envisioned that reinventing governance would eliminate overlapping and duplication to increase the speed by which central agencies respond to fast-changing public needs.[13]

Popular usage of the generic term governance spans across a number of other disciplines and sub-fields, i.e., business, political science, economics, sociology, and law. It is also one of the core themes of international aid administration in the 1990s. Within the U.S., private sector governance, more specifically known as corporate governance, refers to the framework of laws, regulatory institutions, and reporting requirements that condition the way the corporate sector is managed. Governance became a formal scholarly issue of concern within the American academic community with the publication of *Governance: The International Journal of Policy and Administration* in 1991 which was developed by the Structure and Organisation of Government (SOG) Research Committee of the International Political Science Association. In terms of substantive content, governance deals with contemporary issues on executive politics, public policy, administration, and the organisation of the state from an inter-cultural perspective that goes beyond appropriate administration and management in the United States. Numerous other public administration journals, like *Public Administration Review*, also publish articles covering the various sub-themes of governance.

Governance and the High Performers of East Asia

Academically, much has already been written about the phenomenal growth experienced by selected East Asian nations in the last three decades.[14] All scholars agree that the spectacular economic performance of countries such as Japan, Hong Kong, South Korea, Taiwan, and Singapore since the 1960s has been nothing short of a miracle (considering especially where some of these countries started from). Driven by their never-ending search for panaceas to prescribe to other developing economies, social scientists nowadays have made it fashionable to seek lessons from this remarkable East Asian experience. Lesson-extraction has focused on two areas: (1) the right public policies; and (2) the institutions that are able to craft these miracle-inducing public policies. On the successful reform policies *per se*, the concentration of early works has been on extolling East Asia's policies in sectors such as industry, agriculture, human resource development, trade and investment, etc. Latter discussions, though, have moved to the institutions that are capable of formulating and implementing these effective public policies. In examining these institutions, the focus has been on highlighting broad factors such as leadership, quality of policy-making, cohesion, nationhood, and the role of the state.[15] As the search for lessons continues and expands, a clearer picture of the institutional dimension needs to be portrayed.

On a broader front, and in terms of actual practice, development experts from the World Bank and ADB argue that the high-performing Asian economies (HPAEs) (i.e., Japan, Taiwan, South Korea, Hong Kong, Singapore, Indonesia, Malaysia, and Thailand) provide strong empirical support to their policy position that there is a significant correlation between governance and economic performance.[16]

In the *East Asian Miracle* study, for example, the World Bank team provides a discussion on characteristics of effective public bureaucracies in Hong Kong, Japan, Korea, Singapore, and Taiwan. These important features include: (1) a total compensation system that is comparable with the private sector; (2) recruitment and promotion system that must be merit-based and highly competitive; and (3) ample rewards for those who make it to the top of the administrative service. Moreover, contrary to the arguments of some political scientists who label the regimes in the region as "developmental states," where powerful technocrats in alliance with the leadership insulate themselves from political pressure and implement well-crafted interventions, the World Bank cites that in the HPAEs' governance system there has always been room for much-needed government-private sector collaboration.[17]

At this juncture, mention has to be made of two follow-up book projects that emerged from this larger report and took the analysis further. The first book was written by Jose Edgardo Campos and Hilton Root called *The Key to the Asian Miracle: Making Shared Growth Credible* (1996) which took a subset of the themes presented in the seminal World Bank report and expanded on them.[18] The authors' main argument is that leaders in the HPAEs gained legitimacy for their rule by virtue of the fact that not only did they create and nurture conditions for rapid economic growth, but more importantly, they convinced the people that such growth would be shared. This notion of shared growth is central to the success of these countries. The authors methodically document how these countries have enhanced growth and also how they have utilised wealth-sharing mechanisms. One of the key strategies employed by many of these HPAEs is the creation of what are called Deliberation Councils (committees that comprise of representatives from the public and private sectors, and whose principal task is to assist the government in formulating policies that would enhance the performance of a particular segment of the private sector). It needs to be noted though that such Deliberation Councils are not necessarily a sufficient condition to explain why growth has occurred so dynamically in the HPAEs (as evidenced by the growth of Taiwan, for example, that does not have a system of Deliberation Councils).

Furthering the discussion, Root authored another book called *Small Countries, Big Lessons: Governance and the Rise of East Asia* in late 1996 which brought out lucidly the need for an in-depth look at specific East Asian country experiences in the context of governance.[19] Economics aside, the growth has been a result of appropriate policy formulation and implementation frameworks and discussions on these fall squarely in the realm of governance.

Root also - like others before him - concludes that replicability of the East Asian model of development is not assured given the specificity of the applications of such a model in individual East Asian countries. This might - to some - pose some concerns in accepting the external validity of arguments on governance, but as a point of reference, both the books provide a strong foundation on which to base further research.

International Conference on Governance and the IOG

Research on governance to date has fed from, and spawned on its own as well, numerous national and international fora on its practical applications. One such forum for the discussion of what 'governance' is, can, and should be, was the International Conference on Governance Innovations held on October 20-23, 1996, in Manila, Philippines, organised by the Institute on Governance (IOG) in partnership with CIDA, Philippine Civil Service Commission, the Economic Development Institute of the World Bank, the ASEAN-EC Management Centre, and the UNDP.[20] The IOG is charged with the important task of crystallising this concept of 'governance' and showcasing the best and most innovative practices in the Asia-Pacific region as models of good governance especially for other developing countries.[21] A key element of the conference was a stream of papers that focused on the critical interface between the theory and practice of governance. Practitioners and scholars from the Asia-Pacific region and the rest of the world brought out not only the conceptual bases of 'governance' but also its practical applications as well as issues that are inherent in governance reforms with reference to a host of country experiences.

It is the result of this practitioners-scholars discussion sessions that forms the core of this volume. The book consists of edited papers presented at that particular section of the conference, along with the requisite revisions as the authors saw fit based upon the feedback they received during the conference. The book is structured in such a manner as to take the reader from the general macro-based issues related to governance all the way to the specific micro-based issues of capacity building of state agencies at the local level. In between, the book deals with the following themes: bureaucracy and leadership (considered to be key elements of governance), citizen-business-government linkages (the fundamental basis on which the notion of governance rests), accountability, corruption and enforcement (the necessary converse of the prior-mentioned linkages), regulation and information (the upcoming theme in governance), and capacity-building at the local level (considered by many to be the weak link in the study of governance). The book ends with some thoughts on the synergy that exists between the state and society and also focuses on the future of governance including identifying further areas for research.

The debate on what constitutes good governance - and more importantly, how to attain it - is not new. It has been going on in academic and practitioner circles for some time now. As mentioned earlier, the elusive - and particularistic - nature of governance ensures that much more needs to be studied about the specific incidences of good governance before a unifying theme on how exactly to develop a universal framework of application of governance can be finalised, it at all. It is in this context that this book is being brought forward for it seeks to fill a vacuum in the theory-practice dichotomy that has dominated the debate on governance thus far.

The book makes a deliberate attempt at marrying academic rigor with illuminative practical experiences. Written by some of the most well-known and noted scholars and practitioners in the field of governance and covering a wide gamut of topics, the book should provide a policy recipe for practitioners, government policy-makers, aid managers, and others involved in the pursuit of good governance and effective public policy and management. It will be relevant not only to academics and practitioners in the developing world, but also in the developed world where discussions about the role of State, Market and the Community are taking hold. Initiatives to rediscover 'local communities', to increase community building and participation, and to activate 'social capital' testify to this. The book will provide another spur to the thinking and crystallisation of what 'governance' and 'good governance' are. It brings out the historical context of the emergence of the concept of - and debate on - 'governance' while at the same time charting the future paths that this debate might take.

Findings from the IOG Conference and Structure of the Book

Part 1: Introduction

The focus on governance starts out with an exposition of the traditional areas of emphasis which concentrated on public sector reforms (e.g., civil service structure and functions, personnel pay and promotion, tax administration, budget and finance) that international organisations such as the World Bank and CIDA advocated during the 1960s and 1970s. It has now shifted into areas as diverse as bureaucracy and public sector leadership, citizen-business-government partnerships, accountability and the control of corruption, regulation and information, as well as capacity-building and local administration. In Part 1 of the book, the editors highlight these issues.

Taking the issues further, it further, and based on his evaluation of three interesting cases, John Page argues that governance undoubtedly does matter to development. Page first presents new evidence from cross-country data on the relationship between government performance and growth at the national level. He finds that institutional capability has an important impact on economic growth both through higher levels of investment and through improved productivity. He then reports on recent work undertaken by some of his colleagues at the Bank who have been investigating the relationship between the rates of return on development projects and some indicators of beneficiary participation. The bottom line is: participation results in better project outcomes. Finally, Page illustrates how government commitment affects the resolution of co-ordination problems which can inhibit economic growth, using the specific example of export promotion. His findings indicate that credible commitments to an export push, and effective contests to implement it, are central to the rapid expansion of manufactured exports, and hence economic growth.

Part 2: Bureaucracy and Leadership

One of the themes that Page says is integral to continued growth - government commitment - has as its core, the elements of strong bureaucracy and leadership. These two points are further discussed by Koh and Lam in separate pieces. Koh offers an insight into the reforms of a public service for development, but she also explores the need for further reforms and reorientation of the public sector leadership after the first efforts at state-led development have actually been successful. She cites the case of Singapore and starts from the argument that its development has been the result of a strategic political resolve to 'catch up' effectively translated to action by a generally competent and incorruptible bureaucracy. However, with the initial global and local conditions under which that initial development was possible no longer obtainable, new realities present challenges to further economic and social development and hence, to governance in Singapore. In response, administrative reforms have been introduced to create a public service that is innovative, responsive, and has a strategic orientation to change while trying to maintain a high-level of accountability to the political leadership and the public. Modern management tools and practices have been adopted but there are also arguments that this 'generic management' perspective may be inadequate for effective governance. Nevertheless, Singapore continues to be a model of good governance especially to developing countries in the East Asian region

Lam takes the argument posited by Koh further and explores the dilemmas faced by the public service leadership during a period of critical political transition with specific reference to the impact of the reversion of Hong Kong to China. In the process of reunification with China in 1997, the public service in Hong Kong faced rapid political changes including the intrusion of the Chinese government into the governing processes, and the emergence of an alienated political culture. This, it is argued, seriously undermined the leadership of the colonial public service. Adaptation of the public service to changes is absolutely essential to provide leadership for the community and to maintain a responsive administration. Lam analyses two main leadership issues of the public service in Hong Kong: (1) democracy versus convergence; and (2) autonomy versus dependence. Based on a survey research on the administrative culture of the public service, Lam concludes that the responses of the public service to the leadership challenges are basically more "piecemeal adjustments" than "prototyping", "imitation", or "recombination." As one of the most dynamic transitional societies, the experience of the Hong Kong public service could perhaps shed light on the leadership and adaptation of the bureaucracy of the transitional societies. Even with the change-over from British to Chinese rule, Hong Kong's public service will continue to be a key source of lessons for other developing countries.

Part 3: Citizens, Business and Government

One of the key tasks of an effective bureaucracy is to initiate and sustain strong Citizens-Business-Government (CBG) relationships. The effective linkages in this triad has come to symbolise the new wave of governance. One such model is provided by Bolongaita where he offers an innovative model for government-citizen relations employing the business management tool of Total Quality Management (TQM), and based on actual pilot studies that have been conducted at the local government level in Manila, Philippines. The business management literature on TQM continues to attest to the impact that customer satisfaction has on corporate success. Yet, while private enterprise has made leaps and bounds in customer satisfaction, much remains to be done in the ways government deals with its people.

Bolongaita argues that most national and local governments in the world still view their people only as *subjects* (who pay taxes and obey laws), not as *citizens* (who deserve to be treated equally regardless of rank or status) or *customers* (who deserve to be served well). With this as a context, the author explains the model developed by the Politics and Governance Desk of the Asian Institute of Management Policy Forum to adapt TQM to government. Called Total Quality Governance (TQG), this model aims to promote bureaucratic performance and foster political accountability to the end-users of government services - the *citizen-customers*. According to Bolongaita, this TQG model can be customised to apply to various forms of public sector organisations, such as national government agencies, local governments, and government corporations.

Cole and Parker exemplify the partnership discussed by Bolongaita by employing the political economy approach to show how such partnerships can lead to successful implementation of policies on reforms. In their paper, they also address the question of what foreign donor organisations can do to contribute to capacity-building for effective policy reform. The traditional paradigm, the technical approach to policy reform, invited foreign assistance in terms of the sharing of technical expertise and aid in helping to expedite the reform process. This left the beneficiaries of the reform - the local communities and true stakeholders - passive and uninvolved in the process. The authors offer a different paradigm, termed the political economy approach, where focus is on political will and on engaging active participation of key stakeholders in implementation of mutually agreed-upon policies. They offer some tentative lessons stemming from The Asia Foundation's recent experience of assisting in the strategic project of the local deregulation of small business policy in Indonesia. They also talk of facilitating the

Evolving context of governance in the Asia-Pacific region 13

emergence of a broad public-private sector dialogue and coalition in support of policy reform in addition to the aid agency's more traditional role of offering timely and well-targeted expert technical assistance and policy research for effective programming.

The role of the government in the enhancement of governance, and of the linkages inherent in CBG, is also succinctly brought out by Vorachith who focuses on the process of administrative reform in a transitional economy, namely that of Lao People's Democratic Republic. Now that Laos has joined ASEAN, there is great interest in the role that Government is playing in liberalising the economy, and Vorachith specifically hones in on governance innovations that will promote synergistic partnerships between the state and the business community. Vorachith offers useful details of Lao's Public Administration Reform Programme, the work of the Lao National Chamber of Commerce and Industry, and the four other government agencies tasked with promoting business, viz. the Ministry of Commerce, the Ministry of Industry and Handicrafts, the Ministry of Finance, and the State Bank. Vorachith ends by highlighting the issues that will shape the prospects of administrative reform and capacity building for governance and development in Laos.

Part 4: Accountability, Corruption, and Enforcement

Perhaps one of the most negative traits to emerge from this triad (i.e., CBG) relationship - and one that is universal in its incidence - is that of corruption and the concurrent slippage in government accountability. Business-government relations in all the countries of the region are very strong (particularly given the fact that business has fuelled much of the region's phenomenal growth), and governments throughout the region have had to put up with serious incidences of corruption in the public sector. The four chapters that are presented in this part each takes the issue further by looking at how governments are beginning to tackle this issue, and what specific counter-corruption schemes they could employ.

Klein first proposes a perspective for analysing the problem of counter-corruption programming in a country by focusing on The Asia Foundation's four principles that guide decisions on development programming by donors. These four principles are: Constituency and Coalition Building, Access Creation, Structural Reforms, and System Strengthening. The first two are normative and refer to the demand side for accountable governance, and the latter two refer to the supply side and serve to deliver good governance. Use of these four (in tandem or separately) will depend on country-specific situations. According to Klein, it is essential, however, that substantive, country-specific analysis of corruption be the first step in determining the variables that donors must work with in each country. It is also quite clear that no one principle will be adequate in combating corruption. Rather, an array of variables that influence corruption must be addressed simultaneously and in a co-ordinated manner to have true impact.

Phongpaichit, on the other hand, focuses on how the citizenry can force the pace of accountability and hence strengthen state capacity and trust between these two key actors. This chapter documents one particular example wherein citizen accountability contributed in some way towards good governance. Phongpaichit highlights the fact that in Thailand corruption is not only a political problem but also a social and an economic one, and opines that corruption is now at the forefront of political debate in Thailand as a result of a series of studies conducted by researchers at the Political Economy Centre at Chulalongkorn University. The studies not only focused upon corruption but on also the larger issue of the illegal economy. All study results were first discussed behind closed doors with appropriate stakeholders. There was considerable popular support for the studies and the average citizen came to support the researchers when they received death threats and were subject to other forms of harassment. Finally, Phongpaichit suggests that one key way of fighting corruption is through public awareness - which this study sought to highlight.

One such public awareness method is discussed by Osborne. In his chapter, he dwells on the use of seminars as a way of identifying action plans of officials to combat corruption. He argues that seminars about the prevention of corruption help public servants and others become more effective through the exchange of ideas and the development of skills. There are few measures of long-term success, but dialogue between organisers, participants and their managers has helped clarify the objectives and identify appropriate methods and content. The specific objectives of a number of recent seminars have been to increase the awareness and motivation of participants to help them develop suggestions for policies and methods of management and investigation relevant to their own situations, and to help them establish a network of contacts. The content covers the terminology and literature, the practice of leading institutions, sharing experiences with others, and reflection to identify and take ownership for good policies and management as a basis for action. To encourage action, participants prepare reports with recommendations for their own organisations, and action plans for themselves.

Finally, Sahgal and Burns offer their ideas on the strengthening of Supreme Audit Institutions (SAIs) as catalysts to enhance governance and combat corruption. The authors suggest that they can do this by promoting ethics in public service in conjunction with support from the international financial institutions. They argue that independence and objectivity of SAIs are key success factors. They add that strong and widespread support of civil society is key to such an enhanced role for the SAIs. Some of the recommendations that are made in their paper are: the strengthening of reporting and communication strategies particularly in the areas of ethics; playing a role in raising the public's consciousness about ethics and corruption; and the need for the international financial institutions to use their clout to finance the efforts of developing countries and those of their institutions in strengthening leadership in the war against corruption.

Part 5: Regulation and Information

An emerging issue in governance that is only now being extensively tackled by researchers deals with the linkage between regulation and information. Regulation, as is well known, is what governments do to steer the rudder of the country's political economy. In that process, they seek to use information in a manner that will enable them to formulate informed policies. But information itself can be regulated. At a time when communications among peoples are fast superseding what was deemed possible - and in that process forcing governments to keep up with the information flows and to be more open - governments find themselves in a position where they have had to take a long hard look at how far they can take their control over information processing and dissemination.

Afsah, Laplante and Wheeler put forth the argument that one of the key functions of government in public affairs - that of regulation - should change fundamentally in view of the rise of the new information age. Governments should allocate fewer resources to setting rules that impose standards of behaviour and more to collecting and disseminating appropriate information. This new view of regulation puts much more weight on the process that leads to efficient levels of consumption and production. It is operationalised by the Public Performance Audit (PPA) System approach which analyses, rates, and publicly discloses the performance of government agencies, public utilities or private firms. PPA systems can increase both the transparency and accountability of public institutions. Afsah and his colleagues illustrate the PPA concept by referring to a system recently adopted by Indonesia's

Environmental Impact Management Agency for controlling industrial pollution. Inspired by Indonesia's example of public information in action, the governments of the Philippines, Colombia, Mexico and Brazil are also now moving rapidly toward developing their own public disclosure programs.

Lal picks up on one aspect of the information age and focuses on the Internet. She highlights the fact that while the Internet is generally thought of in terms of a "global" information infrastructure, its networked structure allows for local components and for the provision of local information content. She further asserts that the Internet can help governments achieve specific policy goals. The author proposes the idea of electronic "city streets," that employ an Internet infrastructure - either telephone- or radio-based - to develop open communication between the government, the private sector, and citizens and citizen bodies, thus strengthening the CBG triad discussed earlier. Through such an Internet-based network, local or municipal governments can offer e-mail service, electronic news service, direct access to the municipal World Wide Web sites (connected to other local, national and international servers), as well as databases and Internet navigation to citizens. This tripartite network promotes collaboration in decision-making, and enhances administrative transparency and accountability, as well as the exchange of knowledge and resources. As illustrations, she refers to usages of local government World Wide Web sites around the world.

Part 6: Capacity Building and Local Governance

The final area of governance focus that this book highlights has to do with local governance with specific reference to capacity building (CB). CB has long been at the forefront of development management and technical assistance in Less-Developed Countries (LDCs) of the region. Yet, ironically, just at a time when governance has emerged as a key concern around the world, CB is no longer given the prime role it used to - and should - be given. The three authors whose chapters appear in this part argue that CB continues to be of relevance to governance, particularly at the local level.

The key idea that Bhatta brings out in his paper is that, to date, governance has been discussed predominantly in a macro or upstream context, and that the focus on local level governance tends to be neglected. Since governance encompasses not only the political realm but also the economic (in particular, opportunities for people to partake in sustainable development activities), the relevant question in this regard should be: how does governance take into account opportunities for - and capacities of -

people to be involved in increasing their standards of living? Bhatta argues that it is inadequate merely to resort to one of the most widely used tools of governance - enactment of decentralisation laws - to enable local authorities to participate more fully in development. What is also needed is providing them with the capacity to be able to use these legal frameworks to engage in development. In building capacity at the local level, enabling community members to participate in development activities by co-opting local institutions and leaders provides a sound base for effective governance. The other need for capacity building at the local level is action-based training on planning, mobilisation and utilisation of resources.

Brillantes takes the CB issue further by putting it in the context of the Philippines. He argues that the enactment of the Philippine Local Government Code (LGC) in 1991 drastically transformed the nature and power structure in the politico-administrative system when it devolved substantial powers and authorities to the local government units (LGUs). Under the regime of local autonomy, LGUs were thrust to play the central role in local governance. According to Brillantes, it was within this context that a framework for the conduct of capability building programs in the country was adopted by the President through Proclamation 284, resulting in the Integrated Capability Building Program (ICBP). Brillantes also provides an overview of the Philippine local government system, and a discussion of the basic features of the Local Government Code of 1991. The ICBP is also described including an overview of the Galing Pook Program that aims to document best practices at the local level. Finally, other approaches to capability building that are discussed include cross visits among LGUs (Lakbay Aral Program), establishment of LGU Innovations Laboratories, and the Radio Program/Barangay School-On-the-Air (BSOAP) program.

Finally, touching on the issue of local governance, Phimphisut looks at the contribution of local citizen participation in successful development programming by taking two case studies of the management of community forests in Nakhon Ratchasima Province, Thailand. The author contrasts the effective management of important environmental resources through active peoples' participation in one village, with the ostensibly less successful experience of a top-down, state-led, centralised approach where the local population was disengaged and disinterested. Apart from the environmental conditions, the people factor is shown to be integral to how it shapes the other key factors in the management of community forestry, viz., awareness about environmental conservation and skills for doing so, the nature of community leadership in the village, and the broader question of ever-evolving social values, customs and traditions of the community.

Part 7: Conclusions

The overarching theme of governance and civil society that this book dwells on is encapsulated in Peter Evans' piece on how formal bureaucratic organisations of the state can work with local communities in a synergistic fashion to achieve developmental goals. Since governance has at its core a community focus, this synergy takes on a deep importance. Evans opines that there are many ways in which the State and Society can complement one another to achieve developmental goals. This is where local communities offer indigenous expertise, active participation, and 'social capital' to promote the success of a programme. It is also where state agencies have to have the strong system of control, performance, and accountability to engage local constituents in the programmes without being 'captured' by local interests. Evans argues that, paradoxically, the effective engagement and mobilisation of local communities for development projects demands robust and sophisticated bureaucracies while organised communities with high levels of social solidarity are also to the advantage of the functioning of government bureaucracies. In this way, Evans ends by taking us to the leading edge of thought on governance in both the developing and developed world today.

All the chapters in this book emphasise that good governance is critical to effective social and economic development. However, they expose a number of areas that could be the focus of further research and experimentation by both development scholars and practitioners. For instance, care must be taken with regards to replicating some of the success stories highlighted here. The cross-country cases illustrate that cultural and demographic factors need to be examined with care and sensitivity. Additionally, governance innovations need to go beyond mere public sector reforms but more importantly take on board new ideas about how to enhance CBG partnerships. These are often relationships characterised by mistrust. How can this be overcome? Can these three key actors identify a mutuality of benefits and create synergies in pursuing common goals? Or are these necessarily competitive actors in which case, allowing each to thrive is a question of opening-up enough 'space' and creating a clear division of labour and work to achieve optimal results in development? Political will and bureaucratic vigour have also been cited as essential to successful reform implementation. Furthermore, there seems to be a heavy concentration on national-level reforms as opposed to community-level innovations. Hence, there is a need to look seriously into the key issues raised regarding local leadership, local level capacity building, and stakeholder participation in development processes. The clear challenge then for development experts is to refocus some creative energy to these understudied dimensions of governance.

Notes

[1] J. L. Gonzalez, "Development Governance," in Jay M. Shafritz (General Editor), *The International Encyclopaedia of Public Policy and Administration* (Boulder, CO: Westview, 1997); see also J. L. Gonzalez, "Governance, Socio-Economic Development and the East Asian Miracle: Some Lessons for the Philippines," *Asian Journal of Political Science* 4, 1 (1996): 36-63.

[2] D. Brautigam, *Governance and Economy: A Review* (Washington, DC: World Bank, 1991); see also A. Campbell, "Civil Service Reform as a Remedy for Bureaucratic Ills," in F. Lane (ed), *Current Issues in Public Administration* (New York: St. Martin's Press, 1982), and L. Hammergren, *Development and the Politics of Administrative Reform* (Boulder, CO: Westview Press, 1983).

[3] World Bank, *Governance and Development* (Washington, DC: World Bank, 1992), and World Bank, *Governance: The World Bank's Experience* (World Bank, Washington, DC, 1994).

[4] World Bank, *Sub-Saharan Africa: From Crisis to Sustainable Growth* (Washington, DC: World Bank, 1989), and Asian Development Bank, "Report of the Task Force on Improving Project Quality" (Manila: ADB, 1994). The following World Bank governance reports were also conceived by Bank staff to help reverse the dismal trend of development assistance effectiveness especially in Africa: M. Dia, *A Governance Approach to Civil Service Reform in Sub-Saharan Africa* (Washington, DC: World Bank, 1993); L. Adamolekun and Coralie Bryant, *Governance Progress Report: The Africa Region Experience* (Washington, DC: World Bank, 1994); and R. F. Pinto, *Projectising the Governance Approach to Civil Service Reform* (Washington, DC: World Bank, 1994).

[5] "ADB Told Not to Link Loans to Good Governance," *The Straits Times* (Singapore), May 6, 1996, p. 19.

[6] See, for instance, USAID, "Governance and Local Democracy (GOLD)," Project paper (Manila: USAID, 1994); United Nations, *Fiscal Decentralisation and the Mobilisation and Use of National Resources for Development: Issues, Experience, and Policies in the ESCAP Region* (Bangkok, Thailand: ESCAP, 1991); and United Nations, *The Lessons of East/South-East Asian Growth Experience* (Bangkok, Thailand: ESCAP, 1995). The IOG, with the support of CIDA, intensified its governance-related activities in East Asia through its new regional office in Kuala Lumpur, Malaysia. The Ford Foundation and Asia Foundation are also in the process of redefining and rechanelling resources to this resurging

development theme. Recently, UNDP Administrator, James Gustave Speth, announced that the UNDP would set up a US$36 million pilot programme to promote "good governance" in developing countries (*The Straits Times* (Singapore), "UN Sets Up Fund to Promote 'Good Governance,'" July 30, 1997).

[7] From the IOG's conference brochure on an *International Conference on Governance Innovations: Building Government-Citizen-Business Partnership*, Manila, Philippines, October 20-23, 1996.

[8] World Bank, *Governance and Development* (Washington, DC: World Bank, 1992), and World Bank, *Governance: The World Bank's Experience* (Washington, DC: World Bank, 1994).

[9] Central Office of Information, *Britain 1994: An Official Handbook* (London: HMSO, 1993).

[10] Especially very early on as referred to in: F. Mosher (ed), *Governmental Reorganisations: Cases and Commentary* (Indiana and New York: Inter-University Case Program, 1967); L. Meriam, "Concepts of Reorganisation," in J. Shafritz and A. Hyde (eds), *Classics of Public Administration* (Chicago, IL: Dorsey Press, 1987); and L. Brownlow, et al., "Report of the President's Committee on Administrative Management," in J. Shafritz and A. Hyde (eds), *Classics of Public Administration* (Belmont, CA: Wadsworth, 1992).

[11] H. Seidman and R. Gilmour, *Politics, Position, and Power: From the Positive to the Regulatory State* (New York: Oxford University Press, 1986).

[12] See President's Commission on Privatisation, *Privatisation: Toward More Effective Government* (Washington, DC: Report of the President's Commission on Privatisation, 1988); P. Volcker, *Leadership for America: Rebuilding the Public Service* (Lexington, MA: Lexington Books, 1990); and D. Osborne and T. Gaebler, *Reinventing Government: How the Entrepreneurial Spirit is Transforming the Public Sector* (New York: Plume, 1993).

[13] See A. Gore, *From Red Tape to Results: Creating a Government that Works Better and Costs Less* (Washington, DC: U.S. General Printing Office, 1993); B. G. Peters and D. Savoie, "Reinventing Osborne and Gaebler: Lessons From the Gore Commission," *Canadian Public Administration*, 37, 2 (Summer 1994): 302-322; R. Moe, "The 'Reinventing Government' Exercises: Misinterpreting the Problem, Misjudging the Consequences," *Public Administration Review*, 54, 2 (March-April 1994): 111-122; and Donald Kettl, "Beyond the Rhetoric of Reinvention," *Governance* 7, 3 (July 1994): 307-314.

[14] See, for instance: A. O. Krueger (ed), *Export-oriented Development Strategies: The Success of Five Newly Industrialising Countries* (Boulder, CO: Westview Press, 1985); C. Johnson, *MITI and the Japanese Miracle: The Growth of Industrial Policy, 1925-1975* (Stanford, CA: Stanford University Press, 1987); B. Balassa, "The Lessons of East Asian Development: An Overview," *Economic Development and Cultural Change* 36, 3 (April 1988 Supplement): S274-S290; A. Amsden, *Asia's Next Giant: South Korea and Late Industrialisation* (New York:

Oxford University Press, 1989); S. Haggard, *Pathways from the Periphery: The Politics of Growth in the Newly Industrialising Countries* (Ithaca, NY: Cornell University Press, 1990); R. Wade, *Governing the Market: Economic Theory and the Role of Government in East Asian Industrialisation* (Princeton, NJ: Princeton University Press, 1990); E. Vogel, *The Four Little Dragons: The Spread of Industrialisation in East Asia* (Cambridge, MA: Harvard University Press, 1991); and J. Woronoff, *Asia's 'Miracle' Economies* (New York: M. E. Sharpe, 1992).

[15] D. Leipziger and V. Thomas, *Lesson of East Asia: An Overview of Country Experience* (Washington, DC: World Bank, 1993): 3.

[16] See World Bank, *The Lessons of East Asia: An Overview of Country Experience* (Washington, DC: World Bank, 1993), and J. E. Campos, "Leadership and the Principle of Shared Growth: Insights in the Asian Miracle," *Asian Journal of Political Science* 1, 2 (1993): 1-38.

[17] World Bank, *The East Asian Miracle: Economic Growth and Public Policy* (Oxford: Oxford University Press, 1993).

[18] J. E. Campos and H. Root, *The Key to the Asian Miracle: Making the Principle of Shared Growth Credible* (Washington, DC: Brookings Institution, 1996).

[19] H. Root, *Small Countries, Big Lessons: Governance and the Rise of East Asia* (New York: Oxford University Press, 1996).

[20] Valuable local support also came from the Philippine Commission on Audit, and the Philippine Department of Budget and Management.

[21] The Governance Innovations Conference launches a three-year program called the "Canada-ASEAN Governance Innovations Network" (CAGIN). CAGIN links learning activities, pilot innovation projects, and field research.

2 Does Governance Matter?

John M. Page

After half a century of experience with the theory and practice of economic development, economists and development practitioners confront the stark reality that on average the gap in per capita incomes between rich nations and poor nations is widening. Apart from the spectacular performance of a handful of East Asian economies, per capita income growth in the advanced economies of the OECD has outstripped that of the developing countries since 1960. The poorer nations of the world are getting more prosperous, but not sufficiently fast to "converge" to the levels of income per person of the industrial economies.

The economics profession has responded to this bad news in at least three ways. First, there has been a search for new models of economic growth which are consistent with international experience. These "endogenous" models of economic growth describe a process in which the returns to capital accumulation do not diminish rapidly, and they generally emphasise the importance of human and technological learning in increasing the returns to investment in physical capital.[1]

Second, economists interested in public policy have sought explanations for the great divergence in growth performance among developing countries in the choice of economic policies employed by governments. The search for economic policy regimes which can promote rapid growth has relied primarily on cross country case studies and has drawn extensively on the experience of the successful high performing Asian economies for positive lessons and on the economic crisis of the 1980s in Latin America for negative ones.[2]

From that work there is an emerging consensus that at a minimum governments need to put in place policy frameworks that result in macroeconomic stability, sustained accumulation of human capital, effective and secure financial systems, and price signals which reflect economic costs and benefits. There is also a broadly held view that economies which have chosen to develop a high degree of integration with the world economy have grown faster than those which have failed to do so.[3] These "policy fundamentals" are now part of the tool kit of virtually every economist and development agency in the business of advising governments in low and middle income countries.[4] They form the "hardware" of development policy.

What is striking, however, is the extent to which so few developing countries have adhered effectively to the policy fundamentals in the past and the difficulty that many governments and societies have in changing policy regimes to attain these fundamental development objectives.[5] Put more bluntly, some economists in the development policy business have begun to ask themselves, "If our advice is so good why don't more people take it, and why don't those who take it do better?"

This brings me to a third—and I would assert, much smaller—group of economists who have become concerned with the "software" of economic development, the study of how public economic policies are chosen, formulated and implemented. In short, the study of governance. That governance issues are reaching the mainstream of development policy analysis is indisputable. The World Bank's 1997 *World Development Report* will address the issues of state capacity for the first time. The UN system has an interagency task force on governance, and all of us have come to the conclusion that governance matters, but many of us, especially economists— are not quite sure why.

I shall, therefore, try to offer a sample of what the economist's tool kit can tell us about why governance matters for economic growth by focusing on three topics. First, I want to present new evidence for a wide range of countries on the relationship between government performance and growth at the national level. Second, I want to report on recent work undertaken at the World Bank investigating the relationship between rates of return on development projects and some indicators of participation. Finally, I want to present a brief analysis of how government commitment affects the resolution of co-ordination problems which can inhibit economic growth, using the specific example of export promotion.

How Do We Measure Governance?

One reason why many economists have remained shy of governance is that we like to think ours is a measurement-based discipline. But how does one measure, or even define, good governance? The World Bank, for example, tells us that governance is "the manner in which power is exercised in the management of a country's economic and social development".[6] While undoubtedly true and relevant for development policy, that statement is hardly useful in trying to measure the characteristics of better exercise of power or improved management. Nor does it tell us much about how either might contribute to better economic and social development.

There are many dimensions of good governance—political stability, transparent rule of law, competent administration, respect for human rights, participatory political and institutional processes, and democracy, to name a few—only some of which are amenable to quantitative measures. Broadly speaking, they contribute to good governance either through the exercise of power—by affecting legitimacy, accountability, and participation—or through management. My approach here is to focus primarily on measurable dimensions of institutional capability and public management.

I do not wish to dismiss the importance of variables related primarily to the exercise of power. It is simply that they would take me even further afield from my central theme which is that economists hoping to understand why some countries prosper, and others do not, can no longer afford to neglect the institutional and public management aspects of economic development.

Governance and Growth -- Evidence from Cross Country Data

The availability in the last decade of consistent data on such important economic variables as GDP, investment, and educational attainment for a wide range of countries has spawned a cottage industry in the economics profession exploring the determinants of long run economic growth. Surprisingly, however, relatively little attention has been directed toward analysing the impact of institutional capability on growth.[7] Paolo Mauro in a recent paper makes an important contribution to our understanding of the relationship between governance and growth by developing measures of institutional capability painstakingly constructed from the proprietary risk assessments of *Business International*.[8] I want briefly to report on work that combines Mauro's governance measures with World Bank data on growth, investment and productivity change.[9]

The *Business International* indices provide an evaluation for the period 1980-1983 of corruption, red tape, and the efficiency of the judicial system by the magazine's correspondents stationed in about 70 countries. The indices are integer values ranging from 0 to 10 and are scaled such that higher values indicate the presence of better institutions. Substantial effort is made to ensure consistency across countries; the relevance and accuracy of the effort is attested by the willingness of subscribers to pay considerable sums for the survey results. Here I only make use of a composite index which is the simple average of the three individual indices. I call this index the institutional capability index (ICI). [10] Figure 2.1 is a scatter plot of per capita income in 1980 versus the ICI. It makes a simple point: richer countries tend to have better institutions.

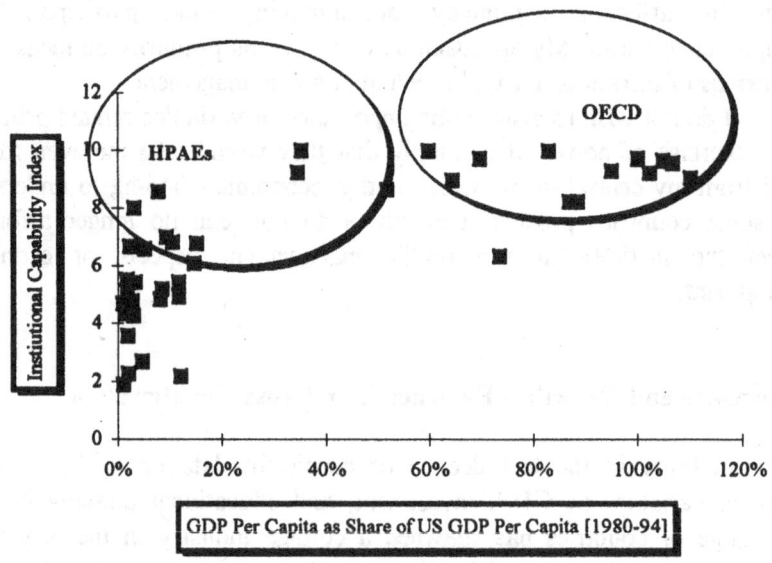

Figure 2.1 GDP Per Capita [as Share of US GDP] and Institutional Capability Index
Sources: World Bank and *Business International*.

The correlation between per capita income and institutional capability is significant at the one percent level. This, of course, begs the question: do better institutions contribute to economic development or are they an outcome of the development process? Figure 2.2 pictures the relationship between the ICI and the rate of growth of per capita income between 1965 and 1995. Here again, the statistical association is strongly significant (at the one per cent level). Countries with higher levels of institutional capability in the early 1980s grew faster from 1965 to 1995 than those with lower levels.

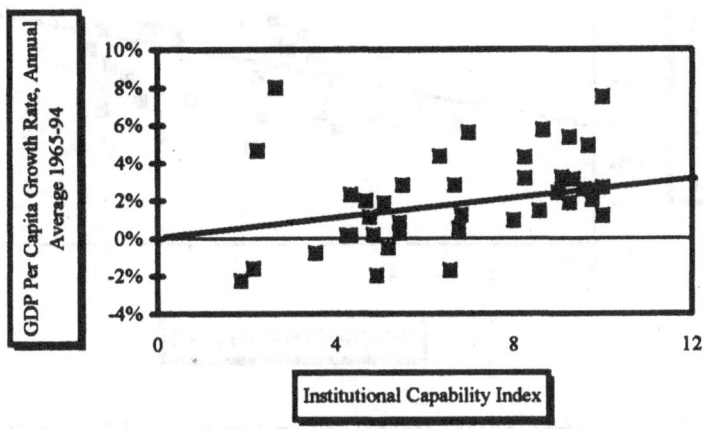

Figure 2.2 GDP Per Capita and Institutional Capability Index
Sources: World Bank and *Business International*.

But why? Economic theory suggests two channels by which governance may affect growth. The first is through investment. Surveys of existing enterprises and potential investors consistently rank the three elements of the institutional capability index as among the major factors determining the attractiveness of developing economies for new private investment.[11] The clients of the *Business International* survey—mainly large foreign investors—pay for that information to help make their investment decisions. Moreover, low levels of institutional capability may lower the marginal returns to investment, discouraging both public and private investment. It would be surprising, therefore, if there were not some relationship between investment and institutional capability. There is a strong positive association between institutional capability and total investment as a share of GDP (See Figure 2.3). Indeed, if the institutional capability index increases by one standard deviation (2.34) the investment rate increases by three percent of GDP.

28 *John M. Page*

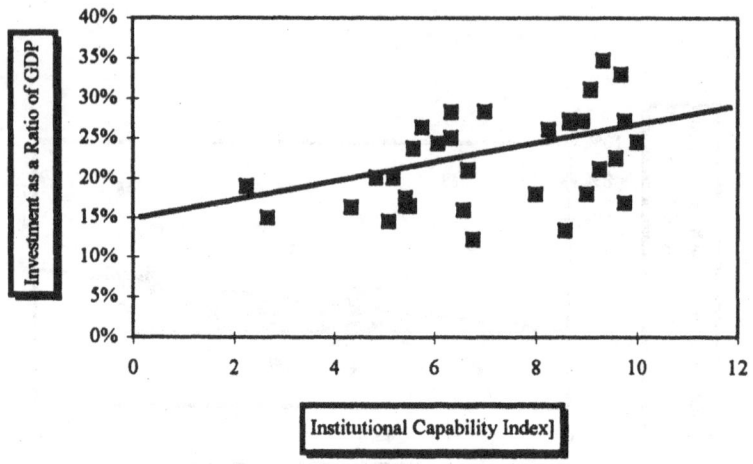

Figure 2.3 Investment Rate Regressed on Institutional Capability Index
Sources: World Bank and *Business International*.

Because private investors rank institutional capability as an important determinant of their behaviour, we might expect that the ICI would be closely related to private investment. Detailed evidence on private investment is scarce. Only twenty three developing economies have data on both institutional capability and private investment.[12] The results are, therefore, suggestive but not conclusive.

We find no statistically significant relationship between institutional capacity and private investment rates, but the statistical results are heavily influenced not only by three outliers—Thailand, Indonesia and Iran—each of which have high private investment rates but low reported institutional capability, but also by the exclusion of the high income countries.

It is, of course, possible that the index of institutional capability is closely associated with other determinants of investment behaviour. If that is the case, omitting them from our analysis may give an erroneous view of the impact of governance on investment. Fortunately, the cross country literature on economic growth has reached a reasonable consensus on other factors influencing the rate of investment. Even controlling for these variables, institutional capability is significantly associated with higher total investment[13] (See Table 2.1). Holding other factors constant, improving institutional capability by one standard deviation increases the investment rate by 4.1 percent of GDP. The meaning here is: governance matters for investment.

Table 2.1 Institutional Capability and Investment

Dependent variable	Total Investment GDP		Private Investment GDP	
Explanatory variable				
Institutional Capability Index (ICI)	++	++	Institution. Capability Index (ICI)	0	+++
Control var.				
GDP in 1960		0	East Asia Dummy		+++
Secondary Enrolment Rate 1960		+		
Pop. growth		0		

Key: Positive and significant at {+=.10++=.06+++.01} Negative and Significant at {-+.10--+.05---+.01}. 0=Not significant.
Sources: World Bank and *Business International*.

Much of the writing by economists about the relationship between governance and economic growth has emphasised another possible channel by which poor institutional capability can affect economic performance. This is through the misallocation of resources. The simplest mechanism by which misallocation might take place is through lack of institutional capability leading to inefficient investment choices by the public sector.[14] It is also possible that low institutional capability—and one of its manifestations, high levels of corruption—may lead to inefficient investment choices by the private sector. Finally, if lack of institutional capability leads to "rent seeking", societies may expend substantial resources not in productive activities but in attempting to capture rents.[15] These efficiency effects of poor governance are unlikely to be captured directly by the relationship between investment and institutional capability.[16] Rather they should be reflected in variations in total factor productivity (TFP), the overall efficiency with which productive factors are used in the economy.

Elsewhere, I have reported economy-wide estimates of total factor productivity change for a sample of 87 high- to low-income economies.[17] These estimates are based on a cross country production function with physical capital, human capital and labour as inputs. The results are summarised in Figure 2.4, which plots TFP growth 1960-1989 relative to level of development in 1960.

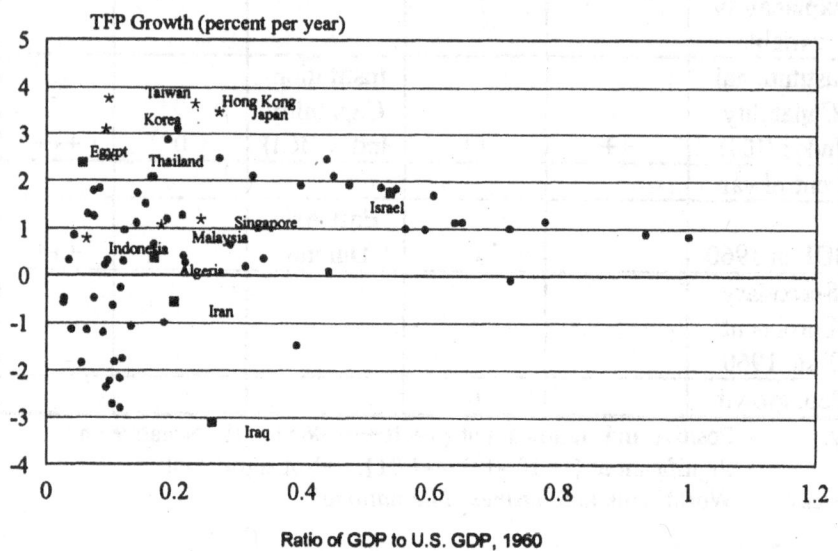

Figure 2.4 Total Factor Productivity Growth, 1960-89, and GDP Per Capita Relative to US, 1960
Source: World Bank.

Two important patterns emerge from the data: (1) nearly one third of the low- and middle income countries have negative rates of TFP growth, meaning that their rates of accumulation of inputs should have yielded higher output growth; and (2) there is very little productivity based catch-up with the advanced economies by low- and middle-income countries.[18] Both of these findings are deeply disturbing for economic development.

The productivity crisis in the developing world is at least partly due to failures of governance. Figure 2.5 plots the rate of TFP growth against the institutional capability index. The relationship is positive and statistically significant (at the five percent level).[19]

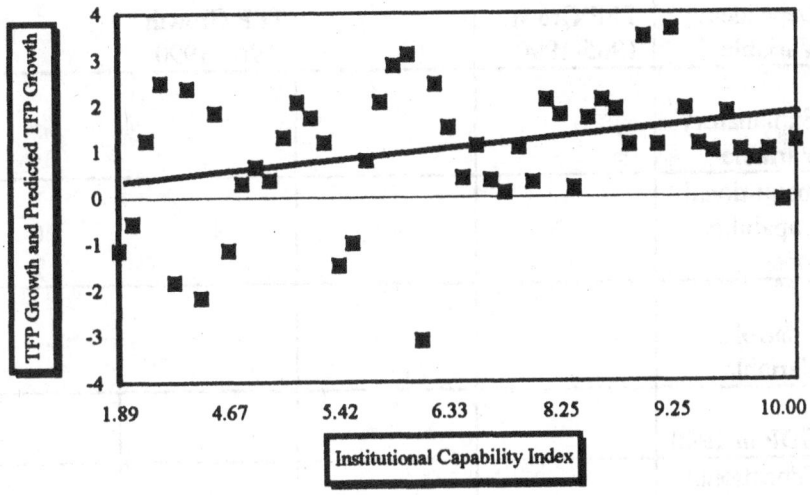

Figure 2.5 TFP Growth Regressed on Institutional Capability Index
Sources: World Bank and *Business International*.

Hence, better governance results in higher total factor productivity growth. A one standard deviation increase in the ICI adds 0.39 percent to the rate of TFP growth. That, in itself, is higher than the recorded TFP growth for one third of the developing countries in the sample. When we control for other possible factors which would lead to intercountry variations in the rate of TFP growth, the relationship is remarkably robust. (See Table 2.2). Even controlling for relative distance from international best practice and educational attainment—two factors strongly correlated with variations in TFP growth rates in cross country studies—the index of institutional capability remains strongly and positively associated with higher TFP growth.[20] In sum, across countries and over time, governance matters for growth. Institutional capability contributes significantly to higher investment and to higher productivity growth. Bad institutions in the past have contributed to present poverty.

Table 2.2 Institutional Capability and Total Factor Productivity (TFP) Growth

Dependent Variable	TFP Growth 1965-1990	TFP Growth 1965-1990		
Explanatory Variable				
Institutional Capability Index	++	++	++	0
Control Variable				
GDP in 1960		-	--	-
Educational Attainment 1960			++	++
Openness Index				++

Key: Positive and significant at {+=.10 ++=.06 +++=.01} Negative and significant at {-=.10 --=.05 ---=.01}. 0=Not significant.
Sources: World Bank and *Business International*.

Participation and Performance: Evidence from Development Projects

It has become conventional for development practitioners and agencies to call for increased client participation in development projects.[21] Yet, despite the widely shared view that participation improves project performance, clear and convincing evidence on the link between participation and project outcomes is surprisingly scarce. Advocates of participation have relied primarily on case studies to document the link between participation and performance.[22] But these are easily dismissed by sceptics because of the small number of cases and the informal testing of the findings.

Recent econometric work undertaken by the World Bank allows us to move beyond case studies, and establishes a robust causal relationship leading from increased participation to improved performance for 121 diverse rural water supply projects.[23] The projects were drawn from 49 countries in Africa, Asia and Latin America and were financed by a wide range of development agencies—including USAID, UNDP and the World Bank—and non-governmental organisations. Project costs ranged from half a million to more than 250 million dollars and the technologies ranged from simple spring captures to power-pumped, piped water systems.

The measure of participation was not simply a measure of whether potential beneficiaries were surveyed for their preferences. Rather, participation was "scored on a continuum, progressing from information-sharing, to more in-depth consultation, to shared decision making, to control over decision making".[24] It was also measured at three different stages in the project cycle—design, construction, and operation and maintenance.

Measured increases in participation are significantly correlated with improved project outcomes, even when the authors correct the data for "halo effects"—the possibility that investigators who believe that participation is good may overstate the level of participation in highly successful projects or overstate the degree of success in highly participatory projects. But as anyone who has suffered through an economic statistics course has had drilled into them "correlation does not necessarily imply causation", it is possible that better project performance may cause increased beneficiary participation, and not the other way around.

Although causality is nearly impossible to establish with certainty, in this case there is a strong argument in its favour. The data permit the measurement of participation at several stages of project implementation. If project success determined participation, we would expect to see no relationship between outcomes that occur prior to project completion and participation. After all, the success of the project could only be determined by the community once it had been completed. Yet, participation is significantly correlated with the quality of project implementation, effectiveness of operations, and maintenance after one year. Moreover, roughly these same results hold when participation at each intermediate stage is correlated with the final project outcome. Participation improves performance.

Rural water would seem to be a particularly good example of the importance of direct beneficiary participation. What about other sectors? Here our evidence is less detailed and our tests are less sophisticated, but cross country evidence from World Bank projects suggests that feedback mechanisms—including but not limited to organised participatory processes—matter for project performance in a wide variety of sectors.

The Operations Evaluation Department of the World Bank conducts retrospective analyses of World Bank projects which attempt to measure project success in two ways. For sectors in which the stream of project benefits can be quantified and valued—infrastructure, agriculture, industry, energy, water, urban, transport, and tourism—an *ex post* rate of return is calculated.[25] For all sectors, including human resources investments where benefits are more difficult to quantify, an overall success rating in achieving development objectives is assigned. Table 2.3 shows basic information about the rate of return and success ratings for more than three thousand World Bank projects evaluated between 1974 and 1993. The average rate of return was about 16 percent, and the percentage of projects evaluated as successful was about 73 percent. There is substantial regional variation.

Table 2.3   Summary Statistics of World Bank Project Performance (1974-1993)

Region	Economic Rate of Return (ERR)		Fraction of Projects rated as "Satisfactory"	
	Average	Number of projects	Average	Number of projects
All	16.1	1824	0.73	3435
South Asia	17.9	235	0.78	439
East Asia	17.7	340	0.83	588
EMENA	17.1	338	0.81	613
Latin America	15.5	364	0.70	701
Sub-Saharan Africa	14	547	0.64	1094

Notes: Includes all projects evaluated by the World Bank's Operations Evaluation Department from 1974 to 1993.

Source: J. Isham, D. Kaufmann and L. Pritchett, *Governance and Returns on Investment* (Washington, DC: World Bank, 1995) Policy Research Working Paper 1550.

Cross-country studies using these data have shown that country structural and policy characteristics are important determinants of project success, as is project complexity.[26] Recently attempts have been made to test the impact of measures of civil liberties on project performance, controlling for the structural characteristics which we know affect project outcomes.[27] Table 2.4 reports the most interesting of these results.

Table 2.4 Participation and Project Performance

Dependent Variable	Economic Rate of Return	Economic Rate of Return	Probability on Project Success	Probability on Project Success
Explanatory Variable				
Freedom House Index	+++	+++	++	+
Control Variable				
Capital-Labour Ratio	--	--	0	--
Project Complexity	---	---	--	---
Terms of Trade Shock	0	0	0	0
Black Market Premium		---		---
Fiscal Deficit		0		0
GDP Growth		0		0

Key   Positive and significant at {+=.10++=.06+++=.01} Negative and significant at {-=.10--=.05---=.01}. 0=Not significant.
Source: J. Isham, D. Kaufmann and L. Pritchett, *Governance and Returns on Investment* (Washington, DC: World Bank, 1995) Policy Research Working Paper 1550.

Using the Freedom House indicators of civil liberties which are available for 165 countries between 1972 and 1994, World Bank's researchers find a robust, statistically significant correlation between greater civil liberties and project success.[28] The quantitative impact of increased civil liberties is quite striking. If the measure of civil liberties improves from the worst (a grade of 1) to the best (a grade of 7) the predicted economic rate of return on a project will increase by 7.5 percentage points—nearly 50 percent of the average rate of return. A one standard deviation increase in the index (of 1.47) improves the predicted rate of return by 10 percent (1.6 percentage points). Using the ranking by successful-unsuccessful, a one standard deviation increase in civil liberties lowers the probability of an unsuccessful project by 3.2 percentage points, lowering the predicted failure rate by 16 percent.

How can we interpret these results? Viewed together with the more limited sample of water supply projects, it is intuitively appealing to argue that the civil liberties variable acts as a proxy for participation. It is likely that beneficiary involvement in projects is higher in countries that score higher on a ranking of civil liberties. At least eight of the Freedom House indicators can directly contribute to beneficiary participation and client feedback in projects—no media censorship, open public discussion, freedom of assembly and demonstration, free trade unions and peasant organisations, free business organisations and co-operatives, free professional and other private organisations, socio economic rights, and freedom from gross government indifference or corruption. It is also likely that these factors contribute to greater accountability on the part of public officials. Both greater participation and greater accountability of public officials are encouraged by an environment in which basic civil liberties are present.

Commitment and Co-ordination—The Case of the Export Contest

A primary function of markets is co-ordination. The price system is the mechanism by which the production (and consumption) decisions of the firms (and individuals) that make up an economy are co-ordinated. When markets are incomplete or missing, they cannot perform this co-ordinating function. In these cases there are great potential benefits to sharing information and co-ordinating action. Among firms in advanced economies, formal and informal sharing of information is common but in developing countries, information is often a source of economic advantage and is tightly held. Co-ordination is difficult because firms are willing to share information only as long as they do not lose by doing so. Thus, governments in developing countries can in theory improve economic performance by acting as brokers of information and facilitators of mutual learning and collaboration.

Co-operation raises several problems, however. First, co-operation may become collusion if firms act together to raise prices or seek other economic advantages. Second, co-operation may inhibit competition, leading to managerial slack or a more general loss of efficiency. Third, business-government co-operation may lead firms to seek special favours from government, expending scarce resources in non-productive "rent-seeking".[29]

Economists are, therefore, nervous about promoting co-operation. While theorists frequently make their reputations working out cases in which government-led co-operation will improve economic welfare, most public policy analysis done by economists - at least for developing countries - has shown that attempts by governments to solve co-ordination problems in practice have reduced national well-being. Indeed, it is conventional for economists to contrast unfavourably the potential gains from correcting market failures with the costs of "government failures."[30] In this view, efforts to solve co-ordination problems are most likely to succeed when they are "institutionally light", displaying the following characteristics:[31]

- applying simple/uniform - rather than selective/differentiated - rules;
- endowing bureaucrats with few discretionary powers;
- containing safeguards against frequent, unpredictable alterations of the rules; and
- keeping firms at arm's length from policy formulation and implementation.

Whether or not governments can play a market enhancing role depends on their capacity to combine co-operative behaviour - including sharing of information among firms and between the public and private sectors, co-ordination of investment plans, and promotion of interdependent investments - with competition by firms to meet well-defined economic performance criteria. Elsewhere, we have called the institutional structures which combine co-operation and competition economic contests, and have argued that they were a key element of the success of public policy in the rapidly growing East Asian economies.[32]

Economic contests differ fundamentally from the arm's length policy regime described above. As practised in East Asia, they frequently involve complex and non-uniform rules, give bureaucrats substantial discretionary power, and depend on interaction between firms and the public sector for policy formulation and implementation. They are institutionally intensive.

Governance is critical to contests and governments must be credibly committed to the objectives of the contest. Without that commitment the players are likely to ignore the game. The key elements of any contest - athletic or economic - are the three "Rs"—rules, referees and rewards. Rewards must be substantial enough to elicit broad participation and energetic competition. Rules must be clear-cut so that contestants know which behaviour will be rewarded and which will be punished. Having competent, impartial referees is critical. This is nothing but a shorthand for institutional capacity. Where contests have succeeded—as in the economies of Northeast Asia—these three elements have all been in place.[33] But as the history of unproductive subsidies in developing economies makes clear, rewards in the absence of rules/referees do not improve performance.

Support for exporters is one of the most pervasive public policy interventions by governments. Economists have rationalised export promotion in a number of different ways. The arguments that are most persuasive are that participation in international markets facilitates learning and productivity change, both because it brings firms into contact with international best practice and because it is a form of competitive pressure. This learning is not limited to the exporting firms alone, but spills over into the domestic economy, leading to a generalised improvement in productivity. For example, in a recent empirical study of total factor productivity (TFP) growth in a broad cross section of countries, Pack and Page find a significant positive relationship between the economy-wide rate of TFP growth and the share of manufactured exports in total exports[34] (Figure 2.6). A simple interpretation of this result is that the higher the probability that an incremental export will be a manufactured good, the higher the economy-wide rate of productivity growth.

As exporting firms cannot charge others for the learning they facilitate, economies will tend to underinvest in exports. Indeed, because there are potentially high costs to creating a country's reputation in the export markets, there is a classic co-ordination failure, and a strong rationale for government action. The policy regimes which individual governments have used to encourage exports range from simple, uniform subsidies on the value of exports to highly elaborate schemes involving access to credit, foreign exchange, and publicly provided services. In a recent paper, Professor Dani Rodrik reviews the effectiveness of export promotion efforts in six countries—Korea, Brazil, Kenya, Bolivia, Turkey and India—and comes to what for most economists is a surprising conclusion.[35]

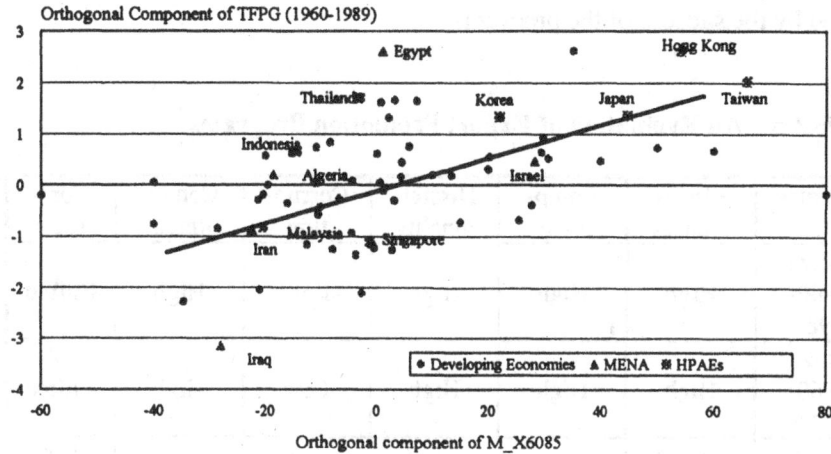

Figure 2.6 TFP Growth Rate and the Share of Manufactured Exports in Total Exports
Source: World Bank.

The two most successful programs of export promotion—those in Korea and Brazil—were highly complex and selective, gave bureaucrats substantial discretionary powers, changed rules frequently, and depended on close interaction between bureaucrats and firms. The two least successful, those in Kenya and Bolivia, consisted of simple, uniform, and non-discretionary subsidies.

I was less surprised. Brazil and Korea created effective export contests; Bolivia and Kenya did not. Table 2.5 summarises the essential elements of the export promotion programs in each country, together with Rodrik's evaluation of their success.

The first notable difference between the programs is in the level of commitment of the political leadership to the program goals. Korean President Park Chung Hee's commitment to export promotion is by now legendary. Exports were monitored on a daily basis and monthly meetings were held with the President attended by ministers, bankers, and the more successful exporters, large and small. In the Brazilian and Turkish cases, the commitment was less personalised in the President but was, to use Rodrik's words, "clear and unmitigated". Credible, public commitment was important because it communicated to firms and to the bureaucracy that *both* would be judged by the success of the program.

Table 2.5 An Evaluation of Export Promotion Programs

Country	Effect-iveness	Comp-lexity	Discret-ionality	Corrup-tion	Comm-itment	Cont-racts
Korea 1960-1980	High	High	High	Low	High	Enfrcd
Brazil 1960-1985	High	High	High	Low	High	Enfrcd
Turkey 1980-1986	Moderate	Moderate	High	Moderate	High	Not Enfrcd
Kenya 1975-1990	Low	Low	Low	High	Low	Not Reqd
Bolivia 1987-1992	Low	Low	Low	Moderate	Low	Not Reqd
India 1960-1970	Moderate	Moderate	Moderate	Moderate	Moderate to Low	Not Reqd

Source: Author's evaluation based on D. Rodrik, "Taking Trade Policy Seriously: Export Subsidisation as a Case Study in Policy Effectiveness," *NBER Working Paper #4567* (Cambridge, Massachusetts: National Bureau of Economic Research, 1993).

In contrast, the export promotion programs of Bolivia and Kenya lacked public commitment from the top leadership. The implementing agencies in each country correspondingly lacked conviction that they would be judged by their success in building exports. The Kenyan case is particularly disheartening. While on paper, implementation was simple, uniform and non-discretionary, in practice, firms often waited for payments for longer than six months from the date they filed their claims; applications were rejected for trivial reasons, for example, according to one observer, "one because a date had been inadvertently omitted on a form and (an)other because the quadruplicate instead of the sextuplicate copy of the Export Entry form had been submitted with the claim".[36] Delay and unpredictability undermined any incentive effect of the program.

One reason why the export promotion efforts in Bolivia and Kenya lacked high level political commitment was that the political leadership was unable to resolve the conflict between competing policy objectives, export promotion and fiscal restraint. As both schemes involved direct fiscal costs, they ran up against the strongly-held objective of reducing expenditure. More importantly, however, governments in both countries designed the programs to counter anti-export bias, not to create an export push in the sense of the Korean, Brazilian or Turkish programs. Export promotion was regarded as an "add-on" to an orthodox economic stabilisation program, not as a strategic, growth-enhancing objective.

The complexity of the rules and the multiplicity of rewards of the Korean and Brazilian programs tend to mask an element common to both successful contests. Firms and the government entered into enforceable contracts regarding export performance. In addition to the rewards for compliance under both schemes, there were also sanctions for non-performance. Competition was thus encouraged by the forward-looking nature of the contracts and by the government's lack of willingness to renegotiate them in response to changing firm-specific circumstances. The success of the Turkish scheme was blunted in part because performance contracts between the government and firms were not enforced. In the cases of the Bolivian, Kenyan and Indian schemes, contracts with individual firms were not sought. Rather, the rewards were proportional to past performance, and there were no sanctions for failing to achieve program goals.

Ultimately, the success of the Korean and Brazilian programs depended on the governments' ability to resist pressure from organised private interests. Cheating, on the other hand, was one of the hallmarks of the other four countries' experiences with export promotion. The autonomy of the referees in Brazil and Korea was sufficient to ensure broad compliance with the program rules, despite substantial incentives for cheating. The origins of that autonomy—especially in Brazil which has been characterised by its inability to achieve autonomous macroeconomic management—are difficult to describe. Even Korea was not regarded as a model of bureaucratic competency before President Park's era. Historical and structural factors undoubtedly played a role in insulating the export bureaucracy, but the scrutiny of the political leadership and its commitment to the export objective must also have heightened accountability and perhaps the perception by bureaucrats of the risks of favouritism.

In evaluating the effectiveness of export contests I have said nothing about the economist's traditional concern with efficiency. Both Korea and Brazil may have spent more of the public's resources on their export promotion programs than was justified by the benefits to society of the exports that they generated. Both programs, however, were clearly superior to those of Kenya and Bolivia which used public resources without any discernible results.

Conclusions

Does governance matter? In each of the three cases I have presented, the answer is clearly, yes. Institutional capability has an important impact on economic growth both through higher levels of investment and through improved productivity. Participation results in better project outcomes. Credible commitment by governments to implement a planned export push, and effective contests, have contributed to the rapid expansion of manufactured exports.

But these results raise as many questions as they answer. By focusing on measurable characteristics of governance and asking how they affect economic outcomes, I have avoided the question of how institutional capacity is created in the first place. In describing the characteristics of effective institutional structures, I have said nothing about their efficiency. This raises an important cautionary note. Effectiveness in the pursuit of economic goals is a necessary—but not sufficient—condition for public interventions to be socially beneficial.

Hopefully, this paper has illustrated how some of the economist's tools could be used to establish that good governance matters for economic growth. If the economists wish to get at the causes of lagging economic development, they will have to expand their search for answers into areas which have been traditionally found to be unfamiliar and uncomfortable. Governance innovations are not just interesting, they are essential to understanding the dynamics of economic development. Of course, I chose to answer the easy question. The much harder one—how does a society achieve better governance—remains for all of us to answer.

Notes

[1] H. Pack, "Technology Gaps Between Industrial and Developed Countries: Are there dividends for latecomers?" *Proceedings of the World Bank Annual Conference on Development Economics* (Washington, DC: World Bank, 1992), and P. Romer, "Increasing Returns and Long-Run Growth," *Journal of Political Economy* 94, 5 (October 1986): 1002-37.

[2] World Bank, *World Development Report 1991* (New York: Oxford University Press, 1991); World Bank, *The East Asian Miracle: Economic Growth and Public Policy* (New York: Oxford University Press, 1993); and S. Edwards, *Crisis and Reform in Latin America: From Despair to Hope* (New York: Oxford University Press, and the World Bank, 1995).

[3] World Bank, *Global Economic Prospects and the Developing Countries* (Washington DC: World Bank, 1996).

[4] There is much less consensus among economists, however, on whether the industrial and financial policy interventions characteristic of the rapidly growing Northeast Asian economies were central to their success. See, for example, A. H. Amsden, *Asia's Next Giant: South Korea and Late Industrialisation* (New York: Oxford University Press, 1989); R. Wade, *Governing the Market: Economic Theory and the Role of the Government in East Asian Industrialisation* (Princeton: Princeton University Press, 1993); and World Bank, *The East Asian Miracle: Economic Growth and Public Policy* (New York: Oxford University Press, 1993).

[5] See, for example, M. Naim, "Las Instituciones: El Eslabon Perdido de las Reformas Economicas en Latino America," in M. Aparacio and W. Easterly (eds), *Crecimiento Economico: Teoria, Instituciones y Experiencia Internacional* (Bogota: Banco de La Republica, 1995).

[6] World Bank, *Governance and Development* (Washington DC: World Bank, 1992).

[7] The one exception to this assertion is that many studies have attempted to measure the impact of political variables—such as changes in government, coups, riots, etc.—on growth. These are surveyed in R. Levine and D. Renelt, "A Sensitivity Analysis of Cross Country Growth Regressions," *American Economic Review* 82, 4 (Sept. 1992): 942-963. J. E. Campos and H. Root, *The Key to the Asian Miracle: Making Shared Growth Credible* (Washington, DC: The Brookings Institution, 1996) report on other attempts to explain variations in growth rates using measures of bureaucratic efficiency which largely yield similar results.

[8] P. Mauro, "Corruption and Growth," *The Quarterly Journal of Economics* 110, 3 (August 1995): 681-712.

[9] Here we extend Mauro's (1995) work. His economic data end in 1985, approximately coincident with the surveys on which he bases his index. Thus, he reports results which reflect the impact of institutions at the end of the period on growth and other variables from earlier periods. Ideally, we would like to do the

reverse: assess the impact of institutions at the beginning of the period on growth in subsequent periods. Because we are able to extend the data series, we can at least move toward that ideal by getting closer to the midpoint of the economic data.

[10] As Mauro (1995) reports, all of the indices are highly correlated with each other. This means that the simple average of the three may be a reasonable proxy for institutional capability (or as Mauro calls it 'bureaucratic efficiency'). I find his term somewhat misleading in that none of the indicators attempts to measure the quality of the bureaucracy directly.

[11] See, for example, the Private Sector Assessments conducted by the World Bank for more than 30 developing countries.

[12] The data on private investment are from G. P. Pfeffermann and A. Madarassy, *Trends in Private Investment in Developing Countries*, IFC Discussion Paper 14 (Washington, DC: World Bank and IFC, 1992).

[13] The regression results are presented in schematic form for ease of interpretation. Only the sign and significance of the parameter estimates are presented. Full statistical results are available from the author on request.

[14] See, for example, Lant Pritchett, *Mind Your P's and Q's: The Cost of Public Investment is not the Value of Public Capital* (Washington, DC: World Bank, 1996).

[15] Anne O. Kreuger, "The Political Economy of the Rent Seeking Society," *American Economic Review* 64, 3 (June 1974): 291-303.

[16] They may be indirectly reflected to the extent that they lower the marginal product of capital and reduce investment demand.

[17] J. M. Page, "The East Asian Miracle: Four Lessons for Development Policy," *NBER Macroeconomics Annual* (Cambridge, Massachusetts: MIT Press, 1994).

[18] B. Bosworth, S. Collins, and Y. C. Chen, *Accounting for Differences in Economic Growth* (Washington, DC: Brookings Institution, 1995) have recently made similar TFP estimates and find similar patterns.

[19] This result differs fundamentally from that of Mauro who, using a cross country growth regression framework, is unable to find a significant association between his bureaucratic efficiency index and growth, independent of investment.

[20] J. M. Page, "The East Asian Miracle: Four Lessons for Development Policy," *NBER Macroeconomics Annual* (Cambridge, Massachusetts: MIT Press, 1994). The ICI is positive and significant in all specifications except when the index of openness is included as an explanatory variable. The ICI and the openness index chosen are highly collinear, however. This suggests a possibly interesting relationship between governance and integration with the global economy.

[21] See, for example, United Nations Development Program (UNDP), *Human Development Report 1993* (New York: United Nations, 1993), and World Bank, *The World Bank and Participation* (Washington, DC: World Bank, 1995).

[22] For example, J. Briscoe and D. de Ferranti, *Water for Rural Communities: Helping People Help Themselves* (Washington, DC: World Bank, 1988).

[23] J. Isham, D. Kaufmann, and L. Pritchett, *Governance and Returns on Investment*, Policy Research Working Paper 1550 (Washington, DC: World Bank, 1995).
[24] *Ibid.*: 178.
[25] The *ex post* rate of return is normally calculated about two to three years after project completion. At that time project investment costs are known and somewhat better estimates of project operating costs and benefits are available. In general, *ex post* rates of return are lower than the estimated rates of return in project evaluations, but exceed the actual rate of return calculated at the end of the project lifetime.
[26] *Ibid.*; J. Isham and D. Kaufmann, *The Forgotten Rationale for Policy Reform* (Washington, DC: World Bank, 1995), and D. Kaufman and Y. Wang, "Macroeconomic Policies and Project Performance in the Social Sectors," *World Development* 23, 5 (May 1995): 751-765.
[27] *Ibid.*
[28] The researchers use several other published indicators of civil liberties as well. The results which are broadly consistent with those reported here are available in Isham, Kaufmann, and Pritchett (1995). The Freedom House indicator is a composite numerical rank ranging from 1 (low) to 7 (high). The individual items in the ranking are: media censorship, open public discussion, freedom of assembly and demonstration, freedom of political organisation, non-discriminatory rule of law in politically relevant cases, freedom from unjustified political terror, free trade unions and peasant organisations, free business and co-operative organisation, free religious institutions, personal social rights (e.g., property, travel), socio-economic rights, freedom from gross socio-economic inequality, and freedom from gross government indifference or corruption.
[29] A. O. Kreuger (1974).
[30] World Bank, *World Development Report 1991* (New York: Oxford University Press, 1991).
[31] This list is from Dani Rodrik, "Taking Trade Policy Seriously: Export Subsidisation as a Case Study in Policy Effectiveness," *NBER Working Paper* #4567 (Cambridge, Massachusetts: National Bureau of Economic Research, 1993). It is similar to other presentations of desirable public policy regimes in the economics literature.
[32] World Bank, *The East Asian Miracle: Economic Growth and Public Policy* (New York: Oxford University Press, 1993).
[33] See World Bank (1993) for a summary of some of the contests employed by Asian governments.
[34] H. Pack and J. M. Page, "Accumulation, Exports and Growth in the High Performing Asian Economies," *Carnegie-Rochester Conference Series on Public Policy* 40 (1994): 199-236.

[35] Rodrik (1993) is careful to point out that he is reviewing the effectiveness, not the efficiency, of the programs. Efficiency could only be determined by a careful comparison of the costs of the export promotion scheme with its benefits in terms of increases in social welfare.

[36] P. Low, "Export Subsidies and Trade Policy: The Experience of Kenya," *World Development* 10, 4 (April 1982): 293-304, cited in Rodrik (1993).

PART II

BUREAUCRACY AND LEADERSHIP

3 Bureaucratic Rationality in an Evolving Developmentalist State: The Case of Singapore

Gillian Koh

Singapore has been lauded as a story of successful delayed or late development.[1] This has been the result of a strategic political resolve to 'catch up' which has been effectively translated to action by a generally competent and incorruptible bureaucracy. State management assumed the 'aura' of being a science.[2] However, the initial global and local conditions under which the Singapore developmental state was able to engender factor- and investment-driven economic transformation based on borrowed technology, are no longer obtaining. The critical trends impinging on the role of the state and bureaucracy in development are the rise of the 'second wave' newly industrialising economies and other Asian emerging economies, the entrenchment on the new informational economy in the global economy, and domestically, a maturing industrial society. These present challenges to further economic and social development and, hence, governance in Singapore, assuming there are no changes in political regime or system.

In the earlier stages of development, the bureaucracy had a relatively clear and given problem definition of the 'catching up' exercise and the basic universal good of socio-economic development. Now, bureaucratic elites are expected to be engaged in the proactive process of problem definition, that is, of creating a vision of the future of Singapore and building it. A clear distinction is made between a public service that is driven by problem-solving which is the task of system maintenance, and of innovation which is the task of vision building.[3] On the other hand, they will also need to grapple with the implications of an increasingly stratified society in directing how the state will meet its social responsibilities. These issues of distributive justice and a differentiated response to needs question the adequacy of an ideology of bureaucracy that is based on technocratic management.

This is not just some abstract discussion about the necessary and the desirable. There has indeed been much thinking among permanent secretaries and the political leaders on the need to 'gear-up' the Singapore Public Service for the demands that lie ahead. As Mr. Lim Siong Guan, Permanent Secretary in the Prime Minister's Office, put it: "How well-adjusted and positioned are we for the challenges of the twenty-first century?"[4] The stated challenges are briefly, an external environment that is increasingly complex, uncertain and that changes at faster and faster rates, and an internal environment of an increasingly demanding public.[5] One other key element has been the drive to offer bureaucratic elites or officers of the premier Administrative Service market-competitive pay scales in order to 'outbid' the private sector in attracting and retaining talent in the Service.

This thinking and evaluation has culminated in a new wave of administrative reform: the establishment of the Civil Service College in April 1993, the devolution of powers to hire, pay and promote staff to ministry-based personnel boards in January 1995, the introduction of a broad-ranging programme code-named "PS21" for "Public Service for the 21st Century" launched in May 1995, and the introduction of "Budgeting for Results" in March 1996 that is not just an accounting system but an important corollary to the impetus to reforming bureaucratic culture.

In a nutshell, these reforms are expected to effect a paradigm shift in how public servants think and work. Firstly, public servants will be catalysts of change to make for a government that 'works smart', grafting traditional virtues like consistency and continuity with those of flexibility and enterprise.[6] The Public Service should play the role of facilitator and nurturer rather than the more passive, reactive traditional role of regulator and controller, hence, public servants should be output-oriented rather than input-driven. Secondly, public servants will strive for service-excellence at 'street-level' in serving the needs of their 'customers', the public. The Service would avail itself of modern management tools and techniques to improve work, and also to keep the morale and standard of welfare of public servants high. Flexibility and autonomy for responsiveness yet with accountability is to be achieved in personnel and financial management systems of the Public Service. These reforms have been described by a Singapore-based academic as adding up to a 'managerialist revolution' in the Singapore Public Service.[7]

The Prime Minister, Goh Chok Tong, had advocated in 1991 that the Singapore Public Service be run along private sector principles and processes with the caveat that its goals remain different. While a company would be revenue- and profit-oriented, the goal of the Public Service was to provide services that were cost-efficient and affordable and that its accountability was to the Government.[8] What are the limits to which 'managerialism' can or should be extended to the Singapore bureaucracy or a public bureaucracy?

There are those who are wary of the utility of the 'generic management' perspective in which a public organisation can be conceptualised as a business organisation and run on the basis of private sector professional management practices.[9] A counter-model is proffered by F. Parkin for the context of democratic societies.[10] If the view of a public servant is one whose duty is to implement a political policy in as cost-efficient a manner as possible then a technocratic ideology of bureaucracy would be adequate. If, however, the view and desire is for a public servant who sees it as his or her duty to be responsive to the needs of the community, as well as to the political leadership, then technocratic professionalism in the public service must be constrained by the even higher mission of being a civic agency driven by substantive social meaning. Agencies would be ultimately judged by their social effectiveness-soft judgement that cannot be captured by the hard measurement of 'performance targets'.

Together, these merit a re-examination of the concept of bureaucratic rationality, and an exercise in trying to encapsulate the nature of what correct and appropriate administrative action among the bureaucratic elites in Singapore has been, is, and will be. How can the demands for a bureaucracy that is forward-thinking and innovative, yet one that is responsive, sensitive to local and particular demands, be reconciled and met? This is the challenge, on the one hand, of strengthening corporate coherence to avoid a hijacking of universalistic state-defined societal goals by particularistic interests, while on the other hand, permitting situational decision-making so that state action is sensitive to the needs of its clients in a specific policy community and is able to develop co-operative relations between government and citizen. This is suggested by Evans, *et al.*[11] This ideal hints at a need to place a heavier emphasis on the role of socialisation, on values and operational principles, and reflective judgement in the *modus operandi* of the bureaucratic elite if the Singapore developmental state is to re-invent itself for the 21st Century.

These issues will be addressed and examined in a progression through the following sections:

- The 'Managerialist Revolution' and Bureaucratic Rationality of the Singapore Administrative Elite; and
- Public Sector Leadership for 21st Century Singapore

The 'Managerialist Revolution' and Bureaucratic Rationality of the Singapore Administrative Elite

C. Offe's concept of bureaucratic rationality offers a way in which to grasp the discussion about the role and mindset of bureaucratic elites of Singapore.[12] One is 'organisational rationality' where bureaucratic action is subsumed by general politically, pre-established formal-legal rules. It is input-driven, a calculable 'reflex' of legal norms, organisational programmes and codified rules and procedures but this hardly guarantees rationality in a functional sense.

The next concept is 'systemic rationality' whose criteria is the bureaucratic fulfilment of the functional requirements of the societal environment; it is driven by goals. Bureaucrats are themselves sensitive to the policy environment and visualise how to meet its needs. They decide what are the requisite resources, and appropriate action. This suspends the input-output orientation of legal norms and weighs their relevance to achieving given goals or functional effectiveness.

This implies, of course, that there may be a blurring of traditional theoretical lines between politics and administration, which means that such bureaucratic action requires extra-legal legitimisation. There may be a need to negotiate and gain a consensus through compromise with societal actors about the required action, and to mobilise them to a consensus. Hence, a third standard of administrative action is, therefore, the ability to generate consensus, support and co-operative relations between the administration and its specific clientele. In the case of Offe's argument about advanced welfare states, he considers the presence of three-tiered, contradictory rationalities a problem for public administration because there is "no available over-arching criterion of rationality that would permit the respective premises of the three levels to be brought into an hierarchical relationship".[13]

In Singapore, however, that singular over-arching criterion as discussed earlier had been development for survival. The state was pragmatic in its choice of development policy, the bureaucracy was fully socialised into the developmentalist values, and the public acquiesced for the sake of this national vision and project. The 'survival crisis' is no longer a plausible legitimisation for these. It could be replaced by the 'problems of the management of success' but this is far less powerful a rallying point. It is uncertain how far the members of the bureaucracy will view what will be demanded of them as being a national project or party politics. An added consideration is the presence of opposition party members in Parliament now.[14] This is the reason why 'nonbureaucratic elements of bureaucracy' become more crucial in shaping the coherence in state policy and action.

The Evans and Rueschemeyer thesis provides a theorisation of how bureaucratic rationality is linked with the issue of state power and state-society relations in the context of the developmental state. Briefly, given the starting condition of relative state autonomy from civil society, the state legitimates intervention as the guardian of the universal interests of the society. With effective state intervention and economic transformation, the increasingly differentiated, and empowered, interest groups of the maturing industrial society will seek to limit the state's potential autonomy over them (or as the case may be, make greater demands on it). Unless the latter effectively co-opts these groups, accepting an erosion of its own autonomy, the aggrieved parties may raise questions about particularistic state action on the larger political arena. After all, states are not likely to be equally capable of intervening in the different areas of the increasingly complex society. This would constitute grounds for questioning the legitimacy of state action and the regime. This dialectic creates the potential of undermining the state's coherence as a corporate actor, and its autonomy.

The implications for a bureaucracy are that as economic transformation progresses, 'non-bureaucratic modes of interrelation' among parts of the state apparatus become increasingly important if the state elites as a unit want to continue to provide direction and maintain coherence. Institution building would be insufficient to stave off these forces. There must be sufficient corporate coherence that allows state actors to carry out 'situational decision-making' in response to the ground. Even if this means forfeiting some level of autonomy, it is still a system that can be managed towards a larger societal project through relatively coherent and stable public policy. Non-bureaucratic elements of bureaucracy or modes of interrelation that Evans argues must be strengthened refer to a bureaucratic corporate identity, to norms, traditions, values, and informal networks within the service that offer members organic solidarity that is centred around the pursuit of the collective ends of the state. In the case of East Asian bureaucracies, these are generally attributed to common recruitment grounds, which are highly selective and meritocratic, and the long term career rewards that create commitment and pride in the Service. This is instead of, say, kinship ties or parochial geographic loyalties that override this internal common identity. Paying bureaucrats well, or somewhat in line with private sector wages, also keeps them independent from unproductive rent-seeking. Together, these give states the ability to resist "incursions by the invisible hand of individual maximisation" and bind "the behaviour of incumbents to the pursuit of collective ends, that state can act with some independence in relation to particularistic societal pressures".[15]

This argument also suggests that strict hierarchical structures of the bureaucracy may have to give way to more organic ones. Each team or division of bureaucrats, given the discretion to understand respective policy communities, deals with demands by moderating centralised policy. That is, it exercises systemic rationality within the context of the overarching metavalues of the state (since we are discussing this in the context of a developmental state). Ascertaining what the intermediate and metavalues are, and socialising bureaucratic elites to them, is a prime consideration if the state is to continue in its role of effectively directing economic and social transformation while accommodating these shifts in the socio-political structure of civil society.

Before looking at how this theorisation anticipates the administrative reform in the Administrative Service in Singapore or offers directions for that, I would like to tease out some other salient arguments on the applicability of technocratic rationality and manageralism in the public sector. These offer another set of considerations which should shape bureaucratic rationality in public sector leaders in Singapore.

On the 'Managerialist Revolution'

Some of the main thrusts of public sector reform over the last decade aimed at strengthening the management capacity of public servants have been summarised as:

- the recognition that government must become more facilitative and catalytic, and involved in steering rather than rowing;
- re-examination of its involvement in economic activities;
- concern about results and results-orientation, emphasis shifting from inputs to performance;
- the need to be customer-driven, providing quality service at all times;
- a decentralisation of decision-making so as to improve service delivery;
- transparency in government decision-making;
- greater levels of accountability in public management; and
- concern for value for money by taxpayers.[16]

Peters and Savoie argue that an underlying assumption in this public sector reform is that management practices in the private sector were far superior than those in government, for instance, empowering public sector managers to feel ownership of programmes and to be responsive to clients' needs. Performance measures were introduced for accountability to the top-level managers, to help them record results and plan activities. Service-orientedness would hopefully make bureaucracies open, responsive, and innovative.[17]

Some important points in their critique is that firstly these measures have been more successfully implemented in agencies that had simple goals and were already well-managed. They were less successful in departments that had many goals and activities that had medium-to-high policy content. Secondly, the pressure of accountability of civil servants upwards to their political masters and downwards, to their clients, actually diminished their autonomy leading to a loss in morale. Thirdly, these reforms took place to the neglect of the policy advice and formulation functions at a time that needed that most:

> The strong emphasis placed on managerialism left unattended the new challenges confronting government. The world of relatively isolated national economies, linearity, discrete variables (and even common sense) inhabited by government officials has given way to a new world. The new order is much more challenging, less deferential. It requires a strong capacity to adapt to change and to deal with a more probing and better informed media, policy communities or interest groups, and the public.[18]

Mintzberg also questioned the assumptions of the applicability of the generic management to governance: specifically, the view in management that particular activities can be isolated does not hold true in public policy that is often interconnected vertically even if some activities can be isolated horizontally in terms of function. Effective public policy must be crafted in an iterative process, with close connection between politics and administration for it to benefit from 'learning' and be effective. Also, many government activities do not lend themselves easily to measurement and in fact, "many activities are in the public sector precisely because of measurement problems".[19] Finally, professional managers cannot be expected to take charge of just any kind of activity because they will be unable to appreciate the constraints, processes, and goals that drive specific and specialised areas of public policy.

Mintzberg recommends that the current wave of managerialism in the public sector should be balanced, if not tamed, by what he terms the 'normative-control model'. It would promote the ideal of public *service* - a commitment and dedication rooted in values and beliefs. Vertical control by the superstructure would be normative rather than technocratic, its motto would be "select, socialise and judge".[20] These would make for microstructures that are more missionary, egalitarian and energised, less machinelike and less hierarchical.

Judgement is a process, or form of substantive rationality, that is so necessary in the type of ever-changing policy environments that face states today, as mentioned by Peters, and as discussed for the case of Singapore. Mintzberg refers to this elsewhere as a form of superior thinking - where the innovative organisation is driven by the process of 'strategy formation' that is based on mental synthesis, 'rich knowledge' that understands the environment deeply, and substantial and intimate experience. This is contrasted with 'strategic planning' that is limited rational analysis, that disengages thinking by reducing problems till they are accessible to given rules and procedures, to a form of *reductio ad absurdum*.[21] This is what Mintzberg refers to as the 'cult of rationality' (organisational rationality of a machine bureaucracy).

A refinement of this concept of judgement or rather the distinction between analysis and synthesis is actually offered by Immanuel Kant as reviewed by F. Parkin. This is the distinction between 'determinant judgement' which is the activity of subsuming particulars under the relevant universal and 'reflective judgement', the act of finding the correct concept with which to apprehend a given instance. Technocratic rationality, however, assumes that the latter is unnecessary because universally accepted substantive goals already exist and the only task is to achieve them. Instead, reflective judgement is exercised when bureaucrats have to concern themselves with weighing the ultimate social ends in policy formulation, implementation and review.

A reason why judgement and intuitive thinking which makes for innovation is unfortunately not more commonly practised in private or public bureaucracies is the fear and avoidance of bias and the need for one to prove one's case. Might not a public servant, however, defend such judgements on the basis of common and socially accepted values if he or she can claim thick knowledge of it and hence compliance to the decision by the community at the end of the day? What PM Goh had referred to as 'political sensitivity' to the ground is this kind of reflective thinking or judgement which is also the basis of Offe's second and third concepts of bureaucratic rationality.

Public Sector Leadership in 21st Century Singapore

Now to move on to a small selection of research findings on the Administrative Service and how the Officers view their role. These are based on responses to a mail questionnaire issued to the population of Administrative Service Officers between September 1991 and February 1992. This was before any of the reforms that were mentioned in the introduction had been instituted. By then, however, calls were already being made for ways in which public servants could exercise more creative, and sensitive policy-making, and run their departments and ministries more cheaply, efficiently and flexibly, along the lines of a private sector company. Administrative Officers closest to the processes of policy-making in the Public Service had to accommodate Prime Minister Goh's aim of promising more consultative and inclusive style of government. Some of the Officers had already been exercised by the new initiatives in some politically sensitive areas of public policy. Also, there was increased opposition representation in Parliament.

For these reasons, it was a good time to re-explore the question of what guides the bureaucratic action - is it a sense of value commitment to the project of development and nation-building, commitment to the political elites, or a drive towards neutral, technocratic competency and professionalism? It is not that these are necessarily exclusive but what was the prevailing mood among the bureaucratic elites at the time? Administrative Officers were asked in an open-ended question at the end of the survey about the role of the bureaucracy *vis-à-vis* the political leadership in the future or the 'next lap' of development in Singapore. Two responses illustrate the forces of change that impinge on the nature of bureaucratic rationality as perceived by Officers themselves.

The first takes into account the larger socio-political factors maintaining that the Administrative Service should continue to support the government in public policy-making but the top-down element in the relationship between the two should be complemented by a strong bottom-up component. A more developed society and diversified economy means that policies would not be so clear as before. Multiple objectives have to be achieved through a package of mutually-reinforcing policies. The Administrative Service has the responsibility of providing the government with <u>alternative</u> policy directions, all viable, all with their pros and cons. The government's single-mindedness in the past has to be moderated with a new awareness that there are always alternative means, and the civil servants should not just follow orders and implement policy but help identify policy options.

The second response considers the direction of party politics and the nature of the political system in the future arguing that some of the civil servants should be less partisan in considering or making policies. This is especially important given that opposition members in parliament are likely to be a fact of life in the next lap.

The responses were coded into four categories (see Table 3.1): 'Greater involvement' which refers to the desire for Officers to take more initiative in policy-formulation, and a more equal role or partnership with the political leadership in doing that; 'Greater professionalism' which refers to a desire to be impartial, for Officers to 'speak their minds' or those that just mention 'professionalism' specifically; 'Greater sensitivity' which refers to the need to be more politically attuned especially to the constituents of public policy; and finally, an 'Others' category which refers to 'maintaining status quo', assisting the political leadership or to the task of implementing policy. Although these are not necessarily exclusive categories, the goals in coding the responses were to try to record the wordings of these responses accurately. Responses that hinted at change in the nature of bureaucratic action and rationality were carefully noted. The response rate to this question was 88 percent of total respondents to the survey.

As for the specific results, refer to Table 3.1 in the following page. 50 percent of the responses fell into the 'Others' category. This was made up by 21.1 percent of the respondents that said the bureaucracy's role was to 'assist the leadership', 10.6 percent to advise on and implement policy, and 10.6 percent to maintain status quo. Generally, the political leadership was described as being in the driving seat in policy formation and the role of the Officers as helping the leadership achieve its vision, and as implementors of policy decisions. A sample of such responses:

- There is no doubt that the politicians are the drivers in the country. Civil servants become relegated to being implementors. This will continue as long as the government in power remains.
- To implement the government's vision and ensure its fulfilment.

The Administrative Service must play a major role to complement the political leadership. The Administrative Service is the key implementor of policies.

Table 3.1 Officers' Perception of Their Role vis-à-vis the Political Leadership in the NEXT LAP of Singapore's Development

Role of Administrative Officers in the NEXT LAP	Frequency	Percentage	Valid Percentage
Greater involvement (Overall)	(10)		(15.2)
Administrative officers take greater initiative	2	2.7	3
More co-operation, rapport building, and equal relationship	3	4	4.5
Develop partnership in work, i.e. that the work should belong to both politicians and civil servants	5	6.7	7.6
Greater professionalism (Overall)	(18)		(27.3)
Greater professionalism (General)	6	8	9.1
More professional: integrity, being able to speak one's opinion fearlessly	4	5.3	6.1
Greater autonomy to be able to do what the Officers should be doing	3	4	4.5
Less politicised, provide impartial apolitical assessment	2	2.7	3
More professional and politically sensitive	2	2.7	3
More specialised	1	1.3	1.5
Greater sensitivity (Overall)	(4)		(6.1)
Greater sensitivity (General)	2	2.7	3
More politically oriented/attuned	0	0	0
Get more feedback from grassroots	1	1.3	1.5
Close to the ground to recommend policies for 'common good'	1	1.3	1.5
Others (Overall)	(33)		(50)
Maintain status quo	7	9.3	10.6
Advise and implement policy	7	9.3	10.6
Assist the political leadership	14	18.7	21.1
Others	5	6.7	7.6
No Comment/Missing Values (Overall)	(10)		(15.2)
No comment	1	1.3	1.5
Missing Values	9	12	Missing
Column Total	75	100	100

Number of Valid Observations: 66 of 75 (88 %)
Number of Missing Observations: 9 (12 %)

This group tended to take an instrumental view of the bureaucracy, along the lines of the traditional dichotomy between politics and administration and suggests that the status group would be maintained. While it is still challenging work to operationalise and implement policy, it suggests less demand for the kind of reflective judgement discussed above, or for systemic rationality. The responses that offered a more normative stance were recorded in the other three categories.

Among all the respondents who cared to make a comparison between the 'Old Guard' bureaucracy and the present, the impression given is that the former were independent thinkers and considered different from the political leadership but nonetheless equal, and unequivocally committed to the national vision. This independence has been replaced by more organic linkages between the two groups. Since the 1980s, especially the political elites have tended to be recruited from the bureaucracy or would have had a stint in the bureaucracy.[22] Also, there has been a fairly stable, not highly competitive political system, PAP being predominant. Hence, being familiar and comfortable with the work of the bureaucracy, it is said that Cabinet Ministers do take a relatively involved, hands-on approach to policy-formulation and implementation. As such, the political leadership was opined to a very pro-active role in administration. The Administrative Service will end up being in the support role.

If, however, party politics becomes more competitive in Singapore, the Service could play a wider, even more strategic role. If this mindset prevails, will this lead these bureaucrats to tend to act on the basis of anticipated response? Will they be able to question and challenge enough of the precedents in public policy to offer fresh initiatives?

More than 27 percent of the responses was coded under the category of 'greater professionalism' where there are direct references to a need for a clearer distinction between politics and administration. Respondents highlighted the need for bureaucrats to develop a form of courage and 'integrity' to independently arrive at and assess policy options:

> The political leadership has to define the broad directions for the good of Singapore and allow civil servants the necessary room to think out the means to achieve them. Civil servants should have the courage to argue against 'bad' policies.

> There should be clearer division of responsibilities between the two. All too often, politicians are dealing with administrative matters. Politicians

should keep their feet on the ground and their head in the cloud(s), i.e., to know ground sentiments and conceive policies with visions of "tomorrow". Civil service should then translate their policies into administrative schemes. There is a need for clearer definition of political policies and policies of administration.

This group of Officers would favour playing a greater role in being idea generators, rather than merely being implementors; they would like a clearer division of work between the two groups; and more opportunities and the climate in which Administrative Officers as a Service can have frank and open exchanges with their political masters. Elsewhere in the survey, Officers were asked about the areas in which their training could be improved. A majority, 69.1 percent indicated the area of 'strategic thinking, administrative science and public policy' and 11.8 percent indicated the need for training in the more 'technical, specialised skills' (see Table 3.2).

Table 3.2   Areas of Training Which Can be Improved

Areas For Improvement	Frequency	Percentage	Valid Percentage
Strategic Thinking, Administrative Science, Public Policy	47	62.7	69.1
Technical, Specialised Skills	8	10.7	11.8
Sociology And Politics	7	9.3	10.3
Attitudinal Training	5	6.7	7.4
Others, not listed	1	1.3	1.5
Missing Values	7	9.3	Missing
Total	75	100	100

Number of Valid Observations: 68
Number of Missing Observations: 7

The establishment of the Civil Service College[23] is very important in helping senior bureaucrats identify the core tasks, competencies and values for the Service, honing the group's techniques in policy-making and evaluation, in thinking skills, and in building up a distinct corporate image for the Service. The College will play a critical role in enhancing those 'non-bureaucratic elements of bureaucracy', and informal modes of 'organic solidarity' among Administrative Officers mentioned by Evans. The introduction of techniques like scenario-based planning throughout the Public Service through its leaders (with a scenario planning unit based in the College) offers Administrative Officers a tool through which they learn to consider paradigm shifts in the form of substantive policy initiatives, organisational structures and processes. There is also a very strong political commitment to effecting these reforms which is important for success.[24]

To put it briefly, the College serves an instrumental function of values transmission, role orientation, developing thinking and management skills (which have also become important with the devolution of responsibilities for personnel recruitment and management in January 1995), and also presents opportunities for networking with the elates of the policy communities in the private sector in a 'think-tank' environment. It has an expressive function where tradition is preserved and identity is built, and corporate bonding can take place among Officers. Finally, it has a visibility function, which builds the outward image of the Service, indicates what the members of the Service do, and also will serve to attract people to join the Service at a time when the competition for talent with the private sector is severe. The Civil Service College has also been placed under the ambit of the Prime Minister's Office which signals political commitment to reforms in the higher bureaucracy. It could also serve to prevent the threat of a displacement of goals.

Two related issues, therefore, emerge: on the professionalisation of the Service, and the possibility of the displacement of goals that could result. In that context, the dissemination of the mission or goals of the Public Service becomes very important so that its members should always have some sense of the metavalues of the public and society at large to what and how they act. The 'managerialist revolution' in public service is to be applauded in how it moves this sector away from an obsession with rules to the achievement of particular outcomes. Outcomes will tend to be short-term and quantifiable and the techniques of accomplishing them will be all-important. The more abstract goals, less easily quantifiable ones like 'public interest', should not, however, be neglected in policy-making especially at this time when the more abstract levels of values have become more important in Singapore.

The Service should be seen to be driven by the social effectiveness of what they do in order to build up, not lose, the trust of the people in state agencies. Besides, 'community empowerment' of state agencies can only add to success of a public policy programme. Another benefit is that of giving social meaning to what they do can also serve to motivate bureaucrats more deeply than merely pecuniary rewards.

Hence, a professionalisation of the Singapore Service must proceed, I think, in tandem with the promotion of some *contextualised* version (suited to the political economy of a developmental state, that is), of F. Parkin's list of the civic virtues that apply to his concept of the 'citizen-technocrat': [25] radical tolerance, civil courage, solidarity, justice, *phronesis* and rational communication where bureaucrats create and uphold channels for dialogue within the organisation and with the public and policy community.

All of these are values very different to those generated by a technocratic rationality. These are metavalues set above the intermediate goals of technocratic public management, imbued with the power to focus action in tune with the life-world of common humanity.

The Singapore Public Service has indeed adopted the above as its general mission statement and the mission statement of the PS21 reforms. The second issue is one that is more practical: whether the demands on senior Administrative Officers to take on the tasks of personnel management will detract them from their policy-making functions. The conditions of the policy environment in almost all spheres of public policy require an enhanced policy-making facility within individual ministries and across them.

It is perhaps the mission of the Service, and the civic values of the 'citizen-technocrat', that the last group of respondents had in mind. For example, 15.2 percent referred to a need for bureaucrats to get a better feel of the needs and sentiments of the constituents of the state, to be 'politically sensitive', or to 'play an equal role of partnership' with the political leadership. They opined that "they should be close to the ground and recommend policies that could contribute to greater social happiness and greater prosperity without the ills of social indiscipline and moral turpitude (found) in many advanced countries ... the Administrative Service should be politically sensitive on one hand, but not compromise on independent efficiency and professionalism".

When the responses were cross-tabulated with rank as a proxy for indications of generational change in the views of their role, the proportion of the most senior bureaucrats suggesting that the bureaucracy should continue to 'advise and assist the political leadership', and 'greater involvement' were larger than the proportions within the other rank groups (see Table 3.3).

'Greater professionalism' featured more frequently within the other rank groups even if only equal or second to 'advise and assist the political leadership'. 'Greater sensitivity' was not overall a very important consideration, and none of the Rank III Officers among the respondents mentioned this at all. To reiterate, one caveat is that these categories are not exclusive and it could well be that 'greater involvement' in policy-making is equivalent to 'advise and assist the political leadership'.

Table 3.3 Officers' Perception of Their Role vis-à-vis the Political Leadership in the NEXT LAP of Singapore's Development by Rank

	I	II	III	Row Total
Greater involvement	3 [30%] (13.6%)	1 [10%] (5.3%)	6 [60%] (24%)	10 (15.2%)
Greater professionalism	6 [33.3%] (27.3%)	8 [44.4%] (42.1%)	4 [22.2%] (16%)	18 (27.3%)
Greater sensitivity	2 [50%] (9.1%)	2 [50%] (10.5%)	0	4 (6.1%)
Others; Maintain status quo; Advise & assist political leadership	10 [30.3%] (45.5%)	8 [24.2%] (42.1%)	15 [45.5%] (60%)	33 (50%)
No Comment	1 [100%] (4.5%)	0	0	1 (1.5%)
Column Total	22 [33.3%]	19 [28.8%]	25 [37.9%]	66 [100%] (100%)

Number of Valid Observations: 66 of 75 (88 %)
Number of Missing Observations: 9 (12 %)
Notes:
1. Rank Of Officer
I = Administrative Assistant and Senior Administrative Assistant
II = Assistant Secretary and Principal Assistant Secretary
III = Deputy, Senior Deputy, Permanent Secretary
2. Percentages in round brackets are valid percentages, those in square brackets are valid row percentages.

A clearer distinction among the categories can be drawn between these and 'greater professionalism' which suggests a delineation between politics and administration unlike, say, under the category of 'greater sensitivity'. Not many chose to say that greater 'political sensitivity' should drive their work perhaps because of the risk of being viewed as partisan. But the demands of the more complex political environment are that the bureaucracy must increasingly be able to empathise with the concerns of people and to be able to anticipate their anxieties and accommodate the exceptions within a general framework of the rules and regulations.

This is not confined to front-line or street-level bureaucracy but the senior and middle levels of bureaucracy need also to set the tone.[26] Courtesy and compassion can be just as valued as competence and efficiency in the bureaucratic ethos, and contribute to enforcement, compliance to policy, and its social effectiveness. How can these 'civic virtues' be promoted and routinised? Parkin made the following recommendations:

- the efforts should focus on middle management, not the elite;
- the civic agency must be sensitive to the methodological and structural issues associated with the concepts of 'community' (of interested parties) and the 'public' (interests at large);
- the civic agency needs more positive engagement with the community through action research, surveys, meetings and committees; and
- modes for rational communication need to be created for upward influence and resolution of upward and downward power flows.[27]

These need to be adapted to the Singapore context although there are already initiatives to communicate with respective policy communities and the public, and hence engage them. It is not certain if this is true beyond the highest ranks of the Public Service though. Administrative Officers are also to receive more exposure through secondments to government-linked companies, statutory boards, private-sector business concerns, etc. In addition, apart from understanding and utilising technocratic policy aids, bureaucrats should be trained in the areas of ethics, political philosophy, sociology, public organisational theory, communication skills, critical thinking, and argument construction. In this sense, it has been right that the Administrative Service is recruiting more Officers from the humanities or giving them scholarships to read these subjects. Technocrats are still always welcome (see Tables 3.4a and 3.4b). Advanced training (i.e., postgraduate studies in technocratic policy aids), is offered to potential high flyers of the Service as well.

Another factor is the internal socialisation through modes of formal interaction among Administrative Officers - the Service is a generalist Service where Officers are rotated among different portfolios so that eventually all begin to take on a global view of public policy in Singapore.

Table 3.4a Nature of First Degree of all Administrative Officers (1991)

Type of Degree	Frequency	Percentage	Valid Percentage
Specialist	55	30.1	30.4
Arts and Social Sciences	91	49.7	50.3
General Sciences	27	14.8	14.9
Combination: Specialist and Arts and Social Sciences	5	2.7	2.8
Not Applicable	3	1.6	1.7
Missing Values	2	1.1	Missing
Column Total	183	100	100

Number of Valid Observations: 181
Number of Missing Observations: 2

Table 3.4b Percentage of Specialist and Non-Specialist Personnel in the Administrative Service (1983)

Type	Subjects Include:	Percentage
Specialist	Engineering, System Analysis, Law, Psychology, etc.	45
Non-Specialist Arts and Social Sciences	History, English, Political Science, Geography, etc.	34
Non-Specialist General Sciences	Chemistry, Physics, Mathematics, Botany, Zoology	21

Sources: D. Tan, "The Singapore Civil Service: A Study of Specialist Administrators In Two Ministries." B.A. (Hons.) Academic Exercise, Dept. of Political Science, National University of Singapore, 1984, p. 36. Information is based on an interview with the Director of Personnel Development, Public Service Division, July 13, 1983.

This facilitates an integrated approach to policy-formulation. In some cases of non-programmed policy-making, review teams are drawn not along

Bureaucratic rationality in an evolving developmentalist state 67

formal organisational lines but according to the individuals' qualities and areas of competence. It makes for a bureaucracy that is likely to exercise 'systemic rationality', and higher up, more reflective in its operation. Tables 3.5 and 3.6 indicate that Administrative Officers would frequently organise themselves into highly organic, responsive administrative adhocracies when initiating and evaluating policies rather than being highly centralised and hierarchical.

Table 3.5 Intra-Ministry Interaction among Administrative Officers

	I	II	III	Row Total
Collective Discussion in Conference of all Relevant Officials	3 (10.7%)	4 (21.1%)	4 (16.7%)	11 [15.5%]
Discussions of Relevant Heads	6 (21.4%)	9 (47.4%)	5 (20.8%)	20 [28.2%]
Meeting of Ad hoc Committee of Officials w/Relevant Areas of Competence	10 (35.7%)	4 (21%)	11 (45.8%)	25 [35.2%]
Discussion & Eval. Independents, Decentralised Among Different Depts /Divs.	7 (25%)	1 (5.3%)	2 (8.3%)	10 [14.1%]
Others, Not Listed	1 (3.6%)	1 (5.3%)	1 (4.2%)	3 [4.2%]
Not Applicable	1 (3.6%)	0	1 (4.2%)	2 [2.8%]
Column Total	28 (100%)	19 (100%)	24 (100%)	71 [100%] (100%)

Number of Valid Observations: 71 of 75 (94.7%)
Number of Missing Observations: 4 (5.3%)
Note:
1. Rank of Officer
I = Administrative Assistant and Senior Administrative Assistant
II = Assistant Secretary and Principal Assistant Secretary
III = Deputy, Senior Deputy, Permanent Secretary
2. Percentages in round brackets are valid column percentages and those in square brackets are valid row percentages.

Table 3.6 Inter-Ministry Interaction among Administrative Officers

	I	II	III	Row Total
Collective Discussion in a Conference of all Officials and Ministers in all Relevant	2 (7.1%)	4 (19%)	3 (13%)	9 [12.5%]
Meeting of *Ad hoc* Committee of Officials Whose Competence Areas are Relevant[a]	17 (60.7%)	14 (66.7%)	14 (60.9%)	45 [62.5%]
Discussion and Evaluation Independent, Decentralised among Officers of Different Ministries Who Each Report to their Own Senior Officers Who Then Meet Among Themselves	4 (14.3%)	2 (9.5%)	3 (13%)	9 [12.5%]
Others, Not Listed	4 (14.3%)	1 (4.8%)	2 (8.7%)	7 9.7%]
Not Applicable	1 (3.6%)	0	1 (4.3%)	2 2.8%]
Column Total	28 (100%)	21 (100%)	23 (100%)	72 [100%] (100%)

Number of Valid Observations: 72 of 75 (96%)
Number of Missing Observations: 3 (4%)
Note:
a. This includes contributors from the private sector.
1. Rank of Officer
I = Administrative Assistant and Senior Administrative Assistant
II = Assistant Secretary and Principal Assistant Secretary
III = Deputy, Senior Deputy, Permanent Secretary
2. Percentages in round brackets are valid column percentages, and those in square brackets are valid row percentages

In intra-ministry consultation on policy proposals, the most common was to organise flexibly according to areas of competence or specialisation 'regardless of level' - listed by 35.2 percent of the respondents (Table 3.5). This trend towards a flexible organisation around areas of competence was even stronger in inter-ministry level consultation. 62.5 percent of all respondents chose this as their preferred descriptor (Table 3.6).

One other factor that influences the level of elite and value cohesion among Administrative Officers is related to the practical matter of attracting and retaining enough people to be in the Service. Due to the competition from the private sector for such personnel, and crusting at the highest ranks of the Service, where movement into the highest ranks is restricted because the incumbents are relatively young, a review in 1989 of Service strength indicated that it was haemorrhaging from among its middle ranks. This led to the introduction eventually of pay schemes for Administrative Officers that are pegged to private sector wages,[28] the devolution of the powers to promote and reward Officers to the heads of individual ministries, and the broadening of the recruitment pool to civil servants in other streams and sectors in the Public Service (dual career, 'Corps of Senior Administrators' scheme, etc.), and to those with some years in the private sector.[29]

Actively recruiting officers from the private sector, and at mid-career levels could potentially erode the elite and value cohesion of the Service although there is a lot of stated caution to recruit those who are younger and those found to have the appropriate mindset because the civil service has a different culture. Each decision carries a whole range of implications and is intertwined with many different issues.[30]

In a way, the adoption of private sector management techniques in the Public Service allows for this kind of movement but the role of socialisation of Administrative Officers becomes even more critical if the unique bureaucratic values and ethos are truly to be maintained. This would similarly apply to the move to second bureaucrats to, say, private sector companies in order for them to understand their policy environment better. These are good measures to bring into the bureaucracy a knowledge-base and experience, and an operational frame of mind, but as discussed, an entrepreneurial mindset or culture driven by monetary results rather than welfare results or public *service* will be incongruent in state bureaucracy. There should be a clear idea given to Officers on secondment of what they should bring back to their work in the Public Service after their stint outside.

Hence the Civil Service College - a mission focus that is centred on the civic goals of public service and a political leadership deeply committed to a civil service ethos with its distinctive values - is crucial for routinising the developmentalist spirit in the higher bureaucracy and the Public Service at large.

The key for the future is to temper the need for managerialism with its benefits of creativity and flexibility and accountability with an overarching orientation towards the civic virtues of the nation. This builds trust from citizens towards state agencies and helps the Singapore State build an even more durable basis for legitimacy that is beyond the personal authority of political leaders and (even its enviable) performance.[31]

Conclusion

To conclude, the basis of the Singapore developmental state was a mission-oriented bureaucracy that was organised like an efficient, machine bureaucracy. The top bureaucrats were certainly reputed to be independent thinkers but this was not an autonomous group. It adopted the overarching metavalue as defined by the PAP leadership of development for survival.

Progress itself, a more differentiated and discerning public, changes in patterns of international business and the global economy, the need to adopt market practices, and forms of accounting in the Service have led to a 'managerialist revolution'. Since salaries of top bureaucrats are benchmarked to those of top professionals in the private sector as a way to compete for the best talent for the Service, it was also an important corollary to specify performance targets to which remuneration and advancement could be linked. In this way, 'private sector pay' would be seen to be linked to private sector-type performance standards and appraisal. Accountability to political leaders and the public is maintained.

This would lead to a bureaucracy that is less oriented towards rules and structure, to one that is oriented towards process and performance. There are, however, areas of the Public Service where cost accounting and performance measures will be difficult to apply especially because public policy often requires a multi-agency network, and some public sector 'goods' are difficult to measure. The Service could suffer a displacement of goals, and managerialism and technocratic rationality may become the goal itself and dictate the bureaucratic mindset, thereby alienating the public from the agency.

To maintain the public's trust and to promote sensitive policy-making through differentiated policy framework and discretionary policy application, the Service will need to enhance its engagement with respective policy communities and the public as well as with the political leadership.

Maintaining the ideal of a public service is important, so that senior bureaucrats will weigh their actions not just by the productivity, efficiency or profitability of their offices and policies, but also by their social effectiveness. This necessarily means that they will have to strengthen the concept of the social goals of state action, and that they are adequately motivated by these goals and engaged with the constituents without being captured by particularistic interests. A 'performance-control' model of governance in the horizontal structures of the Public Service must be adequately balanced or linked to the 'normative-control' model of governance in its vertical superstructure. In Singapore, institutions like the Civil Service College are, therefore, the critical corollary to 'managerialism' because of its potential role in honing policy-making skills, in the socialisation of Administrative Officers, and in its potential for 'institutionalising' networks with at least to the key representatives of various policy communities which will together develop judgement, dedication and service-orientedness in the public sector leaders of Singapore.

Notes

[1] The term 'late development' refers to the industrialization in continental Europe in the late nineteenth century after the early industrialisers, notably England. In England, industrial change had been evolutionary, and spontaneous. The economies in Europe (and the United States too) lagged behind but leapfrogged by borrowing existing technology, and with the state providing the level of social coordination, stimulation of industry, innovation and capital that was necessary. The late development of East Asia has required yet heavier doses of government support and direction for the economies to adopt the more complex industrial systems and make available the necessary capital in order to overcome their conditions of underdevelopment in the post World War II era. See A. Gerschenkron, *Economic Backwardness in Historical Perspective* (Mass.: Harvard University Press, 1966) on late development; A. Amsden, *Asia's Next Giant. South Korea and Late Industrialization* (New York: Oxford University Press, 1989): 11-23, as applied to South Korea; and E. Vogel, *The Four Little Dragons: The Spread of Industrialization in East Asia* (Mass.: Harvard University Press, 1991) on the East Asian experience which includes Singapore.

[2] Chan Heng Chee, "Politics in an Administrative State: Where has the Politics Gone?", in C. M. Seah (ed), *Trends in Singapore* (Singapore: Singapore University Press, 1975): 51-52.

[3] This was first systematically articulated at the National Marketing Workshop organized by the Economic Development Board in 1989. There was a call by the top economic bureaucrats for the civil service to make a strategic shift into becoming a 'third wave' service that would facilitate Singapore's move into a knowledge-based, service-oriented, informational economy.

[4] S. G. Lim, "The Public Service," in *Singapore: The Year in Review 1995* (Singapore : Institute of Policy Studies and Times Academic Press, 1995): 36.

[5] S. G. Lim, "The New Public Administration: Global Challenges, Local Solutions," in *Ethos* (Singapore: Civil Service College, 1996): 8.

[6] *Ibid.*: 37.

[7] "Public sector budgeting: A high bar pushed higher," *The Straits Times* (Singapore), March 1, 1996.

[8] "PM wants Civil Service run more like private sector firm," *The Straits Times* (Singapore), August 6, 1991.

[9] H. Mintzberg, "Managing Government, Governing Management," *Harvard Business Review* 74, 3 (May-June 1996): 75-83, and B. G. Peters and D. J. Savoie, "Civil Service Reform: Misdiagnosing the Patient," *Public Administration Review* 54, 5 (Sept.-October 1994): 418-425.

[10] F. Parkin, *Public Management: Technocracy, Democracy, and Organisational Reform* (Aldershot, UK: Avebury, 1994).

[11] P. Evans, D. Rueschemeyer, and T. Skocpol, "On the Road Toward a More Adequate Understanding of the State," in P. Evans and D. Rueschemeyer (eds), *Bringing the State Back In* (Cambridge: Cambridge University Press, 1985): 44-77.

[12] Offe referred to these as three-tiered contradictory concept of rationality, decisive for administrative action under the conditions of advanced capitalist welfare state (see C. Offe, *Disorganized Capitalism* (Cambridge, Mass.: MIT Press, 1985): 300-316).

[13] *Ibid.*: 316.

[14] In 1996, there were two opposition members of Parliament since the 1991 General Elections. The PAP command over total number of votes has been on a gradual decline and stood at 61% from 63.2% in 1989. There were five marginal seats that were won by the PAP, i.e., that the PAP won these seats with a less than 5% lead.

[15] P. Evans, *Embedded Autonomy: States and Industrial Transformation* (Princeton, NJ : Princeton University Press, 1995): 58-59. See Chapter 3.

[16] H. Shafie, S. Rajagopal, and M. Z. Mohamed, "Notes on 'The Public Service' - New Strategic Dimensions for the 21st Century," *Public Administration and Development* 15, 2 (May 1995): 186-187.

[17] G. Peters and D. J. Savoie (1994): 418-425.

[18] *Ibid.*: 424.

[19] H. Mintzberg (1996): 79.

[20] Selection of people by values and attitudes, rather than qualifications, socializes them to ensure that the membership is dedicated to an integrated social system where guidance is by accepted principles rather than imposed plans, vision rather than targets, all members have a shared sense of responsibility, and finally performance is judged by experienced people, including recipients of the service. *Ibid.*: 81.

[21] H. Mintzberg (1989): 342-373.

[22] As a quick indicator, of the 1968 Cabinet, 6 out of 10 Ministers were from the private sector; in 1994, this figure was 3 out of 14; and of the 1996 Cabinet, the proportion was 4 out of 16.

[23] The Civil Service College was established in April 1993 as a 'staff college' for Administrative Officers. It brings under its roof basic training of new officers, development programmes for officers on 'threshold grades', and other public sector leadership training. It organizes public policy discussion groups and, more importantly, comprises the Scenario Planning Office. Scenario-based planning has been adopted as a strategic tool for creating a bureaucracy that anticipates and is a catalyst for change. It is said that the Public Service is currently running a wide scenario-planning exercise which will seek to identify the driving forces that will bring change in all aspects of governance and life in Singapore. The former Head of the Civil Service, Dr. Andrew Chew, describes its function (*Ethos*, First Quarter (Singapore: Civil Service College, 1994): 2):

> The College will provide an institutional focal point, a catalyst for new ideas and innovations and the meeting place for discussion on public administration and management. It should also imbue in the senior levels of management an acute sense of corporate purpose. It must nurture the shared values and facilitate its transmission from one generation of civil servants to the next.

[24] J. S. T. Quah, "Commentary," in *Singapore: The Year In Review. 1995* (Singapore: Institute of Policy Studies and Times Academic Press, 1996): 53-54.

[25] According to F. Parkin (1994): 91-92, these are:
- radical tolerance, that a public servant should strive to correct any institutional discrimination, say, based on race, religion, etc.; upholding civic liberties;
- civic courage, that is, speaking up for an unpopular cause will not be prohibitively costly as long as it is set in a rational dialogue based on widely accepted moral principles;
- solidarity, that is, empathy for the 'hard-done-by' to fight oppression from the ineffectual, because of personality or social situation;
- justice: civic courage and solidarity can be abused without this, methods must be fair and transparent;
- *Phronesis*, which is the exercise of good judgment for a plan to be accepted and legitimated, but once agreed upon, the decision should be based on rational judgment, not passion or prejudice; and

- rational communication, where channels for dialogue within the organization and with the community should be used and upheld.

[26] The Finance Minister, Dr. Richard Hu, in commending autonomous agencies (similar to the British model of the executive agency) stated that since information technology had taken the routine functions out of the hands of civil servants, this would free them to exercise greater autonomy, and be responsive to demands of a more discerning and demanding public. What was required, he added, was, therefore, "confident, mission-driven organizations" rather than "rules-driven organizations". Chua Lee Hoong, "Dr. Hu on changing role of civil servants: Managing expectations; less routine work," *The Straits Times* (Singapore), March 5, 1996.

[27] F. Parkin (1994): 123.

[28] Two benchmarks for the level of salaries of senior bureaucrats in Singapore :
For Officers of Staff Grade 1, the highest grade in the Civil Service, the pay is 60 percent of the average principal earned income of the top four individuals from each of six selected professions: bankers, accountants, engineers, lawyers, local manufacturing companies, and multinational companies.
For Superscale G, the lowest rung on the superscale ladder, the pay would be the average principal earned income of the 15th person aged 32 from the same six professions.
In the latest round of revisions, the monthly salary of the benchmark Staff Grade 1 Officer is $36,700 and that of the Superscale G officer is $12,400.

[29] Chua Mui Hoong, "Private sector execs sought for govt admin jobs," *The Straits Times* (Singapore), March 23, 1996.

[30] These people are likely to be in their early 30s, and will join the service at Deputy Director or Director levels and put on scales ranging from Principal Assistant Secretary (the fourth rung in the ladder of the Administrative Service) to superscale. *Ibid.* See also Chua Mui Hoong, "Opening door to private sector," *The Straits Times* (Singapore), March 2, 1996.

[31] C. O. Khong, "Singapore: Political Legitimacy Through Managing Conformity," in Muthiah Alagappa (ed), *Political Legitimacy in Southeast Asia: The Quest for Moral Authority* (Stanford, CA: Stanford University Press, 1995): 135.

4 Public Service Leadership and Political Adaptation of the Hong Kong Civil Servants

Jermain T. M. Lam

Introduction and Context

Leadership is the "ability" of the leaders to make others do what they presumably would not have done otherwise and to mobilize human resources in pursuit of specific goals.[1] Leadership can also be perceived as the "process" by which leaders induce followers to act for certain goals that represent the values and the motivations of both leaders and followers.[2] During the process of the decolonialisation and reunification with China in 1997, the colonial public service in Hong Kong has been facing rapid political changes: the intrusion of the Chinese government into the governing processes, the emergence of an alienated political culture, the introduction of elections into the Legislative Council, and the rise of political parties. These changes have seriously undermined the leadership of the colonial public service.

Adaptation of the public service to changes is absolutely essential to maintain a responsive administration and to provide leadership for the community. This applies to both developed and developing societies for the goal of public administration is to formulate effective policies and to render efficient implementation of policies.[3] As the political, economic, and social environments are constantly changing, new demands and interests are continuously emerging from the society. The public service needs to adapt to the changes in the open environment so that new problems can be resolved and old problems can be controlled. Easton puts forward the theory of system analysis to examine how an open system maintains stability and equilibrium and to account for a system's instability, disruption, and breakdown.[4] The survival capacity of a system, according to Easton, depends on its adaptability. In the words of Deutsch, the adaptive ability of any decision-making system to invent and to carry out fundamentally new policies to meet new conditions is related to its ability to combine items of information into new patterns in response to a repeated external stimulus.[5] Deutsch regards the growth of adaptability, rather than power, as the most important dimension of the growth of a political system. The task of public administration is, therefore, to accelerate needed innovation, to adjust its position with respect to the environment, and to achieve the changing goals of the society.

Hong Kong is a good case study to examine the adaptability of the civil servants in the political transition from a British colony to a Special Administrative Region (SAR) under Chinese sovereignty in 1997. The colonial administration is the real governing body of the government, with no institutional checking by other political actors.[6] Members of the elite are co-opted into the colonial administration as appointed members of the Executive and Legislative Councils as well as various advisory committees to serve, rather than to oppose, the bureaucratic regime. The society is depoliticised in the sense that politics is absorbed by administration.[7] Decisions are made by administrators rather than elected politicians and the decision-making process is a sort of administrative consultation rather than party politics. The senior civil servants working for the policy branches and executive departments are not only administrators who implement policies but are also decision-makers who control the functions of resource allocation. They dominate the decision-making process and play an active role in initiating and drafting policy proposals. As a result, political power has been concentrated in the hands of civil servants who constitute the dominant actors and are almost immune from institutional checking by other political actors.[8]

Under such an executive-led and centralized system, Hong Kong civil servants exhibit a distinctive set of administrative behavior. For instance, Lau generalizes several behavioral tendencies of the Hong Kong civil servants as "complacency, defensiveness, formalism and legalism, inflexibility, technicalism, and personalism".[9] Lui observes that the civil servants in Hong Kong are typically "introverted, technocratic, conservative, apolitical, and amoral".[10] Lui further points out a set of bureaucratic values prevailing among Hong Kong civil servants. First, ordinary citizens are usually suboptimised and short sighted. They need to be guided into accepting what is genuinely in their best interests. Second, the power relationship between the bureaucracy and the public should be founded on paternalistic and hierarchical assumptions based on the superior knowledge possessed by the bureaucracy. Third, administrative decisions should be made by civil servants. Citizens' participation in the administrative process should be kept to a minimum. Fourth, civil servants should only concern themselves with their official duties. It is both undesirable and unnecessary for the civil servants to become engaged in public matters which may tarnish their image of impartiality. Fifth, administrative organizations should remain stable as far as possible. Changes should only be made when necessary and only to the extent that a crisis can be averted. The bureaucracy should adopt a reactive attitude towards external pressures for organizational changes. Sixth, a civil servant owes his loyalty to his superiors who should be the sole judges of his conduct and performance. Civil service morality is, therefore, a matter of administrative evaluation confined within the hierarchy. As a result of this set of bureaucratic values and behavior, Hong Kong civil servants have been responsible only to their superiors within the administrative hierarchy, and not to political actors outside the administration. Administrative accountability, rather than political accountability, is the dominant value within the civil service. This colonial character of the civil service is congruent with the static political environment in Hong Kong in the last three decades.

Yet the Hong Kong civil servants have been challenged by various political changes outside the administrative hierarchy since 1991. The introduction of direct elections into the Legislative Council has created a more representative legislature which has demonstrated its will to exert influence on the administration as far as possible. The Legislative Council has been moving away from being a passive to an active chamber of discussion, from a dependent to a more independent legislature, and from an obedient to a critical partner of the executive. The development of representative government has also led to the emergence of a number of political organizations and politicians. As channels and opportunities are open for accessing political power, political parties are formed to consolidate support and politicians are recruited to gain political power. The elected politicians, based on their popular mandate, are claiming their right to make decisions for the Hong Kong government. In addition, the issue of 1997 has created a series of confidence crises among the general citizens towards the British-Hong Kong and Chinese governments. The general citizens have become more conscious of whether their interests are being sacrificed by their existing and future sovereign masters, hence articulating more demands on the administration. Furthermore, China has indicated its intention to participate more in the internal affairs of Hong Kong in the last phase of the political transition. China has regarded itself as the vanguard of the people of Hong Kong, thus exercising tremendous influence on major policies going beyond 1997.

As a result, senior civil servants of Hong Kong are facing political pressure exerted from various sources during the transfer of sovereignty from Britain to China. They are no longer the only decision-makers immune from monitoring by other political actors. Although the senior civil servants of Hong Kong still hold the governing power, they are now encountering the scrutiny of the Legislative Council, the challenges from political parties and politicians, the public demand for more public participation, and the intrusion of China into the decision-making process. Such political circumstances will certainly affect the political leadership of senior civil servants. It also raises the question of how the civil servants are adapting to the political changes during the transition to 1997 and beyond. The senior civil servants' orientations to political adjustments are particularly important to a stable and smooth political transition.

Under this political context, the aim of this chapter is to examine the leadership dilemmas and the adaptability of the public service in Hong Kong during the political transition.

Political Adaptation: Framework of Analysis

With respect to the concept of political adaptation, Christopher Hood offers an analytical framework to examine how the public service handles change. In Hood's words, adaptation is defined as "the ability to spot material changes in circumstances, and the capacity and disposition to respond appropriately to those changes."[11] Thus adaptation comprises three essential elements: (1) the capacity to recognize change; (2) the capacity to respond; and (3) the disposition to respond. The capacity to recognize change is important for failure to do so may result in serious consequences. If the public service is not able to recognize actual changes in the environment, the public service is unlikely to adapt to the new environment by providing new services or modifying the existing policies. The incongruence between the new demands and the old policies would grow large, resulting in the deterioration of problems or the retardation of development. Adaptation is commonly hampered by failure to distinguish material changes from random disturbances, to identify the turning point in a cycle, to recognize the speed at which change is occurring, and to allow for reactive or strategic change.[12]

The capacity to respond refers to "the ability in some way to introduce variations into behaviour or structure". Hood (1986) identifies four possible modes of adaptation:

- <u>Piecemeal adjustment</u> is referred to as "a slight modification of the existing rules and practices to accommodate the new development" and requiring minimal demands on engineering capacity and administration disruption. It has the advantages of low cost, minimum risk, and convenience.
- <u>Recombination</u> denotes "the making of minor modifications to each of a set of well-established elements, rules, routines or operations, so that then added together, a completely different effect is produced or a quite different purpose served." This approach incorporates piecemeal adjustment and is mainly a repackaging exercise of producing a new service using similar but modified input materials. It demands a higher administrative engineering capacity, yet the potential disruption to existing operations remains low.
- <u>Imitation</u> is "the copying of a basic design which has shown itself to be workable elsewhere." This approach requires a relatively low administrative engineering capacity since a formula is just copied and put into operation from one context to another. However, this may involve the abolishment of the old system and the installation of the new system, hence leading to a higher degree of potential disruption to existing operations.
- <u>Prototyping</u> is "the creation of an original design all at once as a self-contained and purpose-built unit." It does not involve significant copying or modification to an existing system. This adaptive approach makes heavy demands on administrative engineering capacity since tremendous effort and energy is required to invent and to test a new system through trial and error. It also causes immense disruption to the existing system as the old system would be totally replaced and uprooted by the new system.

Piecemeal adjustment and imitation involve a lower cost of adaptation in terms of the engineering knowledge and skill required to bring out a change. In terms of disruption to existing operations in replacing some current system by an alternative one, piecemeal adjustment and recombination involve a lower cost of adaptation. These four modes of adaptation are summarized in Table 4.1.

Disposition to respond is referred to as the desire or motivation to alter behaviour or structure in accordance with the changes. The possession of the ability to recognize change and the engineering capacity to change is not sufficient to bring out a successful adaptation. The will and incentive of the civil service to change constitutes the third element of administrative adaptation. Officials must be motivated to alter their habit to adapt to the new rules and organizational structures. They can be motivated by the internalization of the new values, material rewards, or punishment. Yet the task of increasing the motivation of the civil service to change could be difficult, given the conservative nature of the bureaucracy which is trained to follow complex sets of rules and procedures. The inert civil service may resist change as it would disturb its routine behaviour and operations. Vested interest is another obstacle to the introduction of change within the civil service.

Table 4.1   Modes of Adaptation to Changes

		Potential Disruption to Existing Operations	
		Low	High
Engineering Capacity	Low	Piecemeal Adjustment	Imitation
	High	Recombination	Prototyping

Source: C. Hood, *Administrative Analysis* (Sussex: Wheatsheaf Books, 1986).

Civil servants may reject new change as it would decrease their power or responsibility and would affect the prospect of their careers. In short, the ability to recognize change, the capacity to respond, and the disposition to respond constitute the three essential elements of the adaptation of civil servants. The political adaptation of the Hong Kong civil servants in this study is examined according to this analytical framework and the following research design.

Research Design

In this study, both quantitative and qualitative analyses are conducted to obtain and to compare data on the attitude of senior civil servants towards political adaptation. Information was collected through: (1) sending structured questionnaires to Administrative Officers; and (2) discussing with Administrative Officers their attitude towards political changes during the transition to 1997. The study was carried out in four stages beginning 1993. In stage one, in-depth interviews were conducted. 25 Administrative Officers of different grades were interviewed. The interviews focused on the orientations of the civil servants towards the dynamic changes of the political system. The interviews served the following purposes: (1) to provide preliminary thoughts on the structured questionnaire; and (2) to compare and to supplement the data obtained from the mailed survey.

In stage two, a questionnaire for the mailed survey was designed and tested. The framework of questions was drafted based on Hood's theoretical framework of adaptation. The answers from respondents in the in-depth interviews served as important reference to moderate the questionnaire of the mailed survey. A subsequent step was to test the suitability of the questionnaire by sending the draft questionnaire to those interviewed in the in-depth interviews for trial and comments. The draft questionnaire was then revised and finalized.

In stage three, questionnaires with return envelopes were sent to all Administrative Officers. Arrangement was made with the Civil Service Branch for accessing to information of the Administrative Officers. There were 456 Administrative Officers of different grades as of July 1992. Details of the breakdown of the target population are as follows:

Table 4.2   Structure and Establishment of Administrative Officers

Administrative Officer Grade	Number of Officers
Secretaries	13
Staff Grade A	15
Staff Grade B	125
Staff Grade B	32
Staff Grade C	141
Senior Administrative Officers	88
Administrative Officers	142
Total	456

Source: Staff List 1992, *Hong Kong Government* (Hong Kong: Government Printer, 1992).

A total of 456 structured questionnaires were sent to the Administrative Officers of various grades in June 1993. As 52 Administrative Officers were on leave or overseas, the actual number of questionnaires sent were 402. A total of 142 responses were received with a response rate of 35 percent. As far as the sensitive nature of the questions and the tense Sino-British relation over Hong Kong is concerned, this rate of return can be regarded as reasonable and acceptable. Most of the respondents (78.5 percent) were above thirty years old; 34.1 percent came from the age group of 30-39; 34.8 percent came from the age group of 40-49, and 9.6 percent came from the age group of 50-59. Males occupied a significant proportion (70.2 percent) of the respondents. An absolute majority of the respondents (71.5 percent) were married with children. Another observation was that most (68.2 percent) of the respondents were Chinese in ethnic origin while the rest were Europeans and Indians. In summary, a majority of the respondents were Chinese, middle-aged, male, and married.

In stage four, data was collected and analyzed. The analysis of the orientations of the Administrative Officers of Hong Kong government towards political changes would shed light on the prospect of the development of representative government and on the relationship between Hong Kong and China after 1997. Administrative Officers are the top officials of the Hong Kong government, occupying only 0.03 percent of the total size of the public service. They are the real policy makers of the government, making important decisions on two leadership dilemmas: (1) democracy vis-à-vis convergence; and (2) autonomy vis-à-vis dependence. Their orientations towards the political changes and challenges would be affecting the adaptation of the administration during the transition from a colony to a Special Administrative Region (SAR).

The Leadership Dilemmas of the Hong Kong Public Service

On the dilemma of "democracy" and "convergence", the Hong Kong public service has to decide which value is to be adopted or how to draw a balance between the two conflicting values. Democracy is referred to as the establishment of an open and liberal government with maximum public participation and accountability. Convergence is referred as to the compatibility of the government structure and operation before 1997 with the one confined in the *Basic Law* (the post-1997 SAR constitution). Political pressures are applied on the Hong Kong government from different actors. The scenario of Hong Kong citizens towards the governmental system in the transition is that the SAR government would be a more democratic and representative system so as to protect citizens' interests, liberty and freedom under China's sovereignty. Hong Kong citizens perceive that democracy does not override the provisions of the *Basic Law*, hence it is convergent with the political arrangements after 1997. These views are reflected in their responses to the Constitutional Package proposed by Governor Patten in 1992. Various surveys show that Hong Kong citizens are generally supportive of the proposed political reforms.[13] Results of the surveys send several messages: (1) democracy is thought by Hong Kong citizens to be compatible with convergence; (2) Hong Kong citizens are oriented towards a more democratic and representative government after 1997; and (3) convergence with the *Basic Law* means convergence with the interests of Hong Kong citizens rather than what China wants.

Liberal political groups with democratic orientations share the same opinions with the Hong Kong citizens and lend support to Patten's political reforms. The Democratic Party, for instance, declares its support to the Constitutional Package. The rationale to support the democratic reforms is explained by the Democratic Party as three-fold:[14]

- First, the democrats conceive democratic development as essential to further economic growth in Hong Kong. A fair and open democratic system is thought to be able to balance and to protect the interests of different sectors.
- Second, the democrats believe that Hong Kong citizens aspire for democracy. With a high political and social consciousness, Hong Kong citizens are thought to be unwilling to be controlled by privileged elites.
- Third, the democrats insist that democratization is not aimed at making Hong Kong either an independent state or a pro-British puppet. Democratization in Hong Kong instead is to actualize "Hong Kong people ruling Hong Kong" on the one hand and to achieve a genuine "high degree of autonomy" on the other. Other major political groups of the liberal faction, like the Hong Kong Democratic Foundation and the Association for Democracy and People's Livelihood, have also endorsed the Constitutional Package in the Legislative Council motion debate on the political development of Hong Kong.

The attitudes of the Chinese government and the conservative political groups towards democratization as proposed in the Constitutional Package have been explicitly negative. The Chinese government criticizes that the

Constitutional Package is too radical to promote democracy which should instead be one that advances step by step in an orderly way and is conducive to maintaining the long term stability and prosperity.[15] China has consistently made it clear that stable and peaceful transition in Hong Kong means that there should be no substantial changes to the existing governmental system. In achieving a stable and peaceful transition, China thinks that the governmental system in Hong Kong before 1997 should converge with the system in the *Basic Law*. Thus convergence to China means no radical changes to the existing governmental system; radical political reforms will, however, produce a system that cannot converge with the *Basic Law* and, therefore, cannot continue after 1997. In other words, any major change to the political structure of Hong Kong that would weaken the executive-led administration during the transition period would contradict the *Basic Law*.

This line of thinking is well supported by the conservative and pro-China groups. Strong resistance to the Constitutional Package comes from the business background Liberal Party and the pro-China Democratic Alliance for Betterment of Hong Kong which voted against the Constitutional Package in the Legislative Council motion debate. Both political groups believe that democratization in Hong Kong should be mild and that convergence with the Chinese interpretation of the *Basic Law* should be the most important consideration.[16] They are of the opinion that China will dismantle the political system in 1997 if the Hong Kong government insists on implementing the proposed political reforms. In essence, the public service faces a difficult choice between two evils: democracy that will be crushed by China, or convergence with the Chinese as it wishes which means no democracy.

Another related dilemma is that of between autonomy and dependence. The government of Hong Kong is trapped in a dilemma of whether to follow China's views as a dependent government or to act independently as an autonomous government. Facing the issue of confidence crisis, the public service is left with an option of building up an image of a conscientious government devoted to serve the people wholeheartedly. In achieving this option, the government is encountering an arduous task of convincing the public that Hong Kong's interests are not being sold out to China. China has been expressing her views on Hong Kong's internal affairs and demanding for participation in the decision-making processes, like on the issues of the 1995 Legislative Council elections and the construction of the new Chap Lap Kok Airport. Thus the Hong Kong public service is struggling for autonomy against China's pressure to maintain its leadership to govern in the transition period.

On the one hand, to make concessions to China's views is to admit that China has recognized decision-making power over Hong Kong in the transition period. Thus the public service will have to consult and get approval from China on major policy issues in Hong Kong. The concessions will run a risk of surrendering part of or the whole autonomy after 1997. As such, Hong Kong will then be a dependent territory co-ruled by both the SAR and the Chinese governments. Since the citizens share the concern that China would endanger the interests of Hong Kong before and after the transfer of sovereignty, concessions to Chinese demands may further decrease the confidence of the public on the government for protecting liberties and interests of the Hong Kong citizens. This might deepen the degree of alienation of the citizens.

On the other hand, to act independently of Chinese' demands as an autonomous government may result in negative Chinese responses to the government or even in further intervention of Hong Kong's internal affairs after 1997. The debate between the Chinese and Hong Kong governments on Governor Chris Patten's political reforms proposal is a case in point. China has criticized the Governor's proposal as contradictory to the spirit of the *Basic Law*. China has decided that a new governmental system according to her own interpretation of the *Basic Law* will be implemented in Hong Kong after 1997 to replace the political structures established under Patten's Constitutional Package. Thus the Hong Kong public service has to decide who it is to please: the people of Hong Kong, the Chinese leaders, or both. To please the people of Hong Kong will alienate the Chinese leaders, while to please the Chinese leaders will alienate the people of Hong Kong in return. The Hong Kong public service has to strike a right balance between being an autonomous and a dependent government, in order to get consent and support from both the people of Hong Kong and China.

The Political Adaptation of the Civil Servants

The respondents in the study are a group of experienced Administrative Officers whose ability to recognize change, capacity to change, and disposition to change bear significant impact on the adaptation of the Hong Kong public service. The orientations of the respondents towards change are analyzed as follows.

Capacity to Recognize Change

Since 1980 Hong Kong has been politicized by the question on the future of Hong Kong and on the development of representative government. Conflicting views are expressed about the pace of democratization and the contents of political reforms to be introduced in Hong Kong. The theme of representative government has been initiated by the Hong Kong government since 1984 in the White Paper on "The Further Development of Representative Government in Hong Kong." Consequently, indirectly elected members from selected functional constituencies have been introduced into the Legislative Council which was previously a fully appointed body before 1985. Another dramatic development of representative government is the introduction of directly elected members into the Legislative Council in 1991 as an addition to the indirectly elected and appointed members. The Constitutional Package drafted by Governor Patten in 1992 is another major step that changes the nature of the political system in Hong Kong. The Package proposes to abolish all the appointed membership in the three-tier representative bodies, to expand the electoral franchise in functional constituencies by five hundred times, and to separate the membership and power of the Executive and Legislative Councils. As a result of these political changes, the Legislative Council, political parties, politicians, and the general citizens take up different roles and positions. How much the Administrative Officers have recognized these changes would indicate the political adaptability of the public service in the political transition.

An essential principle that regulates the relationship between the executive and the legislature in liberal democratic governments is that the executive should be held accountable to the legislature and citizens. In other words, the executive officials have to follow the orders and are subject to the control of elected political masters. With respect to the changing relationship between the Hong Kong civil service and the elected Legislative Council, the Administrative Officers tend to recognize political accountability as the important principle practiced in the Hong Kong government. For instance, 57.2 percent and 15.7 percent of the respondents respectively thought that the Hong Kong government should be accountable to the Legislative Council to a "great extent" and "very great extent". Only 20.0 percent of the respondents answered "some extent", 5.7 percent thought "limited extent", and 0.7 percent said "very limited extent". The respondents were further asked to assess how much political accountability of Hong Kong government to the Legislative Council was practiced. According to the results, the Administrative Officers seem to recognize that political accountability is introduced and practiced in the government. For instance, 54.6 percent and 10.6 percent of the respondents respectively replied that the Hong Kong government was accountable to the Legislative Council to a "great extent" and "very great extent". Only 28.4 percent and 5.0 percent of the respondents respectively admitted "some extent" and "limited extent".

The changing status and influence of the Legislative Council, the study shows, is also recognized by the Administrative Officers. Most respondents noted that the influence of the Legislative Council increased after directly elected members had joined the sixty-member legislature since 1991. For instance, 38.6 percent, 18.6 percent, and 35.7 percent of the respondents respectively thought that the introduction of elected members into the Legislative Council increased the status of the legislature to a "great extent", "very great extent", and "some extent". Nevertheless, the Administrative Officers express reservation on the degree of representation of the Legislative Council. They have noted the increasing status of the legislature, but they do not recognize the representativeness of the Legislative Council. In spite of the increasing influence of the legislature, only 5.6 percent of the respondents thought that the Legislative Council in the 1991-1995 session was "very representative" of the interests of Hong Kong people. 58.5 percent and 31.7 percent of the respondents respectively considered that the Legislative Council was "partly" and "not quite" representative. As such, the Legislative Council is considered by most Administrative Officers as not truly representative, hence does not genuinely reflect public opinion. This finding implies that the Administrative Officers still regard themselves, rather than the Legislative Council, as the vanguard of public interest.

As far as the general public is concerned, the study also finds that the new value of public accountability to citizens is widely accepted by the Administrative Officers. For instance, 50.3 percent and 35.5 percent of the respondents respectively thought that Hong Kong government should be accountable to the general citizens to "great extent" and "very great extent". Moreover, 44.0 percent and 18.4 percent of the respondents respectively believed that Hong Kong government was accountable to the general citizens to a "great extent" and "very great extent". These data suggest that the civil service has recognized the concept of public accountability and the changing relationship between government and citizens. Nevertheless, the Administrative Officers do not reckon that there is a widespread demand for democracy among the general public in Hong Kong. The study shows that only 4.3 percent and 25.0 percent of the respondents respectively thought that the general citizens were aspiring for a more democratic government to a "very great extent" and "great extent". In contrast, a significant proportion

(52.9 percent) of the respondents thought that the general citizens were aspiring for a more democratic government only to "some extent". This conservative perception would certainly affect their perception towards the involvement of general citizens in the policy-making process.

With reference to the policy-making process, the emergence of political parties and elected politicians adds a new page to the politics in Hong Kong. They change and transform the model of consensual politics to adversarial and confrontational politics. Differences and opposition raised by political parties and politicians against the administration have become the normal business of the day. The study shows that the Administrative Officers of Hong Kong government recognize the changing style of decision-making and they accept the existence of different views in the society. For instance, 44.0 percent and 36.2 percent of the respondents respectively thought that Hong Kong government respected and tolerated different opinions expressed by various political parties and politicians to a "great extent" and "very great extent". It seems that the top civil service has recognized the existence of divergent interests and the role of political parties and politicians in interest aggregation and articulation.

Aside from recognizing the involvement of political parties and politicians in the decision-making process, the Administrative Officers also recognize China as the newcomer to the political arena of Hong Kong. Although the 1984 Sino-British Joint Declaration has decided that Hong Kong would be a SAR with a high degree of autonomy, China is the future sovereign master of Hong Kong to interpret what public policies and interest will conform to the *Basic Law*. China has explicitly declared that any major policy that will extend beyond 1997 will need the approval of the Chinese government. For instance, China has reiterated that the Legislative Council will be dissolved in 1997 and a provisional legislature will be established for the first SAR government. China further declares that contracts, leases and agreements, unless signed and ratified by the Chinese side, will be invalid after 1997. These two statements from China imply that any major policies on Hong Kong have to be endorsed by the Chinese government. As such, the Administrative Officers will be accountable to the Chinese government which will then become the de facto ruler of Hong Kong both before and after 1997. In fact, 39.1 percent, 21.1 percent, and 10.9 percent of the respondents admitted that the authority of Hong Kong government has been damaged by China's involvement in Hong Kong's internal policy decisions. Perhaps China is the most difficult player among the political actors for the Administrative Officers to deal with as it is much more powerful than the other actors in terms of political, economic, and military resources. As the future sovereign power of Hong Kong, China acts as the overseeing power in preparation for the transfer of sovereignty and political power. The Preparatory Committee established by the Chinese National People's Congress has been working to devise a political blueprint and to appoint the first Chief Executive of the SAR government. Recognizing the increasing importance of China, the Administrator Officers have held regular meetings with the senior Beijing officials to exchange views and to establish a working relationship.

In conclusion, the study shows that the Administrative Officers have recognized the major changes and development in the political system during the transition. In order to adapt to the new political environment, the civil service needs to take certain actions to respond to these changes. The responses of the civil service to the changes would be reflected in the approach taken by the Administrative Officers. The success of political adaptation will partly depend on whether the civil service adopts an appropriate approach towards the changes.

Capacity to Respond

Recognizing these changes, the Administrative Officers make various adjustments for adaptation. With respect to the changes to the composition and the role of the Legislative Council, the Administrative Officers have oriented themselves to accept a more independent legislature. The study found that most of the Administrative Officers supported the reform to strengthen the independence of the Legislative Council by separating the membership of the Executive and Legislative Councils as proposed by Governor Patten in his 1992 Constitutional Package. For instance, 45.0 percent and 16.4 percent of the respondents respectively thought that the separation of executive and legislative branches of Hong Kong government was beneficial to a "great extent" and "very great extent". The Administrative Officers also perceived that the fully elected Legislative Council after 1997 would play a legitimizing role in the future political system. For instance, 34.5 percent, 20.2 percent, and 18.7 percent of the respondents respectively believed that the legitimacy of Hong Kong government would be enhanced by a fully elected Legislative Council after 1997 to "some extent", "great extent", and "very great extent". This implies that the Administrative Officers accept a more independent and representative legislature in the decision-making system.

Nevertheless, the Administrative Officers express a high degree of reservation with respect to the changing role of the Legislative Council in the decision-making processes. For instance, only 2.1 percent and 29.8 percent of the respondents respectively thought that the Legislative Council should play a dominant role in the policy-making process to a "very great extent" and "great extent". In contrast, 44.0 percent and 19.9 percent of the respondents respectively thought the Legislative Council should only play a decision-making role to "some extent" and "a limited extent". In fact, most (52.8 percent) of the respondents admitted that the Legislative Council was only playing a policy-making role "to some extent" and 14.3 percent of the respondents even agreed that the Legislative Council was only playing a "limited role". These findings indicate that the Administrative Officers feel that the executive should continue to dominate the policy-making process. This perception is in line with the Administrative Officers' satisfaction of the current practice of limited accountability.

Given the existing limited political powers of citizens (for instance, general citizens cannot elect a government on the basis of direct election and universal suffrage) and the restricted monitoring power of the Legislative Council (for instance, the Legislative Council cannot increase the expenditure requested by the government in approving budget; it can only advise the government to avoid wastage in resources but cannot instruct officials to follow its suggestions; it cannot compel the executive to adopt a new policy which proposed by a member of the legislature will have the effect of imposing a charge on the government revenue), the Administrative Officers tend to favour the existing system of limited accountability. Most of the Administrative Officers in the in-depth interviews defined the meaning of political accountability as "creative dialogue among the administration, the Legislative Council, and the general citizens." Thus what political accountability means to the Administrative Officers of Hong Kong government is to be able to explain, to consult, and to seek advice rather than to follow the decisions of, and be controlled by, the Legislative Council and the general citizens.

Similarly, the Administrative Officers are highly against the idea of getting endorsement from China before any policy is examined by the SAR Legislative Council. For instance, 65.4 percent and 16.2 percent of the respondents respectively disagreed "totally" and "partially" with the statement that "policies be endorsed by the Chinese government before being approved by the SAR Legislative Council." This suggests that the Administrative Officers do not want to give up their decision-making power to the Chinese government. They are willing to consult and to seek the advice of the Chinese government, but they are not prepared to be totally subordinate to the Chinese counterpart. Instead, the Administrative Officers favour maintaining a regular dialogue with the Chinese government. For instance, 58.2 percent and 29.9

percent of the respondents respectively agreed "totally" and "partially" that the SAR government should regularly report the progress of major policy decisions to the Chinese government. Furthermore, 41.0 percent and 38.1 percent of the respondents respectively agreed "totally" and "partially" that the SAR government should regularly explain its policy decisions to the Chinese government.

On the whole, the Administrative Officers are making piecemeal adjustments as a form of adaptation to the new political environment. Amidst the political changes, the Administrative Officers want to keep the existing executive dominant relationship with the Legislative Council, and they prefer to maintain the same kind of trustee relationship with China as with Britain. The actions taken by the Administrative Officers are just piecemeal changes without altering the basic philosophy of an administrative state with the executive leading the Legislature, the citizens, and elected politicians. The administration would also like to treat China as the same as Britain, seeking to maintain a de facto autonomy. These adaptive strategies do not involve a complete re-engineering, copying of a new model, or recombining changes in every administrative aspect. Governor Patten's threat to veto a bill passed by the Legislative Council that is not regarded as being in the public interest is another indication that the administration is determined to keep the executive-led status quo.[17]

Disposition to Change

As the Administrative Officers adopt a piecemeal approach in response to the changes during the political transition, the disposition to change could be reflected by the Administrative Officers' orientations towards government and politics. In liberal democratic states, the idea of popular sovereignty is generally accepted. Citizens are regarded as the masters of society who delegate their authority to elected politicians to govern. Government officials are accountable to the elected politicians who, in turn, are responsible to the general citizens. Thus government officials are accountable to the general citizens through elected politicians. However, in Hong Kong, the government is not elected by the general citizens but governed by the Administrative Officers. Thus Administrative Officers are structurally not accountable to the general citizens.

In line with this structural relationship, the Administrative Officers express reservations towards the involvement of general citizens in making policies. For instance, a significant proportion (46.4 percent) of the respondents thought that Hong Kong government should involve the general citizens in the policy-making process only to "some extent". Only 3.6 percent of the respondents thought that Hong Kong government should involve the general citizens in the policy-making processes to a "very great extent". This result was in sharp contrast to the previous finding that 35.5 percent of the respondents thought Hong Kong government should be accountable to the general citizens to a "very great extent". Furthermore, the Administrative Officers admitted that at present the general citizens were not very much involved in the policy-making process. For instance, only 22.7 percent of the respondents replied that Hong Kong government involved the general citizens in the policy-making processes to a "great extent", while a significant number (50.4 percent) of the respondents admitted that Hong Kong government involved the general citizens in the policy-making processes only to "some extent".

The orientations of the Administrative Officers towards the role of citizens in the decision-making processes is further reflected in their perception of their relationship with the general citizens. An absolute majority (68.5 percent) of the respondents considered the citizens as their "clients", while only 4.6 percent of the respondents considered the citizens as their "masters". This reflects that the Administrative Officers believe they must serve the citizens, but not necessarily do what the citizens say or want. Citizens are just treated as clients, rather than as masters of the society. Thus the Administrative Officers regard themselves as the producers of public goods for citizens rather than as the servants of citizens. The implication is that the Administrative Officers share the moral responsibility to govern in accordance with the public interest as far as possible, but they are the persons who determine what that public interest is. Though the Administrative Officers recognize public accountability, they still hold the belief that the authority to govern should be in their hands. Thus the administration does not want to introduce too many changes that allow for more citizen participation.

In liberal democratic states, governments allow and tolerate different opinions expressed by various political parties and organizations since respect of differences is the foundation of liberal democracy. However, the study found that the Administrative Officers did not value the operation of party politics under the current system in Hong Kong. For instance, 20.9 percent and 48.2 percent of the respondents respectively agreed "totally" and "partially" with the statement that "party politics was detrimental to the efficient running of the government machinery in Hong Kong." This means that the Administrative Officers exhibit some reservations towards the emergence of political parties and political leaders, and their involvement in the decision-making process. Since the introduction of direct and indirect elections into the Legislative Council in 1985, political parties and leaders have dominated the legislature. Two-thirds of the members of the Legislative Council have affiliations with various political parties and organizations. Political parties such as the Democratic Party and leaders like Allen Lee of the Liberal Party have been active and critical in examining government policies. The decisions and proposals of the executive are very often challenged by these political parties and leaders. Thus the Legislative Council is now full of debates and questions. As such, the Legislative Council is no longer as efficient and orderly as in the past. Moreover, policies and issues have been politicized by political parties and leaders, thus a political element in addition to technical considerations is brought into the decision-making process. These changes have presented a new environment in which Administrative Officers must operate. The findings of the study indicate that the Administrative Officers do not favour the existing role of political parties and politicians in the governmental machinery. Though elections provide the legitimacy basis for political parties and leaders to examine government policies and to hold the government accountable, the Administrative Officers exhibit reservations towards the functioning and role of political parties and leaders. Resistance exists among the Administrative Officers towards the competition for power from political parties.

The practice of checks and balances between the executive and legislature has not been fully accepted by the Administrative Officers in Hong Kong. The study finds that the belief of the Administrative Officers in executive dominance has not been fundamentally shaken by the changing political environment in Hong Kong. As such, the Administrative Officers do not expect a powerful legislature to check and balance executive power. This mentality is reflected in the responses to the question "should senior civil servants of Hong Kong government continue to dominate the decision-making process after 1997?" 42.9 percent and 13.0 percent of the respondents respectively replied that senior civil servants should continue to dominate the decision-making processes to a "great extent" and "very great extent", though 32.6 percent of the respondents thought this should be so to "some extent". This implies that the majority of Administrative Officers have not fully accepted the idea of becoming neutral administrators and of transferring the decision-making power to political parties and leaders, although they accept a more independent legislature and tolerate political opposition.

With regard to the motivation to maintain Hong Kong as a SAR with a high degree of autonomy, the study found that the Administrative Officers exhibited a strong will to achieve a highly autonomous government. For instance, 36.9 percent and 27.7 percent of the respondents respectively thought that Hong Kong civil servants would strive to maintain a high degree of autonomy with respect to China before and after 1997 to a "great extent" and "very great extent". The in-depth interviews indicated that what the Administrative Officers preferred about the relationship between Hong Kong and China after 1997 was to maintain the same kind of relationship as with the British government, that is, little Chinese intervention and a high degree of independence in internal affairs.

According to these findings, the disposition of the Administrative Officers to change is predominantly a conservative one, reflecting a bureaucratic and elitist mentality. The changing political environment does exert some degree of change in the political orientation of the Administrative Officers towards a more open and democratic type of administrative culture. For instance, the notion of political accountability has gained recognition among the Administrative Officers. Opposition and different opinions are also tolerated in the decision-making processes. Yet the changes to the administrative structure of the Hong Kong civil service are limited to the extent that the ruling power and status of the executive is not seriously challenged and totally replaced. For instance, the Administrative Officers accept that the executive should be accountable to the legislature, but they do not think the Legislative Council should dominate the decision-making process. The Administrative Officers think that they should act according to the best interest of citizens, but they do not want to involve citizen participation in the decision-making process to a great extent. The Administrative Officers tolerate and respect the opinion of political parties and leaders, but they do not favour the operation of party politics and distrust the politicians in the decision-making process. The Administrative Officers recognize the role of China in the political transition, yet they do not want to surrender their power to the Chinese officials. This kind of orientation towards change and political adaptation will elicit certain implications for the politics of transition in Hong Kong.

Implications

As the Administrative Officers occupy the central role in government, the political adaptability of the senior civil servants to the changes in the political scene will shape the political development of Hong Kong. If the civil service under the leadership of the Administrative Officers is able to adapt to the new dynamic environment, the stability and prosperity of the society could certainly be enhanced. On the contrary, the administrative system will break down if the Administrative Officers fail to adjust themselves and to adopt appropriate strategies to deal with the challenges. According to the findings of this study, three observations which affect the political adaptability of the Administrative Officers can be noted. First, although the Administrative Officers recognize that the role of the Legislative Council and the political parties is increasing, they seem to underestimate the urge for democracy among the general citizenry. The study shows that the Administrative Officers do not perceive that there is a widespread public demand for democracy. Nevertheless, there is ample evidence that the general public is in favour of a democratic system. For instance, the results of the 1991 and 1995 Legislative Council elections, the 1995 Municipal Council election, and the 1994 District Board election are consistent: the general citizens voted for the outspoken and hard-line democrats who won most of the seats in the three-tier representative system. Various opinion surveys also show that the democrats like Martin Lee and Emily Lau are the most popular Legislative Councilors.[18] Studies on political culture also indicate that the people of Hong Kong are developing a mature form of participatory political culture.[19] Thus the perception of the Administrative Officers towards the public demand for democracy is not in line with the election results, opinion surveys, and academic studies. The failure to recognize the accurate picture of the public demand for democracy could lead to frustration, hence loss of legitimacy of the government.

Another observation is the failure to formulate a comprehensive strategy other than piecemeal changes to handle the political changes. The piecemeal changes taken by the Administrative Officers seem to be superficial actions for expedient purposes. These actions do not respond closely to the actual changes and they lack a long term perspective. For instance, although the administration promises to be accountable to the Legislative Council, the administration is still free to decide whether it follows the suggestions made by the Public Accounts Committee of the Legislative Council on ways to avoid wastage in resources. With respect to the public access to information, the administration has not committed itself to allow the public to get access to government information and documents, although the Governor has reiterated that "the Hong Kong government has a responsibility to account to the people of Hong Kong for the progress made in honouring its commitments...and the public will have adequate information to judge the government's performance, the areas for improvement, and the significance of any shortfalls or delays."[20] Governor Patten refused to allow Legislator Christine Loh to initiate a bill on public access to information in May 1995, on the grounds that it would have the effect of imposing a charge on the government revenue. Instead, the administration issued an internal code of practice to handle the demands of the public for access to government information. As the Legislative Council, political parties, general citizenry, and China are becoming more assertive, the timid and piecemeal responses of the administration may not be able to satisfy the demands of the political actors in general, and to create an acceptable political formula for allocation of values in particular.

The low capacity to respond is related to the lack of motivation of the Administrative Officers to adopt innovative approaches to cope with the changes. Perhaps this reflects the lack of morale within the civil service and the decreasing confidence towards the future after 1997. As the Administrative Officers have traditionally been regarded as the elite and vanguard of the society, they are not psychologically prepared to accept the challenges and criticism brought about by the elected politicians and the general public. The practice of requiring the Administrative Officers to defend government policies and to explain policies in the Legislative Council and in the public is contradictory to their traditional norms in the civil service. The Administrative Officers are trained to be anonymous policy-makers being only accountable to the Governor rather than to the elected politicians. Thus the rise of elected politicians, and the assertion of the Legislative Council as the representative of the people, demoralize the Administrative Officers. The uncertain future of their careers after 1997 also negatively affects the motivation of the Administrative Officers. The fear of political purge initiated by the Communist regime on the mainland discourages the Administrative Officers to take a bold move to invent new changes in the administration. The confidence crisis among the senior government officials due to the problem of insecurity raises the issues of early retirement and emigration of the senior officials. A study has shown that one-third of the Directorate Grade officers intend to leave the civil service after 1997, with another one-third saying undecided.[21] The commitment and morale of the Administrative Officers is seriously doubtful, let alone their motivation to respond to change.

Such a pattern of political adaptability of the Administrative Officers could be detrimental to the continuity of stability and prosperity of Hong Kong during the political transition. This could lead to one of the crises that transitional societies are always facing. Binder suggests that political development of a transitional state may trigger off several crises: legitimacy, participation, and penetration.[22] As the citizens, politicians, and Chinese officials challenge the authority bases of the Administrative Officers, the administration suffers a decline of legitimacy unless it can invent a set of rules to place itself into a proper position vis-à-vis the other political actors. Hong Kong could encounter a participation crisis as there are too many public demands for political participation but insufficient channels. Frustrations of the general citizens could lead to demonstrations, protests, strikes, and eventually chaos. Penetration crisis could also arise as a result of a lack of government-citizen integration. If the Administrative Officers fail to adapt to public aspirations, the general citizens will feel alienated. As such, the government will be isolated from the general public, followed by mutual miscommunication and mistrust.

Conclusion

This study finds that the Hong Kong senior civil servants exhibit predominantly a set of conservative norms of political adaptation. During the political transition to 1997, the Administrative Officers are encountering political changes with long term implications. Democratization and the transfer of sovereignty constitute the two significant political challenges. The senior civil servants are slowly adapting to these political changes. The Administrative Officers recognize the increasing role of the Legislative Council, political parties, politicians, general citizens, and China in the decision-making process. Nevertheless, their responses are basically more piecemeal adjustments than prototyping, imitation, or recombination. The Administrative Officers basically prefer to maintain the status quo, that is, to keep the Legislative Council, political parties, politicians, general citizens, and China at the periphery of the decision-making process while they remain in the centre. In view of the increasing demand for democracy and Chinese participation in the internal affairs of Hong Kong, these conservative orientations and responses will arouse confusion and uncertainties in the politics of Hong Kong. Consequently, a new set of administrative norms oriented towards a more open and democratic government has to be inculcated within the civil service in order to adapt to the changing political environment in Hong Kong.

As one of the most dynamic transitional societies, Hong Kong's experience of political adaptation could certainly shed light on the adaptation of the bureaucracy of the Asian developing societies. As far as the Hong Kong experience is concerned, the Administrative Officers exhibit a conservative disposition to change and adopt a piecemeal approach in response to change. Perhaps it is important to cultivate a stronger and more flexible disposition among government officials to respond, in order to make the administration sensitive and far sighted to changes. As the top decision-makers of society, senior government officials are capable not only of facilitating political development, but also of pushing forward initiatives in the direction that the political system is already evolving. Thus healthy growth of a political system in transitional societies depends on the motivation and determination of government officials to adapt to changes.

Notes

[1] Jean Blondel, *Comparative Government* (New York: Philip Allan, 1990): 278.
[2] James Burns, *Leadership* (New York: Harper and Row, 1978): 2.
[3] David Rosenbloom, *Public Administration* (New York: Random House, 1989), and B. G. Peters, *The Politics of Bureaucracy* (New York: Longman, 1989).
[4] David Easton, *A Framework for Political Analysis* (Englewood Cliffs, New Jersey: Prentice-Hall, 1965).
[5] Karl Deutsch, *The Nerves of Government* (New York: Free Press, 1966): 164.
[6] Peter Harris, *Hong Kong: A Study of Bureaucratic Politics* (Hong Kong: Heineman, 1978).
[7] Ambrose King, "Administrative Absorption of Politics in Hong Kong," *Asian Survey* 15, 5 (May 1975): 422-439.
[8] S. K. Lau, *Society and Politics in Hong Kong* (Hong Kong: Chinese University Press, 1982).
[9] *Ibid.*
[10] Terry Lui, "Changing Civil Servants' Values," in I. Scott and J. Burns (eds), *The Hong Kong Civil Service and its Future* (Hong Kong: Oxford University Press, 1988).
[11] Christopher Hood, *Administrative Analysis* (Sussex: Wheatsheaf Books, 1986): 142.
[12] *Ibid.*: 145.
[13] A survey conducted by Hong Kong Polling and Business Research in 1992 revealed that 56% of the respondents wanted the Governor to push through the Constitutional Package, only 19% disagreed. The survey also found that 73% of the respondents supported the Constitutional Package. Moreover, the survey discovered that 60% of the respondents thought the Governor had gone far enough towards meeting Hong Kong's aspiration for more democracy; only 23% disagreed (see *South China Morning Post* (Hong Kong), October 11, 1992). Another survey conducted by the *South China Morning Post* revealed that nearly half (48.8%) of the respondents agreed that "the democracy plan should proceed even if China objects"; only 14.4% disagreed (see *South China Morning Post* (Hong Kong), October 10, 1992).

[14] Speech made by Mr. Cheung Man-kwong in the Legislative Council debate on the Constitution Package on November 12, 1992. Mr. Cheung is a member of the Democratic Party.
[15] Hong Kong China News Agency, November 15, 1992.
[16] See statement by Mr. Edward Ho who is a member of the Liberal Party and a member of the Legislative Council (for details, see *Standard* (Hong Kong), December 2, 1992). Also see the letter written by Mr. Tsang Yuk-sing, Chairman of the Democratic Alliance for Betterment of Hong Kong, to the Editor of the *South China Morning Post* (Hong Kong), October 11, 1992.
[17] *Policy Speech* (Hong Kong: Government Printer, 1995).
[18] Robert Chung, "Public Opinion," in D. Mcmillen and S. Man (eds), *The Other Hong Kong Report 1994* (Hong Kong: Chinese University Press, 1994).
[19] J. Lam, "The Political Culture of the Voters of Professional and Geographical Constituencies of the Legislative Council: Comparisons and Implications," *Politics, Administration and Change* 19: 40-53, and S. K. Lau and H. C. Kuan, "The Changing Political Culture of the Hong Kong Chinese," in J. Cheng (ed), *Hong Kong in Transition* (Hong Kong: Oxford University Press, 1986).
[20] *Policy Speech* (Hong Kong: Government Printer, 1995).
[21] J. Lee and J. Cheng, *Research Report on a Study of the Bureaucrat-Politician Relationship in Hong Kong's Transition* (Hong Kong: City Polytechnic of Hong Kong, 1994).
[22] Leonard Binder, et al, *Crises and Sequences in Political Development* (New Jersey: Princeton, 1971).

PART III

CITIZEN, BUSINESS, AND GOVERNMENT

5 Total Quality Governance (TQG): A New Model for Government-Citizen Relations

Emil P. Bolongaita, Jr.

Satisfying the customer is fundamental to the success of any enterprise: no customer satisfaction, no successful business. The higher the degree of customer satisfaction, the more likely a business booms. Towards this end, customer-driven firms have developed different ways of hearing from the customer, such as customer surveys and interviews, customer follow-up, focus-group discussions, suggestion boxes, and various other means. By listening to customer feedback, these firms receive critical ideas on where, when, and how they can improve their products and services. By responding to customer feedback, these firms not only satisfy and anticipate the needs of their customers, they often can delight their customers.

The literature on Total Quality Management (TQM) continues to attest to the impact that customer satisfaction has on corporate success. Since it was pioneered by Deming and Juran, various processes continue to be invented to listen and respond innovatively and effectively to the customer. Yet while private enterprise has made leaps and bounds in satisfying, even delighting, the customer, much remains to be desired in the ways governments deal with their constituents. As Henry Mintzberg points out, many governments view their people only as *subjects* (who pay taxes and obey laws), not as *citizens* (who deserve to be treated equally regardless of rank or status) or *customers* (who deserve to be served well).[1]

While customer-oriented processes in private enterprise have already been discussed in the literature on the management of government,[2] it has yet to permeate the practice of governments. Few governments in the world, whether national or local, view their people as customers, much less as citizens. Except during elections, when people are courted for their votes, many national and local governments deliver basic services late, poorly, and arrogantly - as if government funds come from their own pockets, and not from taxes paid by the people.

Why People are Rarely Treated as Citizens and Customers

There are at least four reasons why government agencies are in general insensitive, even indifferent, to people's rights to being treated as citizens and customers.[3]

- First, the budget of government agencies is not dependent on citizen-customer satisfaction. Government agencies do not receive their funds directly from the people, but from the legislative assembly and the treasury. When a business displeases customers, sales decline and profits plummet. When a government agency delivers services badly, nothing bad happens to it. Government agencies aim to please not the citizen-customer but the bureaucracy and its bosses. There is no incentive to satisfy, much less delight, the citizen-customer.
- Second, government agencies are monopolies. They have no competition that pressures them to be efficient, effective and innovative. Their employees, in turn, can afford to be arrogant, complacent, and disparaging of the public.
- Third, national and local governments (at least those which are democratic) are only replaced through elections. For the Philippines and other presidential democracies, the terms of office and the timing of elections are fixed. Elected government officials cannot be changed in between elections (save for extraordinary cases). Thus, in between elections, there are no serious incentives for officials to serve the people with efficiency, effectiveness and innovation. Services are more often than not shoddy, wasteful, and more of the same.
- Fourth, the majority of people have historically been accustomed to the poor performance of governments and have not developed a culture of complaint for better service. The long lines in many government offices are accepted as a matter of fact, the arrogance and incompetence of many government employees are considered part of the process, and the sloppy and slipshod services are viewed as something that might as well be accepted. To be served effectively, people know all too well that "pay-

offs" often do the trick (unless, of course, you are "somebody" who can demand special service).

Of these four conditions, the first three remain unchanged in many places like in the Philippines. Government agencies do not lose money when they perform poorly, they have no competition for their services, and the electoral rules of the country still feature fixed terms and regular elections. The fourth condition, however, has shown signs of change, in part owing to growing popular dissatisfaction. Faced with arrogant and incompetent government agencies, many people now bristle at poor service delivery and clamour for change. This is happening in several countries and is now beginning to be evident in the Philippines as well.

Examples of Citizen-Customer Governance

David Osborne and Ted Gaebler discuss cases of successful customer-driven systems in local government agencies in various areas in the United States. The features of these systems are patterned after business practices, such as customer surveys, customer contact reports, customer councils, complaint tracking systems, and many others. These systems were successful not only on the basis of citizen satisfaction, but on other critical aspects as well, namely efficiency, effectiveness, and innovation.[4]

In India, Samuel Paul describes the genesis and development of a "citizen report card" on the delivery of public services in Bangalore.[5] Using a variety of feedback mechanisms - random sample survey, in-depth interviews, focus group discussions, case studies, and documentation of other information - Paul's Public Affairs Centre identified eight different public utilities most often dealt with by the people. The Centre ranked these agencies in terms of citizen satisfaction and analysed the problems encountered by the citizens, such as corruption, excess billing, and poor service. Afterwards, the Centre's report was presented to, and published by, the local press, which apparently pressured two agencies to respond and remedy some of their service deficiencies.

There are signs of citizen-customer governance emerging in the Philippines. The *Gawad Galing Pook* Program managed by the Asian Institute of Management (in co-operation with the Local Government Academy of the Department of Interior and Local Government) has identified cases of excellent programs of local governments.[6] However, as argued above, in the Philippines and in many other developing countries, customer-driven systems are not institutionalised in the operations of national and local governments and public sector organisations. The 1991 Local Government Code called for the establishment of local special councils designed to ensure the incorporation of popular feedback in governance, but these councils for various reasons have not been institutionalised.[7]

Total Quality Governance (TQG): Serving the Citizen-Customer

The revolutionary impact of Total Quality Management (TQM) in improving quality in the manufacturing and service sectors can be adapted to the public sector. The public sector - government agencies and other not-for-profit public organisations - can learn a lot from innovations in service delivery in the private sector. There is no reason why service dimensions emphasised in the private sector - timeliness, accuracy, courtesy, responsiveness, availability, variety, convenience, etc. - cannot be successfully applied in the public sector.[8] The methods for customer feedback used in the private sector, such as customer surveys, interviews, and focus-group discussions, can be adapted by public sector organisations (as demonstrated by Paul's experiences in India and by innovative government organisations in the United States).

In this regard, the Politics and Governance Desk of the AIM Policy Forum developed a citizen-customer feedback system designed to assist public sector organisations in assessing their delivery of services. Unlike previous and prevailing practices where assessment of the quality of service delivery is based on employee reports or some other mechanism, the citizen-customer feedback system would solicit evaluation from the end-user of the service. If in the private sector quality is ultimately determined by the customer, this should also apply to quality in the public sector. The feedback system would enable these organisations to assess specific dimensions of service delivery, such as transaction time, courtesy, responsiveness, and personalised service.

The feedback system was also designed to identify and prioritise city problems and issues based on citizen-customer concerns. More often than not, leaders of public sector organisations rely on subjective mechanisms to identify and prioritise issues that their organisations need to address. These mechanisms, such as informal interviews with key personnel and staff, are likely to be biased, filtered by the prism of the leader's perspective or that of the dominant coalition in the organisation. The feedback system was devised to correct for the biases inherent in a non-scientific approach to identifying and prioritising problems. Considering the technologies of survey research, the feedback system is able to identify and prioritise problems of citizen-customers more precisely than personalistic perspectives could ever hope to do.

The Politics and Governance Desk has coined the term Total Quality Governance (TQG) to describe governance of public sector organisations based on citizen-customer feedback. It is fundamentally based on the principle that service quality is a function of employee empowerment. That is, the greater the participation of an organisational member in formulating organisational goals towards service quality, the harder and better that employee will work to achieve them. However, TQG is not just about empowering employees. It is also about inspiring them through experienced visionary leadership. Just as importantly, it is about ensuring that citizen-customers are involved in the evaluation and judgement of performance.

The TQG model is being developed to apply to various forms of public sector organisations, such as national government agencies, local governments and government corporations. To test this system, the Politics and Governance Desk applied a TQG review of Makati City, the commercial capital of the Philippines.

The TQG review of Makati was designed to measure the performance of local government offices in delivering basic services. These performance measures would, in turn, be used as the basis for benchmarking improvements in service delivery. In addition, the TQG review was also designed to generate a Governance Map that identifies and prioritises problems and issues.[9]

The Database

Data collection was based on a survey of representative random sample of 200 adult male and female residents of Makati City. The sampling followed the survey industry practice of multi-stage random respondent selection. In the first stage, the survey team made a simple random selection of 10 *barangays* in each of the two congressional districts of Makati. In the second stage, the team did a systematic sampling of 10 households in each of the 10 *barangays* selected in each district. In the last stage, the team chose one qualified adult household member using Kish's probability selection key. Thus, there were 100 respondents selected in each district.

The sampling was made by districts to allow for a district analysis of Makati City. It was hypothesised at the start of the project that there might be different citizen perceptions between the two districts because of their different socio-economic characteristics. District 1 contains the affluent *barangays* (such as Forbes Park, Dasmariñas, Urdaneta, Bel-Air, Magallanes, and San Lorenzo), while District 2 encompasses none of the affluent *barangays*. Thus, this survey was intended to be a study of differences in perceptions of citizen-customers belonging to rich and poor districts.

Results of TQG Review of Makati City

Because of space considerations, this paper can only provide an overview of the results of the TQG review.[10] The first part of the TQG survey aimed to find out the usage, efficiency, and service quality of city government offices. The results show that city government offices are visited frequently by residents. However, about a fifth of respondents in District 1 have not visited any office in the past two years! This suggests that the city government should publicise and make available its services to citizens in District 1.

The transaction time of Makati citizens to complete their visits to city government offices varies according to district and office. The results show that District 1 citizens appear to be served faster than citizens in District 2. In this regard, city government offices in District 2 need to improve their efficiency by matching the efficiency rate of District 1. The average transaction time for both districts was about 30 minutes, but the citizens of Makati want to cut this by half. The City Treasurer's Office was found to be the slowest serving office. This inefficiency is most unfortunate, because this is the office where the city earns significant revenues in the form of tax payments and issuance of business permits.

In general, more respondents in District 1 mentioned negative experiences than respondents in District 2. About a fifth of respondents in District 1 said that the employee made them wait while doing something else. Slightly less than a fifth said that the employee passed the buck and sent them to somebody else. Thus, although citizens in District 1 are served faster than citizens in District 2, they have more negative experiences!

To increase citizen-customer satisfaction, positive experience ratings must be pushed upwards and the negative experience ratings reduced. On the positive experiences, the survey identified the following as receiving low positive ratings:

- employee saying "thank you" to citizen customers after their transaction;
- greeting citizen customers "hello" or "good morning/good afternoon"; and
- calling citizen customers by name.

On the negative experiences, the survey identified the following as having high ratings:

- employee making the citizen wait while doing something else;
- employee sending the citizen to somebody else; and
- employee smoking, eating, or drinking in the office.

Problems and Priorities of Citizens Revealed by TQG Review

The second part of the TQG survey aimed to identify and prioritise citizen-customer concerns. Respondents were asked about their rating of severity for thirty-two city services and concerns as well as their perception of the government's response to each of these problems. A *higher priority problem* is one that scores high in problem severity and low in government action. A *lower priority problem* is one that scores high in problem severity, but high in government action. An issue is in the *area of satisfaction* if it is low in severity but high in government action. An issue is in the *area of indifference* if it is not viewed as severe and the government is not doing anything about it.

For District 1, the survey identified 14 problems of high priority, 2 problems of low priority, 15 issues in the area of satisfaction, and 1 issue in the area of indifference. The survey showed that among the problems of high priority, the most important according to citizen-customer perceptions are the following:

        1st Priority: Illegal drugs
        2nd Priority: Illegal gambling
        3rd Priority: Prostitution
        4th Priority: Squatters
        5th Priority: Public Parking

For District 2, the survey identified 12 problems of high priority, 2 problems of lower priority, 13 issues in the area of satisfaction, and 5 issues in the area of indifference. The top five problems of high priority for District 2 are:

> 1st Priority: Illegal drugs
> 2nd Priority: Illegal gambling
> 3rd Priority: Pornography
> 4th Priority: Prostitution
> 5th Priority: Indecent/Bold Shows

Except for several problems (notably illegal drugs, illegal gambling, and prostitution), citizens of District 1 and District 2 identify different priority problems. Pornography is ranked as the third priority problem in District 2, but it is placed as the eleventh priority problem in District 1. Indecent/bold shows is ranked the fifth priority problem in District 2, but it is put as the thirteenth priority problem in District 1. Squatters rank fourth in the priority problem of District 1, but it is not considered a priority problem at all in District 2. Public Parking is ranked as the fifth priority problem in District 1, but it is only in the area of indifference in District 2. Police assistance is considered the fourteenth priority problem in District 1, but it is in the area of indifference in District 2.

Contrary to predictions prior to the survey that traffic would rank high in the TQG survey (Metropolitan Manila, after all, often comes close to matching Bangkok's notorious gridlocks), traffic was not considered a priority problem at all by residents of both districts. Although it is considered a severe problem, residents of both districts viewed the government as already doing a lot about it. Thus, in comparison with other severe problems where the government was viewed as doing little about, traffic was lower in priority.

Conclusion

The TQG review of Makati City showed that customer feedback surveys commonly used in the private sector can be applied to public sector units, such as local governments, to evaluate quality dimensions in their service delivery. The citizen-customer feedback system suggests that total quality management is a transferable technology to assess and improve service delivery in the public sector, in dimensions such as timeliness, courtesy, responsiveness, and availability. The TQG review also identified problem areas that deserve higher and lower priority as well as the areas that are already satisfactory to citizens. For the city government, the TQG review became helpful as a management tool. It informed city officials through a systematic process about the perceptions and priorities of its citizens, which in some areas did not coincide with the perceptions and priorities of city officials. In this sense, the TQG review helped to ensure that supply would meet demand (and thus, result in less wastage of precious resources). Because the TQG review was carried out in an impartial and objective manner, it depoliticised the evaluation of the service delivery process and potentially pushed the city towards more innovation and better service for its citizen-customers.

Notes

[1] H. Mintzberg, "Managing Government, Governing Management," *Harvard Business Review* 74, 3 (May-June 1996), pp. 75-83.

[2] For example, D. Osborne and T. Gaebler, *Reinventing Government: How the Entrepreneurial Spirit is Transforming the Public Sector* (New York: Plume, 1993), and J. L. Crompton and C. W. Lamb, *Marketing Government and Social Services* (Englewood Cliffs, NJ: Prentice-Hall, 1987).

[3] For in-depth interesting and contrasting analyses of why this happens, see, for example, J. Prottas, *People-Processing: The Street-Level Bureaucrat in Public Service Bureaucracies* (Lexington, MA: Lexington Books, 1979), and M. Lipsky, *Street-Level Bureaucracy: Dilemmas of the Individual in Public Services* (New York, NY: Russell Sage, 1980).

[4] See Osborne and Gaebler (1993): 82-86.

[5] S. Paul, "A Citizen Report Card on Public Services: Mixing Barks and Bites?" Paper presented at the Ford Foundation International Conference on Decentralisation, Asian Institute of Management (AIM), Manila, July 1995.

[6] This awards program is patterned after the Ford Foundation's Innovation Awards managed by Harvard University's Kennedy School of Government. The Ford Foundation, together with the Canada Fund, supports the *Gawad Galing Pook* program.

[7] E. Bolongaita, "Rethinking Participatory Governance: The Non-Institutionalisation of Local Development Councils," *Policy Research Paper* No. 2, AIM Policy Forum, Asian Institute of Management (AIM), Manila, January 1996.

[8] For a discussion of service quality issues, see R. Domingo, "Consistency in Service Quality," *The Asian Manager* 8, 6 (December 1995/January 1996): 12-14.

[9] The results of the TQG review were presented at a roundtable conference on May 22, 1996, at AIM, Philippines.

[10] For a full presentation of the results of the TQG review of Makati City, see E. Bolongaita, "A Tale of Two Districts: The Citizen as Customer in Makati City," *Policy Research Paper* No. 3, AIM Policy Forum, Asian Institute of Management (AIM), Manila, May 1996.

6 Small Business Policy Reform: A New Approach to Old Problems

William Cole and Stephen Parker

Small Business Policy Reform as a Governance Problem

By the early 1980s, a rough consensus had emerged among development professionals that the most effective means for reducing the crushing effects of foreign debt and stifling state bureaucracies built up over decades of state-led development strategies was to deregulate economic policy in order to free up private sector initiative, shift from inward to outward-looking trade and investment policies, and privatize state assets. In the ensuing period, macroeconomic reforms and structural adjustment implemented throughout most of the developing world, particularly in Asia, dramatically modernized those economies and laid the foundations for a truly global economy. With the policy fundamentals more or less in place in these successfully developing countries, we are moving to a new generation of reforms needed to maintain the growth momentum and to respond to demands for equity and social justice. In part, this has caused a shift in attention from international competitiveness toward the competitiveness of the many firms operating primarily in domestic markets.

What role did foreign donors play in policy reforms in the 1980s and what is now the best way to assist the reform process given these new challenges? The traditional role for foreign assistance in promoting policy reform was based on what might be called a technical approach to policy reform. Technical experts were placed primarily within government agencies working closely with technocratic allies in an attempt to design appropriate policy responses and to attract the attention of top decision makers. Large donors could pressure for policy reform in return for debt restructuring and/or for new loans. A place at the policy table was sometimes "bought" by smaller donors such as USAID with large, expensive projects, typically involving substantial commodity donations. The in-country beneficiaries of reform were generally treated as "passive" in that they were left outside the policy reform process, especially relative to the foreign assistance strategies. While some of the reforms supported under this approach involved limited administrative changes and passage of new laws with various deregulations related to streamlining licenses and so on especially important for reducing the intervention points by bureaucrats, they generally required minimal involvement in what has come to be called governance reform.

Where governments were willing to pursue sound policy reforms, such technical reform strategies worked well, jump-starting private-sector led growth and the broader structural transformations that underpinned growth. Real progress on the next generation of reform, particularly those related to raising domestic competitiveness, will be much tougher. Why tougher? Most fundamentally because the next generation of changes will require an extension of the deregulatory process to provincial and local levels and they will require transformation of governance institutions, both legal and administrative. In both cases, policy processes, interest groups and government functions are much more disbursed and cumbersome to control than those required for macroeconomic stabilization and export campaigns.

Awareness among economists and other development professionals that "institutions matter" has been growing steadily through the 1990s, and one can begin to see the outlines of a broad consensus on the fundamental need for good governance. This is clearly a positive step forward. The critical next question, however, is: how do we encourage improved governance? There is a potential trap here. There is a tendency to focus excessively on the technical/organizational dimensions of reform, while missing or underestimating the political dimensions of reform. When discussing the challenges of, and successes in, governance reform, there is often an acknowledgement of the need for "political will" but also a tendency to move quickly on to the more technical strategies and tasks involved in the reform process, such as bureaucratic and administrative government reform.

If political will for reform is a prior requirement for success, either for economic or governance reforms, then clearly understanding the process of reform and the prospects for success is largely a political, not a technical, matter. Why are we missing this? One answer is that most of the successful cases of administrative and legal reform, the cases on which we tend to focus and project as lessons learned, almost always involve a national leadership that is strongly committed to reform and where that leadership ultimately has the political power to move the reforms forward legislatively, administratively, and in practice. Under these conditions, it is quite reasonable to focus on the challenges of technical implementation of reforms. The difficulty is that most developing countries do not, in fact, have the advantage of a committed leadership with unrestrained political ability to press forward. And, it begs the question of how countries developed this political will when often it did not exist during earlier stages of national development. As a practical matter, national leaders are constrained actors, limited in action by an array of powerful interests at the national and local levels. Whatever leadership commitments there might be for policy or governance reform, these are in whole, or in part, reduced by realistic political calculations about what is possible in terms of antagonizing entrenched interests that benefit from the status quo. Our conclusion, therefore, is that although sound technical policy recommendations are a necessary requirement for successful economic reform efforts, they are not sufficient. A strategy that incorporates the political dynamics of change, and the ensuing need for fundamental changes in governance capacities, is needed for these second generation development challenges for newly industrializing economies.

What does the practitioner do under these circumstances? Simply waiting passively for the emergence, through whatever means, of a national leadership committed - and powerful - enough to demand implementation of reforms is one approach. A somewhat different approach, what might be called a political economy approach to reform, would pay a great deal more attention to the nature of political will and how various actions can be undertaken to enhance and focus that will in the interest of reforms. We do not yet have a systematic body of literature, a conceptual framework, or even a developed language to facilitate thinking about effective and legitimate ways to engage in the process of building political will for specific policy and governance reforms. Some elements of both the framework and language, however, are taking form.

First, we need to be clear about what is meant by "political will". Real political will for reform must be distinguished from the mere presence of pro-reform actors in specific government agencies or institutions. For several decades under the technical approach to reform, bilateral donor agencies such as USAID sought out individual "reformers" or attempted to create pockets of reformers in key institutions. A degree of technical progress might be made at this level, but a critical point inevitably comes when national leadership has to decide whether the process is to go forward or is to be slowed or even side-tracked -- that is a political not a technical calculation. Willingness of national leadership to back reforms in the face of significant political costs or risks is what we are referring to as political will. An important element of this is the capability for the policy dialogue process to incorporate the often intangible longer-term future beneficiaries of policy reform as a counterbalance to the near-term losses of quite tangible existing vested interests.

Second, in a political economic approach to reform, the beneficiaries of policy or institutional reform need to be conceived of in "proactive" terms. A good governance approach to policy change means that our efforts must be sequenced and positioned to generate a rising, self-generating demand among beneficiaries for further reform. A proactive group of beneficiaries ensures both sustainability of initial gains made and a self-sustaining reform process into the future.

Third, supporting the movement of national leadership in the direction of greater reform, in a political perspective, means reducing political risks for that leadership in supporting reform. This requires building pro-reform coalitions with enough political weight to challenge and prevail against entrenched interests benefitting from the status quo. Generally such a coalition would include interest groups most directly and positively affected by a given change, but it may also be possible and even necessary to draw in other groups that may indirectly benefit in one way or another. While it is clearly impossible to predict with precision what actual alliances may emerge and stabilize around a given issue, it is possible to identify areas of reform in which it is likely to serve different interest groups for perhaps different reasons. It may then be possible to facilitate a process in which these groups explore their potential common interests and define a coordinated reform agenda.

Improving domestic competitiveness and increasing small-to-medium scale firm productivity is an area that poses just the kind of problems best handled with the political economy approach described above. Continued progress requires a new governance dynamic in which feedback from the private sector (or its civil society proxies) and public-private collaboration begins to drive the ongoing policy reform process. At the same time, this area may test the limits of the new thinking - where small and medium business is financially weak, split along size and ethic lines, and not well-organized, the initial voice for reform from that quarter will normally be weak. Under these conditions, a broader coalition of interest based both inside and outside government must emerge to drive the reform process forward.

Our emphasis on the need to incorporate political economic influences into a policy reform strategy, however, in no way reduces the importance for clear technical analysis of the problems, empirical testing of policy solutions, and continual and practical learning-by-doing as the reform process evolves.

The Main Challenges for Indonesian Small Business Development

Indonesia has been relatively successful over the past two decades in reducing absolute poverty, with estimates of those falling under the official poverty line steadily declining from 40 percent in 1975 to 15 percent in 1990. Income inequalities have also declined, at least until recently. Yet, with per capita GDP just over US$1,000, there is a growing public concern that more needs to be done to ensure that the poor share more broadly in the benefits of rapid growth.

As in most low-income developing economies, small and micro enterprises are the main source of employment for the poor outside the agriculture sector. There are some 15 to 20 million medium, small and micro enterprises in Indonesia (excluding farmers). Starting in the early 1950s, the government has used policy and support programs to protect and promote development of an indigenous private sector. A series of policy reforms beginning in the early 1980s, and accelerated in 1986, have been spectacularly successful in generating a cluster of large private sector conglomerates. But these reforms have yielded much less benefits at the small business level.

While Indonesia does have some of the best micro financing systems in the world, by and large, small enterprises have been left to their own devices—hamstrung with poor management skills, low-productivity technologies, limited access to formal financial and capital markets and traditional distribution channels, without the benefit of enforceable contracts, and generally facing a business environment badly distorted by unfavorable regulatory and incentive policies. Some of the most pressing problems for small businesses are related to the slow development of subcontracting and source relationships among small firms and between large and small firms. Market-driven business linkages could go a long way towards reducing problems of low technology and capital shortage, problems most often cited by small business people themselves. The result of these constraints to small business development is an economic structure dominated by the large conglomerates that produce nearly 60 percent of Indonesia's private sector output and a vast group of low productivity small and micro enterprises where most Indonesians find work but which generates perhaps only 15 percent of overall private-sector GDP.

One fundamental problem common to nearly all small businesses in Indonesia is the limited extension of the deregulation process to local levels of government. The most tangible manifestation of this problem is the widespread existence of official and unofficial levies, licensing arrangements, and other implicit taxes on business activity (called "pungutan" in Indonesia, and henceforth referred to simply as "levies" in this paper). Despite Indonesia's impressive record of deregulation over the past decade, thousands of levies remain in place. These levies, most of which are imposed at the local level, are a source of particular hardship for small businesses operating in local markets.

The evidence of the extent of the levies problem is strong, but still largely anecdotal. There has been little systematic examination of the actual costs imposed on doing business in Indonesia. The Director General of International Trade recently stated that 4,000 national, provincial and local levies affect Indonesian exporters alone, in spite of concerted efforts to remove such constraints to export growth. The results of research by the Indonesian Chamber of Commerce (KADIN), Ministry of Labor, and the National Planning Board (BAPPENAS), identified a complex myriad of overlapping charges of various origin, but perhaps the most striking findings were the degree of variation among localities and the lack of clarity concerning the authority on which these charges are imposed. The Chamber estimates that the sum of all levies, including illegal ones, account for up to 30 percent of production costs in manufacturing businesses.

Our discussions with NGOs and leading academic analysts over the past six months have convinced us that levies imposed in various manifestations on small and micro enterprises in the trade and service sectors are of similar magnitude or worse. In addition to the direct drain on firm resources that these levies represent, there is an additional, hard-to-calculate cost of distortion in allocation of firm resources, including cost of scarce management time, as entrepreneurs seek to avoid attracting the attention of local officials. Being successful as an independent business at the local level can be costly. Levies clearly represent a massive constraint, possibly the most important constraint, to rising productivity in smaller firms. Even if the real drain is closer to an average of 10 to 20 percent of all business costs, we are still talking about billions of dollars removed every year at the small business level alone. Clearly the high rates of return that should exist for many small businesses, and that could self-finance technology improvements, training and market experimentation, are being drained off at a crushing rate.

What this means for the structure of Indonesia's firm sizes and the contribution of each to GDP is striking. The largest firms, with protective political connections at or near the top and benefiting from specific deregulatory actions, have clearly been able to cut through much of the burden of official and unofficial levies. For medium-scale firms, primarily operating at the provincial and district levels, the burdens appear to be much greater, except for the few firms that are well connected at that level. This may, in part, explain both the "missing middle" in the firm size distribution in Indonesia as well as the tendency to locate in a few urban areas that have high labor and land costs, but where the levies problem is less onerous because the firm does not stand out so dramatically. The heaviest burden, however, appears to be falling directly on small/micro enterprises that operate entirely at the local level, which face the full force of both national and local levies imposed by a wide array of often unaccountable officials, and that have minimal capacity to resist when hit for payments. From this perspective, larger-scale firms may be achieving faster growth and higher productivity not just because they have received special facilities or because of inherent competitive advantages, as is often argued, but rather because in relative terms, smaller firms have yet to experience significant deregulation and face a relatively much greater implicit tax resulting from the levies.

Making the case for the devastating effects that these payments have on small business development is much easier than doing something about it. Unlike the macro-level deregulation successes in the past, significant results at the local level cannot be achieved through collections of lists of levies followed by top-down policy action by a few committed senior officials in economic ministries at the national level. Sorting through the many layers of levies, licenses and payments at the local level, and then guarding over time against re-implementation of similar payments by thwarted local officials, would involve staggering information and enforcement costs if conducted at the national level, and would require coordination among an imposing range of often unfamiliar economic and non-economic ministries at both the national and local levels with often unclear and overlapping jurisdictions. Moreover, the accelerating movement toward regional autonomy in Indonesia would undermine such a centralized approach in any case. Rather, what will eventually be required will be new and innovative governance mechanisms at the local level that facilitate public-private dialogue and lobbying on these issues, backed up by powerful political demand for reform from the center. What shape those mechanisms might take is not yet clear.

Political Will for Reform -- Reducing the Costs of Levies as a Case Study

Indonesia is only now beginning to tackle the problem of locally imposed levies. Is there political will to address this issue head-on and in a reasonable time frame? Today the challenge has become more pressing on both economic and political fronts. The greatest potential contribution to growth, and to employment generation, is likely to come from medium-scale firms and the larger, more entrepreneurial, firms in the small category. This interest group, however, is fragmented along size and ethnic lines and not organized into strong organizations and sector associations, which makes it difficult for this interest group to articulate and lobby on its own behalf. At the same time, concern is rapidly spreading both in the middle levels of the bureaucracy, and in the public more broadly, about the potentially disastrous consequences of globalization for Indonesia's uncompetitive small and medium scale sector, particularly with implementation of the ASEAN Free-Trade Agreement reforms by 2003. There is thus a weak but emerging "technocratic" lobby, located largely within government, that is calling attention to the levies problem.

Far more substantial pressures could come from what might be referred to as "populist" interests located both inside government and in civil society. Over the past year, the long festering problem of the "wealth gap" (kesenjangan) between those associated with the large and politically favored conglomerates and the poor, most of whom work in small firms in the informal sector, has entered public debate. Popular resentment over this issue has substantially increased pressure on government and the large conglomerates to take more effective action to close the wealth gap. Large in number, but entirely unorganized, small firms are not likely to engage to any significant degree in the process of identifying the problems they face, and are not likely to either act collectively to lobby for redress.

The important and exciting point here is that a strong coalition of interest in reducing levies that is based in part in the government and in part in civil society may be emerging. This consists of a welfare-oriented concern on the part of interest groups with a populist orientation and an efficiency and political expediency concern from the technocrats, in both cases from inside and outside the government. Strong consensus among this coalition that the growth and welfare damage caused by levies and on the need for quick resolution may be enough to move national leadership to undertake serious reforms in this area. Those reforms, again, would involve both policy changes in the form of deregulation, and governance reforms in the form of public-private mechanisms at the local level to identify and press for removal of specific levies at that level.

The TAF Program: Broadening Participation in Economic Growth

We present The Asia Foundation's (TAF) on-going small/micro business program (formally titled Participation, Policy and Micro-enterprise Development, PPMD) as a case study of a political economic approach. This project, working with a range of Indonesian partners, is in the process of developing a political economic strategy for promoting a more conducive policy environment for small and medium enterprise (SME) growth, and in this regard directly tackling the challenge of reducing the costs of the levies, and of developing more effective and responsive support programs such as training and access to financing and distribution channels.

In 1994, we began designing a special assistance program for Indonesia intended to support progress toward an improved environment for small business development. The program, funded by USAID and private-sector sources, was initially built on the assumption, still valid in mid-1995, that political will for attention to the problems faced by small business was growing but had not yet coalesced. The Foundation structured a flexible program to help consolidate political will for change through a series of constraints analyses, policy-oriented workshops, building information networks among public and private analysts, and carefully targeted technical assistance. Implementation of the project effectively began in early 1996.

Since late 1995, much has happened to accelerate Government of Indonesia's (GOI) commitment to policy and programmatic change in this area. Responding to both the challenge of globalization and rising public concern over the wealth gap, the GOI moved with unexpected haste in December 1995 to pass the new Small Business Law (UU 9/95). This law has been widely, though quietly, criticized by senior Indonesian economists and other market-oriented analysts for being protective and paternalistic rather than facilitating of the small business sector. The largest private firms are also showing signs of increased willingness to "assist the small," with some informal inducement from the President. Indonesia's forty largest conglomerates signed the "Jimbaran Declaration" in July 1995, committing funds and promising more effective action to build market linkages to the small-scale firms. Finally, political pressure on capital-intensive, natural-resource extraction companies in the outer islands to assist the development of local small/micro enterprises has increased substantially, particularly following violent disturbances in Iran Jaya linked to the large foreign-owned copper mine.

While the rise in political will to take action is encouraging, the analytical and empirical knowledge to form effective policy in this area and the public-private networks required to deliver sound ideas to the decision makers are not much further developed than they were when TAF began looking at these issues in 1994. There is substantial risk that ineffective, wasteful, or even counterproductive policies, regulations, and programs could be locked in over the next two years as the government develops the administrative actions authorized by the Small Business Law and the conglomerates respond to political rather than business interests.

Based on these changing circumstances, TAF's current small business program evolved to work both inside and outside government: (1) to build knowledge of problems faced by small business as a basis for effective coalition building; (2) to support public-private collaboration on small business policy and programs as a means for facilitating emergence of a broader coalition focusing on, and pressing for, specific changes; and (3) in both cases, to expedite the development of in-country capabilities and dialogue processes while gradually withdrawing from a catalytic role. The issue of levies has emerged as one of the central elements of these efforts.

Key Elements of the TAF Program

Work within Government Providing Technical Assistance to the Ministry of Cooperatives and Small Business (DEPKOP-PPK)

With the recent passage of the Small Business Law, the locus of policy action shifted from the parliament to DEPKOP-PPK. This Ministry now has key responsibilities for drafting implementation regulations, for taking the lead in designing and implementing any new small business support programs, and for coordinating all efforts throughout the GOI in this area. This Ministry has long favored a paternalistic, top-down, bureaucratic approach to development, in keeping with its role in organizing farmers under state management during the green revolution in the 1970s. For reasons cited above, however, DEPKOP-PPK is under intense pressure to generate significant results and to do so soon.

TAF is now working closely with senior Ministry officials and has found a willingness to consider more market-friendly approaches to small business regulations and more direct private sector "for profit" involvement in small business development. We began the relationship by facilitating travel by a senior Ministerial delegation to the United States to help build linkages with the US Small Business Administration and to expose these officials to the dynamics and private/public support activities of the US small business sector. This was followed up with a series of policy papers, policy workshops, and a year-long program of short-term expert assistance for DEPKOP-PPK and other related Ministries. One critical theme running through our work was to focus on the levies/deregulation issue and the need to leverage market forces to spur small business growth.

Work Outside Government: Emphasis Placed on Raising the Analytical Content of Policy Advice and the Enhancement of an Effective Public-Private Dialogue Through a Focus on Priority Policy and Program Issues

TAF is working with a number of Indonesian think-tanks, academic centers, and NGOs to improve the technical analysis and capacities needed to argue for more effective policy and programs. Our approach focuses directly on those issues of most immediate policy concern. A great deal of public-private debate on how best to support small business development is now occurring in Indonesia through workshops, conferences, and the press. There is also a surprising range of research that has been done on the country's small business sector. Both sources, however, often yield results with limited policy relevance, being either too general (descriptive), too theoretical, or too specific (case studies). Project and research results are often not well disbursed or accessible, discussions among analysts are not common, and research is often not well-grounded in practical small business concerns with discussions directly with small businesses. This has limited the ability of the non-government groups to develop sound, empirically-based policy positions that can be advanced effectively in the policy debate and acted upon by government policy makers. Many of the research and academic groups best able to speak clearly and with authority for small businesses are not engaged with policy makers, making it difficult to forge an effective pro-reform coalition pressing for better policy and programs.

For these reasons, our work outside government is concentrated on efforts to assist analysts to develop more policy relevant results and actionable options. We have been expanding the circle of non-government counterparts seeking to strengthen their ability to work together to identify the most pressing areas for policy reform, and helping them improve their ability to articulate actionable solutions to the GOI. Again, a large component of the assistance that we are providing for work outside government is focused on building demand for reform through the levies issue.

Lessons Being Learned

While we are in the early stage of our small business program in Indonesia, we believe some important lessons are being learned. Among these are the following:

Appropriate Role in Policy Coalition Building

As a foreign assistance organization, there are obvious and important limits to the degree to which we can - and should - take an active role in the emergence of policy and governance reform coalitions. What we are learning, however, is that we can play an important role in catalyzing thinking about key policy reforms, in helping various institutions and policy makers to determine more clearly where their interests lie, and in facilitating linkages between these diverse groups with shared policy interests within and outside government. The Foundation's long-standing track record in Indonesia as a partner to both government and emerging civil society organizations, and a commitment to better understanding the concerns and interests of different groups, is critical to establishing the trust necessary to play this facilitating role.

Working on Both Government and Non-Government Sides

Facilitating emergence of a broad and effective coalition of interests supporting small business development requires that we work closely with a range of private sector/NGO actors. At the same time, it is essential to work closely with government officials whose regulations, enforcement and support programs set the environment for small business success. Understanding the problems from both sides, and their respective strengths and weaknesses, helps greatly to better position effective policy dialogue. We found it important in particular to work with key agencies and individuals within the government with a strong interest in small business development, but whose initial approach may not have been oriented toward deregulation and greater private-sector roles but who were open to new and practical ideas that could be shown to be effective in other countries and, in some cases, in specific examples in Indonesia.

Need for Program Flexibility

Being in the right time and place in terms of political will for reform means that events are likely to be moving fast and program opportunities will appear and pass by quickly. Assisting counterparts effectively in this kind of environment requires considerable programmatic flexibility and an entrepreneurial willingness to take risks while retaining a steady vision of overall program objectives. Avoiding over-commitment early on to specific counterpart institutions is critical, which allowed the project to retain a great deal of flexibility as the situation evolved. The nature of our funding sources, a USAID grant mechanism supplemented by corporate assistance, provided critical leeway and quick response capabilities.

Heavy Emphasis on Technical Assistance and Dialogue Facilitation

Our program strategy emphasized three tasks: (1) a continual assessment of the interest of various groups potentially involved in the policy reform process; (2) the timely provision of well-targeted technical assistance and research support; and (3) helping to facilitate private-public dialogue networks focusing on priority policy reform and program support issues. The heavy use of technical assistance working with a range of partners on a flexible and rapidly evolving basis using grant funding differs considerably from the more typical case of relatively long-term, rigid project technical assistance working primarily within a government agency through a contract with profit-making TA delivery firms.

Funding Level Requirements

We are finding that if we properly identify the nature, degree and locus of political will for reform, and build the basic institutional and personal relationships, then the funding levels needed are surprisingly limited -- clearly on a scale far below the funding required for most donor-funded policy reform efforts pursued under the more traditional technical approach described at the beginning of the paper. Despite the current budgetary crunch for DEPKOP-PPK, the Ministry has covered the costs for a wide range of activities related to the project, including the entire travel expenses for the large delegation to the United States mentioned above. Funds are required to support policy studies, workshops, and information clearing houses in the non-government sector, but the funding requirements for this are far less than would be the case for similar inputs by expatriate sources. In some cases, non-government groups enter into partnerships with us that involve modest funding transfers but major inputs, given their commitment to the overall project's objectives. The costs per output for our program, therefore, have been quite low.

Building Local Capacities Expand the Effectiveness of the Project and Ensure On-Going Support

Finally, we entered this project with the goal of working ourselves out of a job over a 2-3 year period, building on the political momentum for reform and facilitating dialogue channels, networks, and building local capacities, all of which combine to add legitimacy and create success that helps to generate in-country, self-financed efforts to further small business development over the long run. When opting for the role as a catalyst where there is political will for reform, a successful foreign assistance project should aim to spur the process and gradually withdraw as the process takes on a life of its own.

Conclusion

These six lessons have served to highlight the impact that TAF has had so far in the development of small business enterprises in Indonesia. We are hopeful that other donor agencies will be able to draw from our experiences and reorient, if necessary, their own programmes of assistance towards sustaining the work of small businesses in a manner that enables these businesses to make maximum impact on economic development in Indonesia.

7 Building a Government-Citizen-Business Partnership: Linking Business with Government in Laos

Sirisamphanh Vorachith

Introduction

The Lao People's Democratic Republic (PDR) emerged from a protracted war as a republic on December 2, 1975, when the Kingdom of Laos was abolished. The history of governance innovations since 1975 can be divided into two stages: the first stage covers the period from late 1975 to mid 1986, and the second period from 1986 up to the present.

A revolutionary political and socio-economic regime was installed in late 1975 in the first stage in order to heal the nation in the aftermath of war and to accelerate the process of development in the country. A regime of people's democracy and a centrally planned economy inspired by the tenets of socialist ideology were established. The role of the public sector was predominant in the economy. Nationalised economic entities, and newly-created ones, operated as basic production and trading units for the society. State-owned enterprises operated more or less like government departments hence the civil service comprised also of those employed in public enterprises. The private sector was insignificant. In rural areas, the government created state farms and farmers' co-operatives. The government solved the unemployment problem by creating jobs in the civil service and the public sector. Though economic incentives were used in a limited manner, the sense of co-operation, mutual assistance, self-abnegation and enthusiasm were fostered in labour collectives.

In Laos, the Lao People's Revolutionary Party makes the policies while the Government is responsible for implementation of the Party's policy guidelines. The multi-ethnic citizenry are the masters of the country in principle through their membership in mass organisations. So in a sense there is a close link between business, citizen and government. Examples of such mass organisations are the Lao Front for Nation Building (LFNB), the Lao Federation of Trade Unions (LFTU), the Lao People's Revolutionary Youth Organisation (LPRYO), and the Lao Women Federation (LWF). The Lao Front for Nation Building during the liberation war was known as the Lao Patriotic Front that mobilised people throughout the country to fight for independence. Nowadays, it brings together the influential personalities of the former regime, representatives of religious organisations, tribal or ethnic group leaders, and personalities in the socio-cultural sphere. The above-mentioned mass organisations reach down to the grassroots levels of local government. They hold a monthly meeting at each level, and these organisations report directly to the Party organisation. This is how the Party collects feedback from the people. The Party itself recruits its members from among the most conscientious, progressive, diligent and influential people. Because democratic centralism is the most important governance principle, the Party and government have gained the people's confidence and political support. This is also the result of the use of participative management and the Party's devotion to the cause of the country's socio-economic development and of the people's welfare.

The decade after 1975 succeeded in establishing peace and in building unity in Laos. However, it still faced many shortcomings in the field of development. In searching for the best way to tackle the problems, the government launched far-reaching and all-round reforms in 1986. This turning point was characterised by the transition from a centrally-planned to a market-oriented economy. The re-emergence of the private sector has contributed considerably to the country's development to date.

Governance innovations in Laos are based on these new thoughts and practices. Perhaps it is worth mentioning here that economic reform preceded public administration reform. The latter reform is treated in greater detail in this paper because it has had a great impact on all other reforms. The government has taken the lead in building the government-citizen-business partnership. In order to establish a better link between business and government, the Lao National Chamber of Commerce and Industry (LNCCI) was created in 1990. This organisation is composed of chief executive officers of various economic entities. Within the organisation, various business groups are formed according to the respective sections of industry.

LNCCI operates mainly under the supervision of the Ministry of Commerce. The objectives of LNCCI, as they relate to the linking of business and government, are as follows:

- To marshal and co-ordinate the efforts of members of the business community. This comprises state, state-private, private and co-operative economic units in the fields of commerce, industry, agriculture, finance, transport, service, and construction. The aim is to promote economic and social development consistent with national objectives and government policies.
- To safeguard and defend the legitimate rights, interests, and privileges of the business community, including those of foreign investors and citizens of other nations trading with and within our country.
- To serve as a channel of communication between government authorities and the business community, particularly to make recommendations for policy changes to government and disseminate information about government policies and programs to members.

Four major government agencies play an important role in promoting business in Laos. The Ministry of Commerce is responsible for applying the law on business operations. The Ministry of Industry and Handicrafts promotes business development. The Ministry of Finance deals with fiscal policy and supervises the observance of enterprise accounting law. The State Bank, together with commercial banks, deals with monetary policy. These four agencies help steer the economy and serve to link business with government.

Let me now move on to describe and examine in greater detail the administrative reforms that have taken place in Laos.

Background to Laos' Transition to Market Economy

The Lao P.D.R. has a land area of 236,800 square kilometres and a population of 4.5 million giving it the lowest population density in East Asia. A landlocked country, Lao P.D.R. is bordered by Vietnam, Cambodia, China, Myanmar, and Thailand with the Mekong River serving as much of the border with Thailand. About two-thirds of the country is mountainous which creates transportation difficulties while at the same time producing many rivers and vast hydro-power potential. Lao P.D.R. is a tropical country, whose climate is affected by monsoon rains from May to September alternating with a dry season from October to April.

Two-thirds of the population live in rural areas of the 17 provinces plus one special zone and 11, 935 villages located in 129 districts. There are up to 68 ethnic groups generally categorised into three groupings: the Lao Loum, who occupy the lowland plains and the Mekong river valley, and constitute some two-thirds of the total population; the Lao Theung, who occupy the mountain slopes, comprise about 22 percent of the population; and the Lao Soung, who occupy the high mountain tops over 1,000 meters and constitute about ten percent of the total population.

On the political scene, the Lao People's Revolutionary Party is the only political party. It is governed by an Executive Central Committee and headed by a nine-person Politburo, the President of which is also the Prime Minister of the Government. The Party organisation coexists parallel with the government administrative structure from top to bottom and its widespread linkages extend downward to the district, village and grassroots state-run economic entities. At senior levels, the Party has separate institutions that are symmetrical to the government administration and also has built-in organs that coexist therein. Lao P.D.R. is a unitary state so the local government structure extends from provincial levels through district levels to the villages. Each province is administered by an appointed Governor.

The Lao Constitution was adopted in August 1991. It provides for the separation of legislative, executive and judicial powers. The Constitution also provides a legal framework for a market-based economic system.

The people exercise their power through an elected National Assembly. The National Assembly approves the annual state budget and plan as well as all laws. Four new laws are vital to the country's transition to a market economy: revised foreign investment law, budget law, taxation law, and the law on business operations. The President is the Head of State, and the main organ of the Government Office is headed by the Prime Minister. The Cabinet, or Council of Ministers, is composed of eighteen members including heads of the ministries, the State Bank, and the State Planning Committee.

Lao P.D.R. is still one of the least developed nations. However, since 1986 when the country started to open its economy, the GDP has grown at a steady rate. During 1986-1990, the average annual growth rate in GDP was 5 percent, while during 1991-1995 it attained 6.4 percent with a GDP per capita of US$ 350 in 1995. The fourth five-year plan calls for the economy to grow at an average rate of 8-8.5 percent per annum up to the year 2000, and in that year the GDP per capita is expected to reach approximately US$ 500.

The government's development priorities are:

- **Food production:** Rice is currently imported. Emphasis will go to irrigated rice cultivation in the country's six major plains with a view to meeting the country's domestic rice needs. Flood, drought, and transportation problems are serious challenges to food production and supply in the country.
- **Stabilisation and reduction of shifting cultivation:** 1.5 million inhabitants are partially or wholly dependent on "slash-and-burn" farming, annually clearing and planting 3,000 square kilometres of land to attain only poverty level incomes. Rural development plans-of-action to be formed for each province in the near future will promote more sustainable agricultural practices.
- **Commodities production:** Improvement of farming practices and development of farmers' commercial operational capability will promote crop diversification while increasing production. The linking of domestic to international markets in the region will provide incentive to increase production since Lao PDR is a relatively small market.
- **Rural development:** Plans for integrated development are being prepared by each of the 17 provinces (as well as the special zone) under guidance from the central government. Foreign direct investment has increased from year to year but income inequality between rural and urban areas has also grown. Rural development is, therefore, necessary not only to solve the problem but also to contribute to national development as a whole.
- **Human resource development (HRD):** Given our small population, the inadequate existing capacity for education and vocational training means the country suffers serious skill shortages, particularly at senior and middle levels of the public and private sectors. A lead Committee of the Party on HRD has been formed to develop a strategic plan for the comprehensive development of the people to their full potential.
- **Expansion of foreign investment:** A legal framework is being strengthened in order to attract more foreign investment. Foreign direct investment is expected to play a more crucial role in the government's open door policy, especially when the country joins the ASEAN community in 1997. This will form a mainstay of our economic development.
- **Infrastructure development:** The government has designated transportation as a top priority in order to improve the socio-economic

status of the rural population and to develop trade with neighbouring countries. Infrastructure development is an essential precondition to foreign and domestic investments.

Overview of Public Administration Reform in Lao P.D.R.

In Lao P.D.R., public administration reform (PAR) has resulted from economic reforms begun in 1986 and referred to as the New Economic Mechanism (NEM). This economic reform proposed to transform Laos from a centrally planned to a market-driven economy. Once economic reform is launched, associated administrative reforms cannot be far behind. That being said, PAR takes many different shapes and paths in different countries depending on the perceived nature of the problem. In some countries, PARs are at the level of tinkering with the internal system, e.g., revising the classification system of the public service, whereas in other PARs, the intervention is much more strategic, e.g., changing the view of what functions properly belong to the public domain and then mounting a privatisation program to divest the public sector of activities that are no longer viewed as within its proper purview.

In the case of Lao P.D.R., PAR has been, and continues to be, not only at the level of improving the internal machinery of the system in such activities as re-organising ministries and improving the personnel management of the system, but also at more strategic levels in such things as reducing the number of public servants, privatising state-owned corporations, and creating new public organisations to meet the needs of a market driven economy, e.g., creation of the Foreign Investment Management Committee in 1988, etc.

Since 1986, the number and scale of public administration reforms has been impressive. In many countries around the world, the scope and pace of Lao's PAR would be considered nothing short of revolutionary. And it is not over yet. This paper describes PAR to date, the nature of the PAR yet to come, and concludes with some suggestions for the future of administrative reform.

Administrative Reforms Since 1986

As stated earlier, public administration reform began in 1986 shortly after economic reform was launched. The early stage of administrative reforms consisted of a series of administrative changes linked to individual economic reforms. More recently, administrative reform has begun to address the limited capacity of the public service by way of personnel management and training reforms. One should mention at the outset that the most important reform in this period was the promulgation of a Constitution in 1991. The Constitution is the basic law of the country. All other laws must be in concert with the letter and spirit of the Constitution.

Articles of the Constitution which relate directly to public service administration are:

- Article 8 promotes the policy of unity and equality among all ethnic groups which means that minorities are to be given equal access, both as clients and as public servants, to public service;
- Article 19 commits the public service to implementing a system of compulsory primary education;
- Article 20 commits the public service to expanding health service and allows private individuals to operate medical services;
- Article 24 states that men and women enjoy equal rights meaning that women should have equal access, both as clients and as potential employees, to the public service;
- Article 28 allows citizens to lodge complaints against, and to propose ideas to, ministries;
- Articles 57 and 60 describe the powers of the government which by extension describe the work of the public service; and
- Article 63 grants governors, mayors and district chiefs powers to supervise all work emanating from ministries and to resolve complaints and petitions from the people.

In sum, the new Constitution has considerable impact on public service affairs which the new reform program will have to address. There have been 20 major organisational reforms since 1986 most of which have dealt with questions of financial management, budgeting and banking functions. The reforms have been a combination of creation of new public organisations (e.g., the Agricultural Promotion Bank and the Committee for Planning and Co-operation), re-grouping of functions between organisations (e.g., assignment of monetary policy control to the Central Bank), or simply re-organisations of existing ministries (e.g., Ministries of Health and Education) with a view to cutting back the number of departments and divisions.

More recently, the government has begun to focus on personnel management reforms through the creation of the National School for Administration and Management (NSAM) in 1991, and the Department for Public Administration and the Public Service in 1992. These administrative reforms recognised the need to strengthen the personnel management system in order to better equip the public service to implement the range of reforms underway.

Another important personnel reform promoted by the World Bank and the IMF has been the cutback in the number of public servants. The World Bank estimates that the public service comprises 1.65 percent of the total population of the country, which it considers excessive. The Bank also estimates that the public service salary cost accounts for 45 percent of recurrent government expenditure which leaves only 55 percent of government expenditure for actual programming. The conclusion has been that there are too many public servants for the task at hand and that personnel cutbacks would free up funds for programming and for increasing the pay of the remaining public servants.

The series of public administration reforms since 1988 was intended to establish a national planning, budgeting, taxation, and personnel management system. Until recently, the provinces and districts operated pretty much on their own with regard to these matters. This clearly hampered the national government's ability to govern the country. It is understood that once the government has these basic financial and personnel systems in place, it will begin to delegate or decentralise certain levels of authority to the provinces and districts, but all this only within the framework of the national system.

The privatisation of state-owned enterprises has also been an important part of the economic reform. Before the reforms, there were approximately 640 state enterprises which employed about 10 percent of the non-agricultural labour force or about 16,000 people. About two thirds of the enterprises were centrally managed by line ministries, while the rest were managed by provincial and district level authorities. The intent of privatisation has been to strengthen the private sector while cutting back on the size and cost of the public sector. During the initial phase of privatisation from 1989-90, about 100 of the smaller provincially-owned enterprises were privatised mainly through long-term leases. Because of inexperience with privatisation, many of these privatised businesses failed. Between 1991 and early 1994, an additional 55 state enterprises were privatised of which 15 were small enterprises (less than 30 employees), 25 were medium (30-100 employees), and 15 were large (over 100 employees). A major cause for the slower than planned pace of privatisation since 1991 has been the shortage of trained public servants to manage the privatisation programme as well as the inadequate policies, strategies, and procedures for privatisation. Questions of how bid documents are to be written, how bids are to be evaluated, how negotiations are to be conducted, etc., are all in need of further definition and refinement, while training of the specialised privatisation staff is also a priority.

Ongoing and Planned Administrative Reforms

Further economic reform is dependent on the capacity of the Lao public service to manage the reform process. This implies a coherent set of policies across the system, a trained cadre of middle and senior managers with authority to use their judgement and to make decisions, and the free flow of information throughout the system so that analysis and decisions are taken on an informed basis. The US$ 3 million nationally-executed (NEX) administrative reform program funded by the UNDP described next is meant to address the fundamental deficiencies of the public service.

The Public Administration Reform Program (PARP) was launched at the beginning of 1994. PARP is meant to build the personnel management structure and systems for the entire public service and to clarify the basic roles and relationships between central government, provinces and districts. The project consists of four related components. The first component is to strengthen the Department of Public Administration and Civil Service created in 1992 in the Prime Minister's Office which is also the central personnel management agency. The Department will issue all personnel policy and will manage the appointment, promotion, discipline, and retirement of public servants. The second component of this project is to mount a pilot operation (involving the Ministries of Health, Finance, and Labour and Social Welfare, and the two pilot provinces of Savannakhet in the south and Oudomxai in the north) whose purpose is to clarify the roles, relationships, authorities and accountabilities among, and between, Ministries, and the provincial and district operations with particular reference to financial and personnel management.

The third component is to conduct a training needs assessment and then to develop a management training policy and a plan. Also envisaged is development of the appropriate curriculum, and eventually implementation focusing on the development of a management cadre for the entire public service. An important element in this component is the development of a new policy and program for introducing more women and minorities into the public service so that their much-needed perspective is considered by the system. The fourth and final component of this reform program is to launch a national dialogue about the public service with a view to making its decisions, operations, and services common knowledge first to the public servants themselves and also to the citizens of the country. In relation to this reform programme, much work has already been done in building the personnel management system and in enhancing the management cadre for the public service.

UNDP also launched a US $200,000 nationally-executed (NEX) project in late 1994 to strengthen the capacity of the Lao public service to execute its own international development projects by upgrading the skills and enlarging the pool of trained senior public servants of technical assistance projects.

Further aid support is planned to strengthen the co-ordinating role of the State Planning Committee (SPC) which is the body charged with developing the State plan. SPC will package proposals and give them to the Prime Minister's Office for approval. Once approved, SPC will oversee and monitor the projects. Financial aspects of the grants will be managed by the SPC while the Ministry of Finance will manage financial aspects of international loans. These changes are being assisted through a combined UNDP/IMF/ADB technical assistance programme.

Continued public servant cutbacks are also planned. However, it is becoming more difficult as most of those receptive to the idea of leaving the public service voluntarily have already done so. With 85 percent of public servants employed at the provincial level where resistance to cutback is most serious, the challenge for this initiative is to move from retirement offers to involuntary severance based on real needs in each ministry and province. In targeting involuntary retirements, the system must make distinctions between those public servants it wishes to keep and those it wishes to retire. Involuntary severance must be combined with a program to prepare public servants to move to the private sector either as employees, as entrepreneurs, or as business partners of their spouses.

Much of the international assistance we receive is either directly or indirectly related to public administration reform. Almost every donor project has one or more of the following reform elements: training, re-organisation, policy development, strengthening of management, establishment of information and other office support systems, and generally making us more aware of modern public administration practices.

Assessment of Administrative Reform to Date

The sheer volume of administrative reforms since 1986 is impressive. There has been considerable success with some of these reforms. For example, the number of non-military public servants has been reduced by an estimated 20 percent between 1989 and 1992. State-owned enterprises have been reduced from 640 to 485. There have been 20 major organisational changes. New ministries such as the Ministry of Labour and Social Welfare and new organisations such as the Department of the Civil Service and the State Planning Committee have been set up. It is difficult to make judgements about the operational reality of these reforms because there has been no analysis and report prepared and, in some cases, it is too early to make judgements about individual reforms. Yet, it is evident that reform efforts over the last decade demonstrate that the Government of Lao P.D.R. is serious about the new directions it wishes to take.

The Future of Administrative Reform

The success of future administrative reforms is dependent on a higher and more cohesive public profile of the effort. It would be helpful if the reform program could form a chapter in the next five-year development plan for the country. This chapter would have specific objectives such as improving the service to the public, motivating and equipping managers to do a better job, achieving more results while economising on budget and personnel, etc. It would describe and work out the cost of future administrative reforms and would describe how these administrative reforms will support future economic reform. This chapter would summarise central administrative reforms such as that for the personnel management system and would include a statement for each ministry's planned reforms over the plan period. To track this administrative reform, it would be helpful if a report was prepared annually to be co-ordinated by the Department of the Public Service which would summarise administrative reform efforts and which would draw lessons from this effort and make suggestions for adjusting the reform plan for the coming years.

Future public service reforms will be more difficult both to implement and to assess. This is because the next stage of reforms must address the more difficult areas of human resource development, such as behavioural change of public servants, transparency and accountability for ministerial decisions, further mobilisation of women and minorities in the public service, etc. This implies that there will have to be careful analysis, planning, implementation, and monitoring, if these more difficult reforms are to be successful. It also implies a longer planning horizon for the administrative reform effort. Building institutional capacity, training and development of personnel, and operating in a more open consultative style are not the kinds of changes that can be slotted into arbitrary time frames of one or two years. These changes may well take a full decade to implement.

There is a continuing and fundamental need for the development of public service personnel. The need, first and foremost, is in general management, i.e., how to plan, organise, execute and monitor programs and projects. Particular training emphasis should be placed on how to delegate tasks, how to motivate staff, how to use information to keep subordinates and the general public aware, and how to view methods and procedures as a means to accomplishing the mission of a ministry as opposed to an end in itself. Those in planning positions are critical to the performance of the public service and they have training needs in project management, macro-economics, market economics, and development planning. Those in technical ministries, such as Communications or Agriculture, have sectoral training needs. Finally, there is a large training task involved in the area of administrative law -- the drafting, application and monitoring of government legislation. Training must not be restricted to Vientiane government personnel. Personnel at the provincial and district levels must also be targeted for training. Indeed, if government policy is truly going to be effective, training must extend down to the village level even though chiefs of villages are not public servants but volunteer elected officials. Finally, training must target women and minority public servants as well so that full benefit is derived from their potential contribution to the country's development.

The current census of the public service should produce an accurate figure which can serve as a solid base for calculating future losses and gains in numbers of public servants. The approach to personnel cutback to date has been driven by an offer of a severance package. There has been no attempt to assess how many public servants are needed to execute the mission of each Ministry. It is probable that some ministries have a surplus of staff while others are short-staffed to execute their mandate. In future, it will be important to gain a better insight into this matter in order to make more informed judgements about the deployment of personnel among the ministries. This means there must be some consulting capability in the new Department for Public Administration and the Public Service, or purchased from the private sector, to analyse ministry mandates, workloads and the number of public servants required, and to make recommendations either for cutbacks or increases of staff according to the analysis.

As to the question of pay, while there have been increases, in some cases up to 100 percent, the levels of pay are still low compared to the private sector. And while it is true that when comparing between countries, in order to figure out the real income, we have to take into account the general level of price which are not considered very high in Laos, it must still be pointed out that equitable pay has a positive motivational effect on the performance of public servants. Low pay can only have a negative effect on their job performance.

What would be helpful to the administrative reform process for the future is a vision of what kind of public service Laos wishes to create. Without such a vision, reform tends to be piecemeal and the overall effect less than it might be. At this point in the development of the country, Laos needs a public service which demonstrates leadership and instils pride in its citizens for its honesty and integrity, its accomplishments, and its commitment to making the country more unified, stronger and richer. To achieve this kind of public service, it will be necessary to imbue public servants with a sense of the highest commitment to the nation so that they feel a deep obligation to, and pride in, serving their country. To do so, it will be necessary to make sure that each public servant knows clearly his or her job responsibilities and, through training, is confident of carrying out these duties. It will also be necessary to delegate authority to the level in the organisation best able to take decisions. Sometimes this means giving middle and low level public officials authority to take decisions on behalf of the ministry. It will be necessary to eliminate all procedures and rules which do not support this vision of a public service. Finally, it will be necessary for the system to treat public servants with respect and show them that the country cares about them if the system is to have a productive and motivated public service. This implies a personnel administration system which pays public servants regularly and on time, which offers bonuses or promotions to public servants to accept new postings in the provinces or districts, which offers training and development opportunities, and which promotes public servants fairly and on the basis of merit.

Conclusion

During the past two decades, Laos has gone a long way towards building a government-citizen-business partnership, especially the linking of business with government. It has succeeded in safeguarding peace, security, national concord, unity, and political stability in the country. This situation has long been sought after by the Lao people. At present, the people enjoy a peaceful life, the freedom to choose their occupations, and to contribute to the development of the country. The Party and Government have gained influence from, and confidence of, the people, and the Government has fostered patriotism, solidarity and co-operation among the people. Laos' national traditions and customs - anchored in Buddhism - have yielded a unique management culture in Asia steeped in compromise, consensus and a step-by-step approach to change and renewal. In that context, the government realises that it needs the participation and support from the people and businesses in order to develop the country and ensure the people's well-being.

The political system functions only when it obtains adequate support from the socio-economic system. This, in turn, must prove itself at all times that it is able to bring about economic growth. The growth of the private sector must be promoted and a regulatory mechanism set out so that the country can benefit from the virtues of the market economy and at the same time solve the problems of market imperfections. Private ownership of productive resources may be blended with substantial planning and welfare systems, or social ownership of resources may be combined with market determinations of what is produced and how production occurs.

Finally, Laos can offer itself as a cross-roads or a viable link between neighbouring countries. Laos' accession to ASEAN, and greater economic linkages, will enhance its economic development. At the same time, it is determined to preserve its unique characteristics as a peaceful and gentle country in spite of the challenges imposed on it by technology and globalisation.

PART IV

ACCOUNTABILITY, CORRUPTION, AND ENFORCEMENT

8 A Strategic Approach for Donor-Assisted Counter Corruption Programs

James R. Klein

There is a growing body of literature which describes the fundamental nature of corruption and which proposes theoretical assumptions about what needs to be done to counter unethical behaviour. It is generally accepted among developing nations that the less accountable ruling elite are to the general public, the more privilege there exists for corrupt practices to flourish, and so the fewer opportunities there are for the civic sector to voice opposition to corruption. Second, as Steve Hanke has suggested, statistically, those nations in which the state has the greatest control over the economy, are those most likely to have a high degree of corrupt practice. This is because there are more opportunities to bribe officials.[1] In addition, however, it is often these same states, where ruling elites have acquired the greatest personal interest in the economy, which leads to an array of unethical practices from kickbacks and the rigging of contract bids to special favours for cronies or nepotism in the award of economic opportunities. Invariably, the judicial systems of these nations have been either politicised or starved of the resources required to develop. As a result, regardless of what laws may appear on the books, corruption is further nurtured because there is little chance of detection or prosecution.

Giving voice to civil society, reducing the state's control over the economy, and professionalising the judicial system are formidable tasks. The fundamental prescriptions for resolving these issues and combating corruption are fairly well known internationally, even if they are not always accepted locally. These measures vary quite broadly from increasing the salaries of police and bureaucrats to the complete overhaul of bureaucratic systems. Other prescriptions stress the need for implementing new laws, administrative rules and regulations - or the simplification and clarification of others - and the adoption of ethical codes of behaviour. What is often distinctly missing from the theoretical literature is a practitioner's perspective which might serve as a practical road map for donor agencies to decide where, when, and how to assist in the counter-corruption process.

To determine "what to do", as well as "when" and "with whom to partner", four basic strategies employed by The Asia Foundation might prove useful to other donors. These are: Constituency and Coalition Building, Access Creation, Structural Reform, and System Strengthening.[2]

The first two strategies - Constituency and Coalition Building and Access Creation - are normative in orientation and contribute to the demand side for accountable governance. In simplest terms, Constituency and Coalition Building activities are designed to rally, and to sustain, the political will required to undertake counter-corruption measures. Access Creation activities are designed to promote broad respect and support for improved ethical standards, the inclusion of non-elites in the policy-making process, and alternate access points to justice.

On the supply side, Structural Reform and System Strengthening serve to deliver good governance. Structural Reform refers specifically to changing "the rules of the game", and is often inherently political in nature. System Strengthening activities, often referred to as institution building and human resource development projects, are designed to provide efficient and adequate systems to implement and enforce counter-corruption efforts.

These four strategies can be used individually or in various combinations and sequences, according to opportunities and needs. The appropriate selection will be determined by the internal situation in a country, such as official openness to counter-corruption activities, the type of corruption which is to be addressed, and the intensity of the corruption. Equally important in determining strategy selection is the level of funding a donor wishes to invest in counter-corruption activities, and the level of risk the donor is willing to assume.

Constituency and Coalition Building

To replace an entrenched tradition of corruption with a more ethical orientation, donors must make significant efforts from the outset to help support the establishment of pro-reform constituencies and coalitions. These voices are critical in the process of holding policy makers accountable and serve as a countervailing force to forge the political will required for sustained efforts in subsequent access creation, structural reform, and system strengthening initiatives. Failure to develop and sustain these constituencies leaves only the goodwill of government officials or the intervention of external, often unproductive, variables to promote counter-corruption measures.

The first step in constituency and coalition building is promoting the free flow of information and open policy debate. This step is essential in order to desensitise the issue of corruption as a public policy issue. Too often, due to cultural or political sensitivities, the issue of corruption is treated like a Victorian secret - no one talks about it in polite company. The lack of information and open public discussion, however, results in ignorance about the real impact of corruption. General complacency to do anything about corruption is a consequence of this ignorance. Complacency, in turn, is one of the most significant factors sustaining the growth of corruption.

In every country, even the common man on the street can provide anecdotal examples of corruption around him. Internationally, there is a growing literature analysing the generic forms of corruption. While such information is a starting point for promoting the free flow of information, it is not necessarily an appropriate locus for public discussion. An essential foundation for such debate is in-depth, country-specific research. This is required because in virtually every country corruption has cultural roots. More importantly, any policy debate, particularly on a sensitive issue such as corruption, must be grounded in fact, not in supposition or innuendo. Stated simply, corruption must be accurately diagnosed if effective remedies are to be designed.

Generic as various corrupt activities may be, corruption is firmly rooted in the social traditions of a society. Through the economic and political development process, social exchanges and practices once considered to be an accepted and honourable part of the local culture, often may have permutated into what are viewed, at least by the international community, to be corrupt activities. At the same time, however, the original social exchange concept may still be revered locally as an essential element of the culture. In Thailand, for example, *sin nam jai* (gift of goodwill) is a traditional form of showing gratitude. The giver provides willingly, and the receiver sets no conditions. To eliminate *sin nam jai* would be to fundamentally alter the nature of Thai personal interactions. On the other hand, to both rural and cosmopolitan Thai, a line has been crossed when the gift is valued in the millions and the receiver extends more than emotional goodwill.[3]

In such cases, cultural relativists might argue that it is improper to impose Western standards of ethical behaviour on another society. It is increasingly understood, however, that the issue is not the cultural roots of a behaviour, but rather the manner in which economic and political developments have corrupted that behaviour. Without detailed research on the impact of economic and political trends on the development - or devolution - of a behaviour, it is difficult to move beyond a purely cultural explanation of corruption to an analysis of what has gone wrong, and what remedial measures might be taken.

In addition, particularly from a donor perspective, substantive empirical research is required because what may be a serious form of corruption in one society may be either less prevalent or less politically sensitive in a neighbouring society. This has important repercussions for donor strategy. For example, in a country where there is a high degree of public and political support for counter-corruption programming, a donor will want to focus resources on the most critical corruption problems in that particular society. However, at the opposite end of the strategic spectrum, where political will is weak or ethics reform activities remain especially sensitive, a donor might decide to focus attention on smaller and less evocative issues in an effort to desensitise corruption as a policy issue, build public interest, and stimulate momentum for the reform process.

Another reason substantive country-specific research is required is that any good public policy must be grounded in sound analysis of an existing opportunity or problem. Simply put, national policies and donor programs are most responsive and effective when based on facts. An example of the importance of research to sound policy is a study prepared by the Political Economy Centre of Chulalongkorn University analysing money laundering in Thailand.[4] A poll of Bangkok residents indicates the popular perception that illegal income from the drug trade constitutes the majority of currency involved in money laundering. To address this problem, the Thai National Assembly has been considering draft legislation specifically to control money laundering related to the drug trade. The Centre's research, however, clearly demonstrates that less than ten percent of black money in Thailand is derived from drugs. More than forty percent is earned through prostitution and trafficking in women and children, while another forty percent originates from illegal gambling activities. The Centre's research has already prompted calls by a number of legislators and concerned citizens to broaden the draft money-laundering legislation to include all forms of money-laundering, and not just that associated with the drug trade.

A second step in constituency and coalition building, and a key to effective anti-corruption intervention by donors, is the ability to sift through all the potential constituencies and coalitions to determine which are likely to have the broadest impact on changing the prevailing national norms which support corruption in favour of values and attitudes more conducive to higher ethical standards. Again, sound research and analysis of the social roots of corruption, as well as the impact of recent economic and political development trends, will suggest constituencies which may be unique to a particular society. Without such prior analysis, it is difficult to provide either a laundry list of potential constituencies or to prioritise their potential importance to anti-corruption efforts.

Experience, nevertheless, suggests that several key constituencies, if they exist in a society, can play critical roles. Among these are a counter-corruption agency with meaningful powers; legislators, particularly those who may serve on budget scrutiny committees or committees designed to promote accountability, such as ethics committees; jurists and legal professionals; the commercial sector, including both representatives of national trade and industry associations, as well as members of foreign chambers of commerce, and public interest organisations, independent think tanks, and a vibrant, professional media. An equally important group of constituents are individuals who, either through their personal connections with policy makers, their expertise, or their locally perceived moral authority, have formal or informal impact on policy decisions as a result of their private counsel to key policy makers.

Access Creation

An important consideration for donors in the selection of constituencies and coalitions to support is the degree to which a constituency promotes access to information and/or to justice. Without access to information, neither citizenry nor bureaucracy is in a position to identify instances of corruption. Without access to justice, expeditious prosecution is impossible.

In promoting the free flow of information and policy debate, a successful counter-corruption strategy will provide a balance of resources to both the civic sector and to the bureaucracy. All too often, donor assistance is focused on building the capacity of bureaucratic agencies, such as a counter-corruption agency or an attorney general's office, to gather and analyse relevant information. While such support is clearly essential to the prosecution side of the equation, it is usually inadequate to foster the public opinion required to forge political will or to vigorously identify specific instances of corruption.

Equal, if not more significant, support should be provided to academic think tanks and public interest organisations to strengthen their capacity to conduct independent and apolitical analysis of corruption. There are two important reasons for this. First, support to such civic sector-oriented organisations helps to nurture a culture in which civic concern for accountable, transparent government is both accepted and valued. This is an important component for building and maintaining the political will required to sustain counter-corruption efforts. It is an essential element in overcoming public complacency toward corruption, and building a society which respects and values high ethical standards.

It should be stressed, however, that independent analysis is most beneficial only when it can be disseminated and thereby contribute to informed public debate. For such dissemination to occur most effectively, there must be a vibrant, independent, and professional media. The irresponsible publication of allegations or simple stories which merely report officially released "facts" are not particularly helpful in this process. Rather, a key role for the media is to help explain the real costs of corruption and thereby provide the incentives required to forge difficult political decisions.

Independent analytical capabilities and a professional media are also important because it is the nature of bureaucracy to curb the free flow of information, especially where potential litigation or political sensitivities are involved. Unless civic organisations have the capacity to conduct their own analyses, and an independent media is able to disseminate such research, the likelihood that information will be made available to the public is greatly diminished. As a result, the pace of general public policy debate will be impeded, thus retarding the process of building the political will required for identification and prosecution of corrupt behaviour.

While non-governmental constituencies can be more effective in raising the level of public debate and forging political will, they are also more open to official criticism, if not suppression. Donors must, therefore, be willing to assume a degree of risks and sometimes the donor must stand behind such partners. For example, in 1993 when the Political Economy Centre of Chulalongkorn University released its seminal study on corruption in Thailand, a prominent member of the then opposition party threatened to sue the researchers for libel. Fortunately, the threat merely increased publicity for the study and prompted even wider public debate on the issue of corruption, which, in turn, generated a broader general understanding of the adverse impact of corruption on Thai society. The party leader failed to follow through with his threat. In a similar manner, in 1996 when the media reported on a draft report by the Centre concerning the financial connections between the police and operators of illegal gambling dens, the head of the national police threatened legal action. Privately, researchers received more direct personal threats. Fortunately, the threats again backfired prompting wider public interest and discussion of the issue.[5] Within weeks of the formal publication of the study, and its dissemination at a national academic seminar and in the media, the head of the national police was abruptly moved to an inactive position, a new police chief was appointed, and serious efforts were made to close down a number of illegal casinos.

If there is access to information, constituents must also have access to justice for a counter-corruption program to function effectively. While well-trained counter-corruption commission staff and prosecutors are essential to litigation, if these are the only access points for justice, it is frequently easy to attempt a cover-up, or for political leaders to use their influence with the bureaucracy to restrain expeditious investigation of a case.

Through such mechanisms as administrative courts, ombudsman, legislative oversight committees, grievance committees, and citizen councils, the civic sector has the ability to independently raise specific allegations of corruption. While it is still ultimately a prosecutor's decision to move forward on a case, because the allegations have been raised through alternative access points, and no doubt with considerable media coverage, the probability that a prosecutor will shy away from a case in the glare of publicity for political reasons is significantly reduced.

Structural Reform

If there are sufficient constituencies to encourage the political leadership to maintain counter-corruption efforts, there must still be appropriate structures to implement and sustain reforms. The Structural Reform required for effective counter-corruption measures refers explicitly to adjusting the fundamental rules of the game, which means altering the fundamental foundations of power relationships. It should, therefore, be clearly understood, and taken into account, that much of structural reform is politics, especially in ambiguous policy and value-laden regulations, policies, and practices which surround the issue of counter-corruption and the vested interests opposed to such reform.

The political nature of Structural Reform makes it the most difficult of the four strategies for donors to assist in designing and implementing. Sustainable, enforceable structural reforms cannot be imposed from outside on the stakeholders. Indeed, unless specifically invited by policymakers to assist in structural reform, any attempts by donors to implement such activities would undoubtedly be viewed as interference in a nation's domestic affairs. For the donor, this means first that stakeholders must buy into, and themselves control, the reform process if decisions are to be sustained; and second, that specific reform issues may be undertaken by a donor only when the political will or interest is sufficient enough among stakeholders to move forward. As a result, it is often difficult for a donor to detail reforms that it will address through a project during a given time period with any specificity.

In spite of these problems, a donor approach which is purely bureaucratic in orientation (see Systems Reform below) will fail to achieve its objectives unless political strategies are effected simultaneously. While donors cannot necessarily press their own agenda, they can help to desensitise the issue of corruption as well as guide local adoption of an agenda through constituency and coalition building exercises. More critically, if a donor has earned the confidence of local policy makers, stakeholders will eventually extend a request to that donor for assistance with Structural Reform activities. It should be noted, however, that policy makers may at the same time appeal to the donor to assume a low profile. This can often be a problem for donors who have their own constituencies to whom they must demonstrate a record of positive achievements. Nevertheless, due to political considerations, or simply to ensure local "ownership" of a project, a low profile should be adopted whenever requested in order to better achieve project objectives.

Central to Structural Reform is the drafting and adoption of appropriate legislation, rules and procedures that promote accountable government and check corrupt activities. Many nations already have counter-corruption measures enacted. If preliminary analysis indicates that these are essentially good laws, an evaluation is needed to determine why they are not effective. In some cases, research may reveal that the problem is merely the result of a lack of appropriate systems to implement the laws. This conclusion would suggest adoption of Systems Reform measures to alleviate the deficiencies. In other situations, however, the problem may be the vexing issue of political will, which will require enhanced Constituency and Coalition Building efforts.

On the other hand, all too often the laws on the books may have been intentionally structured, for political or cultural reasons, to promote less than fully accountable, transparent conduct by officials. Under such circumstances, it may be necessary to draft and implement an entirely new set of rules, regulations and oversight mechanisms more rigorously designed to promote enhanced ethical standards. In many cases, what this actually means is a significant reduction of rules, regulations, and procedures.

Too often, donors attempt to assist in this mode by providing technical experts who do the drafting. While this is usually the quickest method of completing drafts, it is rarely effective over the long-term in managing corruption. This is because no local expertise is developed to draft the inevitable subsequent companion legislation or implementing administrative rules and regulations. More problematic, a consultant draft rarely contributes to the encouragement of intense internal policy debate and public scrutiny which is required to develop a deeper appreciation of the meaning and impact of specific clauses in a piece of legislation. Simply stated, since discussion has been limited, few policy makers or interested citizens fully understand what is included in a consultant's draft, and even fewer understand why certain clauses are included or not included in the draft.

Therefore, in developing a donor assistance package to assist with Structural Reform, it is important to support measures which will ensure that it is the stakeholders who make decisions, and that they and the public fully understand the impact of these decisions. A number of methods have proven useful in assisting policy makers to better understand the complexities of a structure and the systems required to enhance ethics in government. For example, donors may provide copies of counter-corruption legislation from other nations to assist policy makers to study the variety of rules and regulations that other nations have found to be effective, or ineffective. Due to unique cultural and political traditions, it would be clearly inappropriate to adopt another nation's counter-corruption legislation. However, this does not mean that policy makers must totally reinvent the wheel. In combination with short-term advisors and workshops, sample legislation can assist policymakers to quickly narrow down their alternatives and promote timely analysis of the most appropriate options.

Observation programs have also proven to be effective. They enable policy makers to examine first hand how systems in other nations have been structured and function to implement complex counter-corruption efforts. Such programs can be particularly useful when they include a cross-section of constituents, such as a mix of counter-corruption commission members, interested legislators, and representatives of concerned public interest organisations. A multi-constituent observation program can promote better mutual understanding of the issues by all interested parties, as well as advance a healthy working relationship among various constituents. Other useful activities to strengthen Structural Reform are consultants, in an advisory rather than a drafting role, and support for public forum and open hearings to discuss proposed Structural Reform.

Systems Reform

Even if political will is strong and the rules of the game are clearly written, there is no guarantee that reform will be successful unless there are appropriate systems to implement and sustain counter-corruption measures. Programs to strengthen existing systems or to create new ones are traditionally referred to as institution building projects and human resource development activities. These are the type of concrete activities most typically supported through donor aid, and, all too often, these are the first, and the only type of projects to be adopted by donors.

Systems Reform activities have high potential impact, and an equally high price tag. Unfortunately, they usually fail to fully achieve their desired results because they have not been sufficiently linked to prior development of Constituency and Coalition Building, Access Creation, and Structural Reform. Thus a system may have been created, at great costs and effort, but it is essentially non-functional or dysfunctional. The proverbial "paper tiger" has been created.

Conclusions

This chapter has been intentionally short on identifying specific counter-corruption project activities in which donors might invest, particularly institution building and human resource development activities. Analysis of such activities would be better served in a separate series of papers which examine the various types of corruption which are generic to the major branches of government (executive, legislative, and judicial), as well as more narrowly within the police and the bureaucracy, or outside government proper in the form of white collar and organised crime.

The purpose of this chapter has been to propose a perspective for analysing the problem of counter-corruption programming in its many aspects and complexity. Four strategies have been offered as a framework through which difficult decisions can be made by donors in determining which of many timely and important project activities should be considered and how they might be properly phased.

Through Constituency and Coalition Building activities, donors can assist to increase the capacity of beneficiaries, both within the government and in the civic sector, to affect policy formulation and implementation. Through Access Creation efforts, meaningful participation in exposing instances of corruption and seeking justice can be promoted. Structural Reform activities assist in the formulation and drafting of beneficial policies. System Strengthening efforts contribute to implementation or enforcement of good counter-corruption policies.

Substantive, country-specific analysis of corruption is the first step in determining the variables that donors must work with in each nation. That analysis will undoubtedly suggest to donors that no one strategy is sufficient for addressing corruption. Rather, an array of variables must be addressed simultaneously and in a co-ordinated manner to have true impact. Rarely will System Reform activities on their own resolve the issue; even more rarely should System Reform be a donor's first line of attack.

Notes

[1] Steve H. Hanke, "The Curse of Corruption," *Forbes*, July 29, 1996, p. 103.

[2] These strategies have been adapted from approaches outlined by the Office of Evaluation of the U.S. Agency for International Development (see Harry Blair and Gary Hansen, *Weighing in on the Scales of Justice: Strategic Approaches for Donor-Supported Rule of Law Programs*, USAID Program and Operations Assessment Report No. 7 (Washington, DC: USAID, February 1994)). This report drew extensively on The Asia Foundation's development of strategies and programs during the 1980s to promote legal and judicial reforms.

[3] Pasuk Phongpaichit and Sungsidh Piriyarangsan, *Corruption and Democracy in Thailand* (Bangkok: The Political Economy Centre, Faculty of Economics, Chulalongkorn University, 1994): 125. This is the seminal research on the cultural roots and the political economy of corruption in Thailand and its impact on the democratisation process.

[4] Pasuk Phongpaichit, Sungsidh Piriyarangsan, and Nualnoi Treerat, "*Phap Ruam Setthakit Nok Kotmai Nai Prathetthai*" [Overview of Illegal Economic Activity in Thailand], Bangkok, 1996. Additional information is based on the author's notes from a workshop on Money Laundering held by the Political Economy Centre, Faculty of Economics, Chulalongkorn University, Bangkok, Thailand, on October 3, 1996.

[5] Of significance, in both instances, was the fact that support for these studies, backed by a respected international donor, provided part of the shield protecting the researchers from adverse consequences. While this factor may not be of importance to certain regimes who downplay the importance of international opinion on domestic policies, for those governments seeking to attract international investments, the wiser course of action is to avoid publicly escalating the issue.

9 Methodology for Evaluating Dimensions, Characteristics and Costs of Corruption

Pasuk Phongpaichit

Introduction

"Corruption in Thai politics is nothing new". With these words, we began a study on 'Corruption and Democracy in Thailand', initially made public in 1994. We did not embark on that study with the aim of rousing public opinion. But the study created a small furore; is still being regularly quoted in the local press; has just been reprinted by local demand; and has led on to further research on the subject.

The same group is now close to completing another study on the extent of the illegal economy. The preliminary results of this study have already been widely reported, and has led to considerable controversy. I want to draw some lessons from this experience.

The problem is that corruption in Thai politics is nothing new. Across the region, rumours and reports about corruption among politicians and bureaucrats are a daily occurrence. We have become desensitized to the issue. Corruption is part of the political fabric, so deep-rooted that it is felt that there is little we can do about it. Our studies broke through this inertia. And I want to reflect on why that was so.

Context of Corruption in Thailand

The rise of corruption as an issue in Thai politics in the late 1980s was not simply the result of an increase in the incidence of corruption. Indeed, the sums involved appear to have been small in comparison with the loot extracted by the military regimes from the 1950s to the 1970s. The rise of democratic institutions including parliament, press, and public opinion have closed many of the simplest and most lucrative avenues of political corruption.

The rise of corruption as an issue was more a function of increasing competition for political power and corruption revenues between the old power-holders in the military and civilian bureaucracy, and the new challengers in civilian politics, particularly those with a business background.

The prevalence of bureaucratic corruption stems from the system of self-remuneration in the traditional bureaucracy. Officials were expected to remenerate themselves by taking a cut from revenues they collected, and extracting fees for services performed. In the transition to a modern *form* of bureaucracy, these practices were never erased. Meanwhile, the systems for imposing moral and conventional limits on the *extent* of such self-remuneration have tended to decay.

Sections of the bureaucracy such as the police are riven with corruption syndicates which at the bottom collect fees for performance or non-performance of their duty, and which redistribute these sums right up to the top levels of the service. The practice of corruption has become embedded in the sub-culture of such government departments.

Corruption in the bureaucracy has shaped corruption in politics. Many of the provincial businessmen who came to dominate parliament and political parties in the 1980s owed their wealth, and hence their political base, to their ability to exploit the flexibility of the bureaucracy. They made super-profits by colluding with local officials to profit from government contracting, and to run semi-legal or criminal businesses. Then having bought votes to enter parliament, they continued to view politics as an extension of business, as an opportunity to make money.

Public opinion remains far from clear or coherent on the issue of what is corruption. The attitudes and vocabulary from the old traditional systems of official self-remuneration persist. Many forms of payment to officials are still rationalised as *sin nam jai*, the 'gifts of good will' from the public to men in power. The boundary between *sin nam jai* and bribery, extortion, and corruption is not clearly marked.

The businessmen, officials, and politicians who are most involved in such transactions are more likely than the average to condone them as gifts of goodwill. They also argue that the resulting flexibility and collusion actively promotes economic growth.

Two other social groups display a stricter attitude. Many middle-class groups wish to impose a stricter concept of public office which would outlaw all forms of self-remuneration on principle. Many lower echelon groups are growing increasingly aware that they are the ones who bear the cost of such systems of corruption. These two lobbies argue that the benefits in terms of economic growth are far outweighed by the social costs in terms of wasted resources, distorted distribution, environmental damage, and social inequity.

Keeping the background and context of corruption in Thailand in mind, a group in the Political Economy Center of the Faculty of Economics in Chulalongkorn University, including myself, Sungsidh Piriyarangsan, Nualnoi Treerat, with help from Teeranart Kanajan-uksorn, and many others, embarked on a path-breaking study on corruption in which we were mainly interested in studying why corruption had become an issue in political debate, particularly since the late 1980s.

Study on the Illegal Economy

Our study for the first time attempted to quantify the illegal economy in Thailand in terms of value added to the economy. We focused on certain specific parts of the illegal economy, including drug trafficking, the contraband in arms, smuggling of diesel oil, international trafficking in women and labour, prostitution, and underground gambling. The study analysed the impact of these activities on money laundering, accumulation, speculation, and the financial stability of the economy; the relationship between the 'big bosses' of these activities and 'money politics'; and the impact on Thai society. Lastly, the study addressed the issue of appropriate public policies such as anti-money laundering legislation to help combat activities like drug trafficking, arms contraband, and trafficking in labour and prostitution; the reform of politics and the judicial system; rethinking about defence spending; repealing the anti-prostitution law but strengthening the laws about trafficking; and rethinking about the outdated anti-gambling law of 1935.

To undertake an analysis of this mammoth and all-pervasive problem, we did some proper and rigorous research: we documented research on the historical roots of Thailand's political corruption; on the amounts involved over recent decades; and researched the political background and the legal framework surrounding the issue. We also used survey research, focus groups and discussions, questions of people's definitions of corruption, attitudes about it, and opinions about reform. Before releasing the results publicly, we exposed them in closed-door sessions to other academics, opinion-leaders, senior officials, and political figures.

Intimidation and Public Outcry

In one of our surveys, we had asked respondents to name the political party which they most associated with corruption. After we held an open seminar, the results were reported in the press. The head of the political party which ranked first on this survey question threatened to sue us for defamation in all 77 of Thailand's provincial courts. The party also threatened to cut off research funding when it next got into power (the same party headed the government which has just fallen after two no-confidence debates peppered with corruption charges).

The story went straight to the front pages, and stayed there for several days. We were besieged by radio phone-ins and TV talk-shows. More importantly, a whole swathe of organizations came out and lent us support - academics, students, NGOs, and pressure groups. Many said publicly that they agreed with our findings, and urged the political party to improve itself rather than issue threats. They urged us to do studies, suggesting we had exposed only the tip of the iceberg. Many people came forward to give us information.

Without any prompting, the university announced that the politician could not sue us personally but would have to sue the university instead since the research was carried out under its auspices. The politician backed down. The issue faded from the media spotlight. But the study had entered into the realm of public debate, and is still regularly referred to in the press.

Recently, we have been through something of a replay. For the last two years, the group has been researching the nature and extent of the illegal economy. The project began when Nualnoi began to wonder about some of the discrepancies in official figures on the economy. We became interested in calculating just how large were many illegal economic activities which normally do not get counted - in particular, drug trading, arms running, oil smuggling, underground gambling, and prostitution. As with the corruption study, The Asia Foundation agreed to support us, and this time the Thai Research Fund also offered its support while the Counter Corruption Commission agreed to support a related project. Both these latter bodies are funded from the government budget.

The illegal economy project is currently between the closed-door session and the public seminar stage. However, a few weeks ago, we released some preliminary results about gambling. Once again, there was a strong reaction, this time from the police.

To collect information on the amount of money involved in the gambling business, we interviewed a sample of gambling den owners and policemen. The interviews were conducted both individually and in groups consisting of gambling den owners and police officers (both were present at the sessions). We covered 10 gambling den owners, large and small. From them we obtained figures on the amount of money involved in the business, and the profit rates. We also found out how much gambling den owners give to the police as protection money. We used this as a base to give a rough estimate of the value-added in the industry, and the likely amount of protection money the police received. We also made an analysis of the link between gambling, protection rackets, and organised crime. In recent years, there has been a shift from private gangs controlled by some members of the police force to organised crime syndicates controlled by some officers in the military.

We reported the results of the study to the public, and sent the study results to the Director of the Police. Some police officers were unhappy. Police station heads held a meeting and resolved to lay defamation charges against us in all 75 of Bangkok's police stations.

Laying complaints like this in multiple or remote police stations is a well-known form of harassment. The charges may not come to anything but the accused are subject to considerable inconvenience. The number of stations where complaints were actually filed reached around thirty. A police officer who heads the police station in an area famous for gambling dens and other vices like prostitution, went on the radio and television talk-shows insisting that there was not one gambling den in his area. He demanded that the researchers apologise and admit that the findings were wrong.

In addition, the police laid siege to the home of Dr. Sungsidh who had carried out the casino research, forcing him to go into hiding; plainclothes police appeared on the campus and loitered around our faculty; our office phone was bugged; and our Center received threatening faxes (pictures of bullets and a death threat).

Also as before, there was an immediate and spontaneous rallying of protests against the police action from academic groups, students, the lawyers' association, NGOs, human rights groups, trade unions, slum-dwellers' associations, and others. On radio phone-in shows, callers insisted on giving addresses of illegal casinos in their neighbourhood. A poll by a TV station came out 9:1 in favour of the research and against the police. The Parliament's Committee on Human Rights invited us to present our findings and inquired whether we felt intimidated.

The issue boiled up so quickly that the Prime Minister came forward to host a summit of the police chief and the university rector to defuse matters.

Key Observations

I would like to make a couple of points about these incidents. But first I want to emphasise that the members of our group are all committed to being academic researchers. Several of us have resisted invitations to get more involved in politics. None is looking for fame or martyrdom. But why did these studies excite such reactions both from those who felt threatened and those who came out in our support?

First, our studies carried more weight than the usual reports and rumours about corruption because they came from a prestigious academic institution. The police tried to undermine the second report, by repeating on radio that 'this is not research', and by appearing on television tossing the report across the table in a dismissive gesture. But this strategy did not work. Chulalongkorn is Thailand's premier university, and that fact carries public weight.

Second, we had carried out some thorough research, and had submitted the research for evaluation by academics and other prominent figures. Obviously working in this area where facts are hard to come by, research is difficult, and our methodologies and results are far from perfect. But in both projects, we have patently used the best professional tools we can find to understand and analyse the data and the issues. The depth of the research adds weight to the findings.

Third, in both projects we have devoted some of the research time and budget to understanding people's opinions about the matter at hand. The opinions we present are not only those of two or three academics. They are distilled from survey work. This was especially important in the case of the corruption research. We had not defamed the political party by calling it corrupt. We had merely reported the results of a survey.

Fourth, the spontaneous outburst of support for our work indicates the depth of popular feeling about these issues. When we recently backed down from the confrontation with the police over casino rake-offs, many of our supporters were quite angry. They wanted a confrontation, in order to force the pace of reform.

Fighting Back Against Corruption

We think corruption is not only a political problem. It is also an economic and social problem. It distorts policies. It distorts the economy. It affects all of us. One way we can help to reduce it is by making the public become more conscious about it and more motivated to fight it. We consider this as one of our duties as members of an academic institution. We believe our studies have given people in the media both ammunition and confidence to expose corruption.

Our success in pressing for public measures to control corruption among the police and elected politicians has been less impressive. We have not been able to press the government to introduce new policy measures to control corruption among politicians. However, we have suggested that the anti-money laundering bill, which is currently with the juridical council, be extended from drug trafficking to include another transnational crime - trafficking in humans for prostitution. This recommendation has recently been taken up by the juridical council.

Conclusion

Our study shows that the control of corruption will require three strategies:

- First, the formal machinery for monitoring officials and politicians needs to be drastically improved. Most of the *means* to do this are already well-known and have been recommended by official commissions. What is lacking is the political *will* to implement them.
- Second, this *will* can only be generated by popular pressure. We cannot expect the bureaucrats and politicians who benefit from the political system to reform themselves. Thus it will be important to bring about changes in the political structure and environment to enable the people to exert greater pressure on the rulers, through freedom of the press, decentralisation of administrative power, more transparency in government decision-making, and reform of the political parties.
- Third, the public must be educated to exert moral and political pressure to outlaw corruption. The mobilization of such public pressure depends on a clearer understanding of the modern concepts of 'public office' and 'public service', and a more widespread awareness of the social costs and political risks which corruption entails.

Thailand now has a parliamentary democracy based on a political party system. But money politics has come to dominate this parliamentary system. People use money to buy their way into parliament, and bargain for cabinet posts. They abuse their powerful positions to make money in various kinds of ways, including collecting kickbacks or commission fees on big public projects which are privatised; channeling government contract works to their own companies or their friends' as well as enlarging the budget size for these contracts beyond reasonable costs; amassing wealth by using loopholes in the laws and government regulations to acquire public lands under their own or their relatives' names; and using their powerful positions to prevent the police and other relevant government officials from cracking down on their criminal activities and those of their friends and associates.

The urgent need to reform this system is now at the forefront of the political debate. Over the last two years, corruption charges have fueled three no-confidence debates in parliament, and has led to the fall of two Cabinets. The issue of corruption is a major theme in the debates connected to the general election which is currently being campaigned for. The need to move rapidly beyond the current stage of political development has placed political reform at the centre of the debate.

Corruption is now at the forefront of political debate in Thailand not because Thailand is necessarily more corrupt than before, or more corrupt than other places. Rather, it is because there is a widespread effort to suppress corruption within the framework of a democratic parliamentary system.

10 Combat Training: Using Seminars to Fight Corruption

Denis Osborne[1]

Seminars on preventing fraud and corruption are arranged and funded as part of the increasing and diverse world-wide efforts to fight corruption. The responsibility for directing such seminars for people from several countries and cultures has led to attempts to clarify the objectives, content, methods and outputs of such seminars. The purpose of this paper is to share these ideas and experience gained through the seminars.

Seminars need to be customised to suit different contexts. This paper is based on experience of seminars lasting from one day to four weeks for international groups in Britain, and seminars for groups from individual countries in their own country, between 1992 and 1996. It takes into account feedback and ideas from participants, from the ministers and officials of several governments with whom they work, and from the representatives of donor agencies and the private sector, including non-governmental organisations. Most of the participants in these seminars have been senior public servants. There have been similarities with other senior management seminars.

Objectives

To start with, the following is a list of objectives of a seminar that is to be held in Britain for comparison with seminars held elsewhere. Taking into account comments on the earlier seminars, the objectives of this one are to enable participants to:

- develop their understanding of the causes and consequences of fraud and corruption;
- examine the policies, management methods, and means of investigation used to combat malpractice, fraud and corruption in public administration;
- appreciate the principles and procedures of control systems in Britain;
- examine the skills and techniques required of control personnel;
- examine the impact of information and computer technology on management systems and the potential for computer fraud and its control;
- assess and transfer relevant good practice to their home situation; and
- build up a network of contacts for information, advice and co-operation.

The objectives for seminars taking place in developing countries or the transitional economies differ from those for seminars in Britain, but there are also many similarities. In several countries, action to prevent corruption is fragmented and participants can benefit from learning about principles and control systems in agencies other than their own. Building networks can be as valuable a product of a seminar in-country as it is internationally. In one country preparation for a seminar on corruption there were revealed gaps between the mandates of different agencies that made it easy for criminals to escape detection of corrupt practice, or to get corrupt benefits (i.e., unfair and unintended benefits) without actually breaking the law.

The objectives place a responsibility on the participants. Research into corrupt practice is difficult because of the secrecy that surrounds it so that there is no clear body of knowledge that can be taught. There is no choice of textbooks on how to beat corruption to match the barrage of books on general management with its fast-changing fashions. Yet, much can be done to motivate people and equip them for the fight.

Whose objectives do we meet? It is helpful in preparing a seminar to distinguish between the objectives of the different stakeholders: the participants, their employers, their governments, the funding agencies (for participants not funded fully by their employers), the host management or training organisation, the director, and the people who lead sessions.

The specific aims for groups and individuals depend on the context. At the start of a seminar, participants are asked to write down their own individual objectives for the programme. They may discuss these if they wish, or keep them private, but participants are reminded to review progress against their personal objectives from time to time and to take any action needed to ensure that they are met as fully as possible. Some revise their objectives during the seminar period.

A few participants are defensive or embarrassed if they think it is suggested that corruption is a problem in their own countries. Corruption is a problem for all countries. The nature of the problem differs from country to country and from time to time. In some countries or organisations, corruption becomes systemic, "everybody does it" and corruption is a fever affecting the whole economy rather than a localised infection in just one part. In others, corruption may be a matter of individual choice and there may be little perceived corruption. But for all countries and organisations there is the threat of an invasion of corruption from foreign business contacts or mafia-style criminal gangs, and in all countries both the *reduction* and *prevention* of corrupt practices are long term goals.

The actions designed to reach those goals have to be cost effective, not only in cash terms but also in comparison with the restrictions they may bring. Excessive reporting requirements may cause delays and expense. Regulations that are intended to make corruption more difficult may make business inefficient, and sometimes provide added cause and opportunity for corrupt practice. Some requirements for accountability and some methods of investigation detract from individual freedoms and rights. In a discussion of management methods and levels of discretion at one seminar, it was suggested that all sensitive decisions should be taken by a committee. Participants had to consider whether such safeguards would be effective (committees can be corrupted too) and what the delays and management costs might be.

Participants

For whom should seminars on preventing corruption be proposed? Management seminars make the biggest impact when the participants are able to communicate ideas effectively after their return to work. Who may do that best? Junior staff get discouraged after any management training when their seniors will not let them make changes or heed their suggestions. Top public servants and senior ministers have little time to spare (and may not remain in office for long before they retire or move to other posts). Senior public servants - the second or third tiers down in most government structures - are probably the best target group. But the exchange of ideas in seminars is more useful with a mix of people, i.e., representatives from the private sector including banks, perhaps, and non-governmental organisations, and from politics (such as members of a Parliamentary Public Accounts Committee or its equivalent). Experience shows that having a few junior staff participating works well. They may be closer to the action, and when it comes to corruption, few want to claim that greater seniority necessarily brings greater expertise.

Klitgaard (1995) advocates workshops for the most senior people, ideally with invitations from a country's President, for "participatory diagnosis" of the problem in order to devise strategies to reduce corruption.[2] The time has been right for these workshops in some countries, but they are likely to be one-off events that lead to new beginnings, perhaps the adoption of new codes of practice or the founding of new institutions. Seminars at other levels have complementary roles and may precede or follow any such presidential initiatives.

Content

It is helpful to consider four main programme components, though many activities contribute to more than one of these and other classifications may be preferred. The four components are:

- **background** - terminology, causes and consequences of corruption, literature, the national and global context, corruption and culture;
- **experience** - participants learn from each other, from visits to - and from - organisations engaged in a fight against corruption, from case studies of action against corruption elsewhere, and from experts in specialist areas such as computers (used for corrupt purposes and used to detect and deter corruption);
- **reflection** - participants evaluate this shared information to derive ideas for policies and management methods that are relevant to their own situations, and thus "internalise" ideas and take "ownership"; and
- **action** - participants prepare reports and recommendations ready for their return to normal work, and personal action plans to follow up the seminar.

Participants have different priorities. Some investigate corruption or prosecute offenders directly, though these are usually in a minority. Most have management responsibilities and wish to reduce the risks of corruption among their staff. Some participants advise on, and formulate, policies for the legislative process, the law, and the institutions concerned with corruption (including those aimed at prevention and education as well those needed for investigation and conviction). All, as citizens, have some responsibilities for national policies and interact with groups in civil society and with the media. The relationship between policies, management and investigation is important for all.

Background

It seems wise to have a session on language near the start of a seminar programme. This is especially useful for participants working in a second language (but many British civil servants would find it difficult to distinguish clearly between bribery, extortion, fraud and embezzlement). However, it is not necessary to get bogged down with attempts to define corruption precisely. Understanding the language about corruption includes modern idiom from different countries - sleaze, ghost workers, air supply, black mist, etc.

Practitioners in organisations seeking to prevent corruption do not always admire the academic literature on the subject. The literature can, however, bring to the lexicon words that describe and classify corruption and indicate possible causes, such as patrimonialism (the abuse of monopoly power by the ruler or the state, as described many years ago by Weber) and clientelism (the effect of monopoly power by pressure groups making demands on the state).

The provenance of these different books highlights the theme of ethics and culture. Inputs on this have been summarised separately.[3] In terms of the earlier classification, this subject may be regarded as background, though it is an area where it is also important for experience to be shared.

Experience

Those who choose to attend such seminars are involved already in a fight against corruption, and the exchange of ideas between participants is always valuable. They are told beforehand that this will be part of the programme and several bring literature about their own organisations for others to see.

Seminars in Britain have included visits to police fraud squads (visiting more than one provokes comparison and helps evaluation), the National Audit Office, Audit Commission, Public Accounts Committee of

Parliament, Customs and Excise, a City Council, and the Stock Exchange. Visiting speakers have told the seminar group of the work of organisations such as the Serious Fraud Office, the National Criminal Intelligence Service, private sector accountants and other private companies, and non-governmental organisations. It has been difficult to get co-operation from banks, leading to suspicions of defensiveness and secrecy about corruption in banking circles for fear of losing public trust.

Before these visits and sessions, the group discusses what they want to know about an organisation, and how they can ascertain staff attitudes and ways of working and co-operation with others, setting objectives for the discussion that go deeper than the information in annual reports and similar documents. Participants respond well to this proactive approach to visits. Most visiting speakers and host organisations respond superbly and say they enjoy the interrogation!

We discuss case studies of seemingly successful action against corruption at different times (with studies for Botswana, Britain, Hong Kong, Italy, Malaysia and Tanzania currently up-dated and available). Different cases are assigned to syndicates. The study notes are available to all and when representatives of the syndicates report back to the full seminar they do not need to describe what had been done but rather give their assessment of what was good and what was bad about the work described - what lessons or warnings it contained. Focusing discussion in that way promotes evaluation and "ownership".

Reflection

From time to time the group would discuss the information gained on visits and from visiting speakers and pass judgement on them. The lessons learned fall into three main categories:

- **policies** - about which decisions are mostly taken at national level and which include decisions on the institutional framework (whether to have a separate anti-corruption agency, for example), the media, and ways to win public support;
- **management** - how to detect and deter corruption by the staff of an organisation or its clients (fraudulent benefit claims, for example), and equally how to motivate staff to seek and maintain high standards; and

- **investigation** - for which it is valuable if investigators, managers and policy makers understand each other's roles - and managers, in particular, know what investigators can do and when they are best called in to help.

In leading these sessions or briefing others to do so, we seek to get participants to provide the ideas. This is part of the effort to help internalise the information gained from visits and discussions and get all to take ownership for ideas most relevant to them. If necessary, a leader can introduce ideas that other groups have discussed, and provoke discussion so that these ideas also, or variants of them, are owned by the group. Participants are helped if they have hand-outs about seminar sessions, but an appropriate hand-out has to be prepared *after* such a discussion rather than before. If they are given material prepared before the session, those taking part perceive this as saying "these are the conclusions you should have reached". But this is an area where experts do not know best: the participants are better able to identify the needs of their own countries and organisations. So there should be no ready-made handouts for this session. However, if there are long delays in providing material, the impetus is lost, and handouts can normally be prepared overnight by editing material used for earlier seminars so that it fits the priorities of the new group. An example of a recent handout on management issues is given as Supplement A and Supplement B. Similar reflection leads to suggestions about policies. Earlier in the programme there is discussion about the perceived causes and consequences of corruption, and a handout on the consequences is given as Supplement C. These examples show the range of the seminar discussions and how these are guided towards concise points for awareness and action.

Action

The long term impact of the seminar depends much on how participants communicate their ideas when they return. Efforts to help with this are described in the next section. In addition, participants in longer seminars make short studies of selected themes of interest to them, visiting or working with a chosen organisation for a day or studying reports and other literature. The results are given as short notes and reported to others in the group as a ten-minute oral presentation after which the ideas are challenged and discussed.

Products

The intended outcome of a seminar is to enable those who took part in it to prevent or reduce corruption in their countries. Such results are not easily measured. The immediate product of a successful seminar is the people - with changed awareness and motivation about corruption, and ideas about policies, management, and investigation. Many participants are ready to undertake sessions with their own staff to share ideas and to train, using for this the handouts and background papers provided during the seminar. They are motivated to structure these occasions so that they listen to their staff and work with them to uncover any particular risks of corruption in their own organisations.

To support this, participants are encouraged and helped during the seminar to prepare written materials to take back with them. When participants from other management seminars were visited some weeks or months after their seminar had finished, it was found that many had been overwhelmed by a backlog of work and decisions when they returned to the office. If participants do not write reports before the end of the seminar, these are much delayed, often for months, and lose their effectiveness.

Because of this, participants in the seminars about preventing corruption write a "Back-To-Office-Report" as part of the programme, with recommendations for action to be taken within their own organisation. The main report is short (two pages of typed A4) so that recipients will read it. A factual description of the seminar may be added as an annex. A description is provided in draft to the group, revised in discussion, and made available for those who wish to use it, either as it stands or after editing to meet individual interests. Participants decide to whom their report should be addressed; this may be a senior manager or a minister, or their colleagues of equal rank, or their junior staff. There may be copy recipients too, depending on the local organisational culture. Hand-outs give guidance for this exercise. Participants are encouraged to write reports appropriate to the culture of their organisation. Some recommend changes, others say only that they were interested in reports of successful measures taken in another country. The reports are typed, checked, edited by their authors, and prepared in final and presentable form before the end of the seminar. The exercise again helps participants focus attention on parts of the programme where they wish to make the ideas their own, and to take that message home.

Participants each write a personal "Action Plan" for their own use, specifying what they intend to do (or do differently) on their return, and how they propose to follow-up recommendations in their report. These short action plans cover the essentials of what, who, how and when. Where target dates are uncertain, participants specify that they will *review* progress by a chosen date, e.g., three months after their return. Personal action plans have special value where participants have been cautious in wording their Back-To-Office-Report.

Participants in national seminars may be given different responsibilities from those in international groups. They may be charged as a group with making reports and recommendations to their Government, an exercise requiring a drafting group and discussion to reach consensus that can make a valuable contribution to the training. A seminar group in Ghana, for instance, was asked to prepare a press report and that preparation served as an excellent training tool that helped build motivation and consensus.

Outcomes

Participants evaluate programmes weekly during a longer seminar and at the end of all seminars. The feedback has been positive and the suggestions and comments have guided further programmes. But there is little information about the impact on fighting corruption over subsequent years. Is this "combat training" effective? Participants in earlier seminars claim that the seminar led to a significant improvement in their work. Attempts are being made to get more feedback from more participants but seminars of the type described here have evolved only recently as part of a learning process about corruption and the associated training needs. The numbers who could give relevant feedback are small and widely dispersed. Funds have not been available to have an impartial investigation made of the results.

An assessment would be made best by interviewing participants from past courses, now back in their own countries. It would help if there were interviews with their colleagues also. Part of the aim would be to ascertain what changes there had been in awareness and motivation, which it would be important to record but difficult to measure. It should, however, be possible to find measures for the information passed on to their colleagues by participants, and to evaluate the reactions to this, and to assess how far recommendations in Back-to-Office-Reports were accepted and implemented. It should also be possible to count the number of contacts with any network members introduced by the seminar. These results from a seminar could be thought of as secondary or "downstream" products that could be valued, albeit in a fairly arbitrary fashion, as contributions to the desired outcome of preventing and reducing fraud and corruption.

SUPPLEMENT A
PAPERS AND HAND-OUTS GIVEN TO SEMINAR PARTICIPANTS
(1996 Seminar in London)

I. **Handouts** were given on: (1) the organisations visited; (2) the presentations given by visitors from different organisations; and (3) seminar sessions.

II. **Reprints** were given of the following papers:

- G. J. Church, et al, "War against Sleaze", *Time*, May 6, 1996, pp. 38 - 43.
- R. Klitgaard, "National and International Strategies for Reducing Corruption," paper presented at OECD Symposium, March 1995.
- J. Mahoney, "Ethical attitudes to Bribery and Extortion," paper presented at the Inaugural Conference of the Centre for Business Values, Hong Kong, 1994.
- D. Millbank and Marcus A Brauchli, "Greasing the Wheels," *The Wall Street Journal*, September 19, 1995, pages 1 and A 16.
- National Integrity Systems - The TI Source Book, draft 1996.
- P.M. Raphael, "Scope of Offences at Common Law and By Statute in the United Kingdom," paper presented at OECD Symposium, March 1995.

III. **Short summaries and comments** on the following books about corruption were also given out:

Alatas, Syed Hussein, *Corruption: Its Nature, Causes and Function* (Aldershot: Avebury, 1990).

Alatas, Syed Hussein, *The Problem of Corruption* (Singapore: Times Books International, 1986).

Carino, Ledivinia (ed*),* *Bureaucratic Corruption in Asia: Causes, Consequences and Controls* (Quezon City: JMC Press Inc., 1986).

Dia, Mamadou, *A Governance Approach to Civil Service Reform in Sub-Saharan Africa* (Washington, DC: World Bank, October 1993), Technical Paper Number 225, October 1993.

Hyden, Goran, *No Shortcuts to Progress: African Development Management in Perspective* (Berkeley: University of California Press, 1983).

Joseph, R. A., *Democracy and Prebendal Politics in Nigeria* (Cambridge: Cambridge University Press, 1987).

Klitgaard, Robert, *Controlling Corruption* (Berkeley: University of California Press 1988).

Noonan, John T, Jr, *Bribes* (New York: Macmillan, 1984).

Osborne, Denis, "Corruption as Counter-Culture: Attitudes to Bribery in Local and Global Society," paper presented at the Fourteenth International Symposium on Economic Crime, Cambridge, September 1996.

Theobald, R., *Corruption, Development and Underdevelopment* (Durham, USA: Duke University Press, 1990).

Thomas, Rosamund T. (ed), *Teaching Ethics - Volume One: Government Ethics* (Cambridge: Centre for Business and Public Sector Ethics, 1993).

IV. Similar summaries and criticisms were also given on books about the general social, economic, government and management context, in particular:

Gellner, Ernest, *Plough, Sword and Book: The Structure of Human History* (London: Collins, 1991).

Hammer, Michael and **James Champy,** *Re-engineering the Corporation: A Manifesto for Business Revolution* (New York: Harper Collins, 1993).

Osborne, David and **Ted Gaebler,** *Reinventing Government: How the Entrepreneurial Spirit is Transforming the Public Sector* (New York: Penguin Books, 1993).

Reich, Robert B, *The Work of Nations* (New York: Alfred A Knopf, 1991).

V. Other documents made available for study included:

- several of the books mentioned above;
- the Fraud and Corruption Audit Manual, Audit Commission, UK; and
- background material on activities to prevent and reduce corruption in Hong Kong, Italy, Malaysia, and Papua New Guinea; in possession with the author.

VI. There were also copies for participants of **relevant British laws**

Prevention of Corruption Act 1906	defines corruption
Prevention of Corruption Act 1916	extends definition
Theft Act 1968	defines theft, fraud, etc.
Data protection Act 1984	protecting individuals from misuse of IT
Police and Criminal Evidence Act 1984	clarifies role of police
Financial Services Act 1986	on auditors, insider dealing, disclosure
Criminal Justice Act 1987	establishes Serious Fraud Office
Computer Misuse Act 1990	new crimes of malicious damage, hacking
Banks and Banking Financial Services 1993, No. 1933, Regulations 1993	money laundering
Proceeds of Crime (Scotland) Act 1995	about confiscation of assets.

SUPPLEMENT B
MANAGEMENT TO FIGHT CORRUPTION

Initial Steps

Awareness
Managers need to be aware of the risks of corrupt practices among their staff, even when they think this is unlikely.

Consultation
Managers should consult their staff and discuss the risks of corruption, the damage it could do, which areas are considered high-risk, and how the risks may be reduced.

Values, Vision, Mission, Code
Managers should aim with their staff to review or express the values, vision and mission of the organisation in fighting corruption. They should adopt, revise or endorse a code of conduct. The code should specify what levels of hospitality or gifts may be accepted and whether these have to be declared.

Objectives
Awareness of the risks facing the organisation should lead, in the light of its values and mission, to objectives and then specific proposals for action. These will differ from one organisation to another and at different times but some examples are given below. Many are simply part of good management practices in search of greater effectiveness, efficiency and economy. The priorities for action will change with time because this is an iterative and learning process. And criminals change their priorities too!

Motivating Staff
The best safeguard against fraud and corruption is properly motivated staff. Motivating staff to work well and achieve quality of service is a primary concern of management. Motivation is improved by:
- customers having direct contact with staff - encourages staff to give good service;
- managers showing an interest in staff, and their work, and their difficulties;
- objectives being set by - and for - staff in consultation with their managers;
- changes, and proposals for change, being discussed by managers and staff, with managers seeking to give their staff a sense of ownership, and explaining changes and the reasons for them *before* they are introduced;
- mistakes being handled by managers in an understanding way, with staff encouraged to report and discuss mistakes, and managers combining any rebukes with offers of training or support;
- promotion based on merit, with the staff confident that this is so;
- pay levels that are adequate - the manager may have little discretion about pay but should know that, while good pay is no safeguard against corruption, falling standards of living may demotivate staff and make corrupt gains more tempting;

- **allowances** should help and encourage staff to do things in line with management priorities; the arrangements should minimise the opportunity for fraudulent claims, not tempting staff to take travel or training visits that should be delegated to others;
- **a physical work environment** that is acceptable, depending more on a shared work ethic ("let's clean this place up" and "making the best of what we have") than cost; and
- **office equipment** should work well and be accessible (sometimes frustration from poor machines can be reduced: erratic telephones, for example, cause less anger if callers - when they make a connection - find the answer quick and friendly).

Appointing Staff

Check references and CVs carefully when recruiting; consult referees or previous employees by telephone if there are "gaps"; ask questions of fact. Examples: What was the sickness record? Do you have you enough evidence to know whether this person is honest? If so, do you think he/she is trustworthy?

Clarify rules, regulations, codes of conduct, and what constitutes a conflict of interest. May staff run their own business? With what restrictions? What are sanctions for breaches of the code? Ask new staff to sign that they have received the code.

Clarify delegation of financial authority, responsibility, and discretion. Staff may sign, for example, "I understand that I may authorise expenditure up to £100,000 but that above that figure, or if there are special circumstances or sensitivities, I recommend to ..."

Train and educate staff about the system, the job, the law, regulations, structures, functions, relationships, etc, and ways to report problems and suspicions.

Management To Prevent Corruption

Ensure all staff are supervised and given clear accountability, especially for work with revenues, expenditures, contracts, and stores;

Allocate separate responsibilities - e.g., staff who check invoices do not sign cheques;

Reduce cumbersome procedures - e.g., simplify processing of expenditures and income;

Hold awareness seminars for staff, possibly also with suppliers or customers on risks of fraud and corruption and means of prevention;

Create or update and use manuals of procedure so that staff know what to do and all can see that it is done;

Transfer staff, sometimes moving those in the most sensitive positions without prior notice, but with due consideration for staff needs where transfer includes changing location - and with advance consultation with all staff whom this may affect - to explain that this protects them from suspicion and demonstrate the organisation's integrity;

Hold regular meetings of managers and staff or of "teams" working on particular projects; let staff initiate topics for discussion;

Establish staff appraisal patterns with training to encourage self-appraisal; help staff identify their own strengths and weaknesses and training needs;

Pay for outputs or results where possible, rather than inputs; check Value For Money (VFM); and

Use outsiders (sometimes foreigners) to make some of the random checks or (in courts) to try fraud and corruption cases, to avoid even the suspicion that local politics or social and family pressures influence decisions. To avoid suspicion that such pressures influence decisions it is best if contracts for foreigners are non-renewable.

Management to Promote Detection

Set up internal audit or inspection teams to check outputs and VFM as well as inputs;

Use random or "spot" checks to examine some contracts, etc., in great detail;

Investigate delays - delays give opportunity for corruption, some indicate corruption;

Seek transparency - publicise fees and prices; give target times for taking decisions;

Check physical security - and check proper procedures are known and followed;

Maintain and check an inventory - with regular *and* random checks;

Ask questions - and don't be fearful of exposing ignorance; in signing authorisations for payment ask to see support papers for one or two items on a random basis, or ask the officer presenting papers to explain one item in detail;

Create a hotline so that suspicions can be made known without damaging relations with management; and

Watch staff lifestyle - ask questions when necessary; if in doubt, seek declarations of how assets were acquired if regulations permit; use or seek authority or get others with that authority to check assets and bank accounts of staff in "sensitive" posts.

Management when Corruption is Discovered

Preparation - be prepared; have a **contingency plan**, know where to get legal advice and what questions lawyers will ask, what records should be kept of how fraud or a bribe was discovered;

Enquiry - hold a preliminary enquiry and seek legal advice; find out the facts and try to ascertain the level of the corrupt act (how much money is involved, what is the loss to the organisation, is it already public knowledge);

Priorities - decide; these may be in conflict but general principles should have been decided as part of the contingency planning; the priorities may include:
- to stop further loss;
- to get lost money back;
- to discourage others by well-publicised punishment of offenders;

- to protect the organisation from scandal;
- to react in ways that are themselves cost-effective and protect the public purse from great expenditure (and public service management from unnecessary effort); and
- to learn lessons for the future, especially about better prevention.

Consider options - that must depend on the level of the fraud or other corrupt acts. Should this be dealt with administratively? Should prosecution be sought?

- Warnings may suffice for minor breaches of regulations. Some agencies claim this is very cost-effective, after the shock of being found out and warned most members of staff do not offend again, but this requires a believable threat that behaviour will be monitored and further misdemeanour will bring punishment;
- Demotion, or loss of salary, may be appropriate if regulations allow;
- Resignation may be welcomed, especially if the case appears not certainly proven, and both the staff member and management wish to avoid costs and inconvenience of suspension;
- Suspension may be necessary pending enquiries or trial (with the disadvantages of salary payments for an unfilled post or a risk in some places of long delay); and
- Dismissal (if regulations allow) may be preferable, despite the risk of legal action by the person dismissed.

Police or anti-corruption agency - decide whether and when to call in the "authorities" after corruption is discovered; if it is small scale fraud - cheating on expenses - this may not be thought necessary but guidelines should be decided as part of contingency planning. In some countries, the law requires that certain crimes must be reported. Beyond that, action should be prompted by accountability to the public. That is a pragmatic requirement as well as an ideal: managers should be aware that everything that is done or not done may become evidence in a court of law or in other ways be subject to media exposure and become public knowledge.

Policy advice - to top management, to the police or an agency, to Government, based on their experience of fighting corruption, is the responsibility of all managers.

SUPPLEMENT C
SOME CONSEQUENCES OF CORRUPTION

Governments suffer from:
- **less revenue** - people pay less tax or customs duty because they pay bribes (a small bribe may lead to a large loss in tax or duty; in some countries, this is thought to be the most serious effect of corruption reducing revenues by up to 50%);
- **higher expenditure** - contractors increase prices to cover the cost of bribes (often 10 to 15% of the total), but costs rise much more when contracts are won by favour not by merit because there is no competition to ensure Value For Money;
- **distorted policies** - decisions are taken for the kick-back and not on merit; and
- **poor regulation** - regulations are not enforced because people pay bribes instead.

Companies suffer too because:
- **there is less money available** for the real work since governments have less tax revenues to spend, and the proportion of the budget paid to cover bribes (15%?) is lost to contractors, leaving a smaller cake for companies to share;
- **the better companies lose out** when contracts are not awarded for the best bids - and the better companies get a smaller share of the smaller cake; and
- **employees get corrupted**, being tempted to accept bribes when placing orders for the company if they know the company itself pays bribes to win business, so that the company gets poor Value For Money on its purchases and bad policy decisions.

Whole nations suffer from:
- **moral outrage** because in all traditions, corruption is thought unfair; hurting people, and increasing inequalities between groups as the rich get richer;
- **economic loss, less development, and poor services** with less money and less Value For Money, and corrupt takings invested abroad rather than within the country;
- **administrative muddle, shortages and delays** as officials seek to maximise corrupt gains;
- **loss of security** when criminals avoid punishment and regulations are not enforced (so, for example, buildings fall down, employees are not protected, the environment is at risk, etc.); and
- **political instability, discontent, unrest, violence** when people get angry.

Global security suffers from:
- increased risks from drug trafficking, terrorism, money laundering, environmental pollution, or high-risk genetic research when bribes to regulators or inspectors, or to a corrupt police or judiciary, allow offenders to escape the penalties for their crimes.

Corruption anywhere threatens everybody everywhere - failures of control have potentially global consequences, justifying international concern and making international co-operation against corruption essential.

Notes

[1] The author wishes to thank the British Government's Overseas Development Administration for supporting a study of development, better government and aid between November 1990 and September 1992, and other governments and donor agencies for contracts more recently. He is grateful for the opportunity to direct seminars on preventing fraud and corruption for RIPA International in London in 1995 and 1996, and for support in preparing for a further seminar for RIPA International in 1997, and for the experience gained helping with seminars on this theme during 1995 in Ghana, Russia and Nicaragua. The author thanks the participants for the lessons learned. The views expressed are personal and do not represent the people or organisations whose help the author acknowledges.

[2] Robert Klitgaard, "National and International Strategies for Reducing Corruption," paper presented at OECD Symposium, March 1995.

[3] Osborne, Denis, "Corruption as Counter-Culture: Attitudes to Bribery in Local and Global Society," paper presented at the Fourteenth International Symposium on Economic Crime, Cambridge, September 1996.

11 Strengthening Legislative Audit Institutions: A Catalyst to Enhance Governance and Combat Corruption

Vinod Sahgal and John Burns

Introduction

This chapter describes how strengthened Supreme Audit Institutions (SAIs) are potentially powerful instruments for promoting ethical behavior, thereby combating bureaucratic corruption and promoting good governance. A strengthened audit function is directly linked to greater accountability, transparency, and improved public sector management. The SAI can be one of the key institutions charged with the responsibility to help combat corruption through preventive measures. The efficient and effective stewardship of the world's resources is fundamental to good governance. Governance has become a cornerstone of development co-operation policy linked inextricably with accountability, transparency, and combating corruption.

Corruption is becoming a constraint to both international trade and development co-operation, and the linkage between ethics and accountability is an area of emerging interest around the world. The role of legislative auditing is discussed here in such a context.

The potential of SAIs as agents for combating corruption by promoting ethics in public service and improving the quality of management is underutilized. Corruption is bad for business as well as government. Business practices in several countries are under review. Cases of bribery and nepotism are being reported with increasing frequency. The full potential of the SAI to address such issues has not been exploited. This may be partly because of lack of visibility in the role played by SAIs in many countries. Or it may be partly because of insufficient understanding of the SAI's potential for combating corruption; there is thus an opportunity to improve the situation. The emerging international consensus on the need to emphasize "good governance", reform certain institutions, and combat corruption suggests the need to explore the role of SAIs.

SAIs have an important role to play in preventing corruption. SAIs can be increasingly involved in examining major issues of ethics and promoting fraud awareness. They are uniquely suited to provide independent views on how ethical practices can be promoted including the quality of public sector management and the extent to which the individuals and corporations operate within stated authorities. When well-equipped with the right tools, approaches and resources, SAIs can serve the public by examining and making transparent the business practices adopted in their countries as well as the performance of projects and programs that are funded by government. The overall objective is to improve both international trade and the sustainability of development projects and programs. Perhaps the International Financial Institutions (IFI) are ideally situated to take the lead in working with SAIs and Governments around the world in this area of Government-Citizen-Business Partnership.

Overview

In this chapter, the authors stress the need to strengthen Supreme Audit Institutions in order that they act as a catalyst to enhance governance and combat corruption. It is suggested that they can do this by promoting ethics in public service in conjunction with support from the international financial institutions. We acknowledge that independence and objectivity of Supreme Audit Institutions are key success factors, and that the strong and widespread support of civil society for an enhanced role for the SAI will also be needed.

The purpose of this chapter is to explore the role of the SAIs for combating corruption by promoting ethics in public service. Promoting ethical behavior is well in line with the existing role of most SAIs. The link between governance, accountability, transparency and legislative auditing is discussed in this context.

The SAIs of all nations, rich or poor, have a moral and professional responsibility to be proactive in helping the efforts of their societies in combating corruption. Recent polls in one rich country indicate that many citizens do not trust their governments to always act in the public interest.

This should be of direct concern to SAIs. The SAIs of developed nations also have to be cognisant of the fact that nationals of their countries may also play a role in contributing to unethical business practices at home and overseas. Thus, the issue of corruption has to be tackled on an international basis. It compromises open and transparent competition on the basis of quality and price and undermines governance. It promotes disparity. It leads to waste and can have several other harmful consequences for society.[1]

Developing countries have much at stake; they could be more active in the search for ways to combat corruption. Corruption increases poverty and can lead to economic stagnation because it diverts scarce resources that might have been used for a country's socio-economic development. The SAIs of developing countries could act as catalysts for promoting transparency and ethical behavior in their jurisdictions. They could assist the effort of others working to minimize the waste of scarce resources for development with far reaching effects throughout society.

The chapter outlines some specific steps that could be taken by those legislative auditors, governments and International Financial Institutions (IFIs) that are willing to work together in this area and are able to take on the challenges ahead. The Auditor General of Canada, for example, examined the question of Ethics and Fraud Awareness in Government in 1995, and his Office believes that it is important to discuss ethics in government and to take action to maintain and promote ethics.

SAIs are well situated to help meet the challenge of combating certain aspects of corruption. They are widely viewed as the independent watchdogs of the public interest. They can build on this inherent advantage. They are mandated and staffed with highly motivated and experienced staff necessary for promoting the public interest. They could make a start by placing greater emphasis on accountability for "ethics in the public service" in the scoping of their ongoing audit work instead of just monitoring compliance with rules and regulations and promoting efficiency and effectiveness.

SAIs have a wide network of professionals with a common set of values located around the world, and they could point to best practices in governance. For example, they could assist governments to design a variety of preventive measures for combating corruption in the public service such as a code of ethics for government and business, adoption of more modern principles of public life, and accountability and appropriate standards of public scrutiny.

SAIs are also ideally situated to monitor the implementation of such corruption-prevention measures. Monitoring the behavior of public officials, and the very threat of public reporting, can have a salutary effect and be a strong deterrent to corruption. In that context, combating corruption will require governing bodies to take a more proactive role in the search for solutions. There is, for instance, need for more "sunshine provisions" in legislation. The public and private sectors will need to forge a stronger partnership on this account if they wish to "make a positive difference".

Finally, International Finance Institutions (IFIs) have the clout and the financing to promote the efforts of developing countries and those of their institutions willing to show some leadership in combating corruption. The IFIs will, however, have to advocate not only the cause of strengthening legislative auditing and promoting greater transparency in the operations of government and commerce on a national basis, but also focus on related changes in the international banking sector. The Banks in some countries may inadvertently be contributing to corruption.

Governance, Accountability and Transparency

Definition of Governance

Governance is generally defined as the exercise of power in the management of resources. It involves the nature and extent of authority, and the control and incentives used to deploy human and other economic resources for the well-being of the general public. The Institute on Governance (a non-profit, private organization founded in Ottawa in 1990 to address governance-related issues) defines governance as "the responsible and responsive exercise of power on matters of public concern. In the public sector, governance comprises the institutions, processes and traditions which determine how power is exercised, how decisions are taken, and how citizens have their say."[2] The World Bank defines governance at the country level as "the management of a country's economic and social resources for development."[3]

From an administrative standpoint, good governance demands sound and ethical public administration of bureaucracies and the policies they carry out. Governing well cannot be achieved without efficient, equitable, and effective public administration; to be fully effective, public administration should support public policy. Thus, the two go hand in hand in making public service more transparent, accountable, and service-oriented. The supreme audit institution is one important component of this process. An effective legislative process, an independent judiciary, and good public service agencies that promote and protect the principle of merit, also advance good governance. Donors of international aid and lenders place special emphasis on these aspects of governance.

From a political perspective, governance also encompasses respect for human rights and adherence to sound ethical principles. A free press and independent election commissions are other important components. Honesty, integrity, fairness and caring are important values. Accountability is at the heart of the issue.

Principles of Good Governance

The Canadian Comprehensive Auditing Foundation has been promoting discussion on good governance from an accountability perspective. Some principles have emerged; for example, governing bodies acting as stewards of public resources must have:

- people with the necessary knowledge, ability, and commitment to fulfill their responsibilities;
- an understanding of their purpose, and of the best interests of their constituencies;
- an understanding of the objectives and strategies of the organizations they govern;
- knowledge of, and access to, the information required to exercise their responsibilities;
- a commitment, once informed, to ensure that the organization's objectives are met and performance is satisfactory; and
- a responsibility to fulfill accountability obligations to those whose interests they represent, by reporting periodically on their organization's performance.[4]

These principles of good governance are fundamental to public administration. They also guide SAIs in their efforts to serve the accountability relationship between those who govern and those who are governed.

Governance is becoming a cornerstone of international development assistance policy. Key governance issues that have been identified, such as the need for combating corruption, include developing institutions that militate against the arbitrary use of power and enhancing the reliability and consistency of public policy and administrative practices.

Transparency and Accountability

Transparency is a key aspect of sound public administration. Governments have a moral and, often, a legal responsibility to report periodically on their performance: those from whom they receive their authority and those to whom they provide a service have a right to know. The essential principle that must be maintained is that the business of government must be transparent, no matter how governing bodies may use the information.

The Auditor General of Canada has argued that transparency allows the rays of light to enter the inner sanctum of government in a way that can have a significant effect on "sanitizing" the management of the public interest. The practice of transparency can be a sound deterrent to corruption.[5]

Transparency focuses on public reporting and availability of information with the objective of making what governments do more visible, holding them accountable for the way they exercise authorities conferred on them, and for meeting expectations they themselves have created. The cost of failing to be transparent, of ignoring the limits to authority, and of underestimating the power of governing bodies, can be high. A lack of transparency can lead to a lack of credibility, mistrust, corruption and poor governance that is not in the public interest.

Accountability runs on information. Simply stated, accountability means holding public officials responsible for their actions, including the provision of appropriate information to the legislature.

In summary, transparency is a powerful tool to promote accountability for the effective stewardship of funds by those entrusted with the responsibility to use them properly and combat corruption. It is rightly recommended as a remedy for social and industrial disease. Hence, sunlight is said to be the best of disinfectants where corruption has taken root.

Link Between Governance, Accountability and SAIs

Political leaders are ultimately responsible to the people for their government's actions, and this means there must be full respect for accountability for stewardship within government. As indicated earlier, accountability basically means holding public officials responsible for their actions, including the provision of appropriate information to the legislature.

In Canada, a prerequisite for the proper functioning of political democracy is that citizens have knowledge about the structure and contents of the public sector's activities. Accountability and sound public sector management are important aspects of good governance. Supreme Audit Institutions, or national audit offices as they are often called, are institutions that promote transparency and accountability on behalf of the citizens of a country, which, in turn, support good governance.

In considering the promotion of good governance through transparency and accountability, some questions arise. For example, is a constitution with transparency and public participation in decision making a part of good governance or a condition preceding it? Can we divide good governance into reasonable components that have logic and consistency? Is there a role for an independent audit function to serve the accountability relationship between governments and legislatures?

The answers to the first two questions can be debated further. The answer to the last question is "yes". However, the SAI must be independent of the government. It must employ qualified professionals with the right mix of skills, possess the required tools for modern legislative auditing, and carry out its audits appropriately to make a positive difference. These qualities are essential to carrying out its responsibility to report publicly on matters of a nature and significance that warrant the attention of the governing bodies they serve.

The argument put forward here is that strong SAIs promote transparency and accountability. Transparency of government programs and operations enables the legislature to hold the government accountable; government accountability will promote good governance and combat corruption.

The Relationship Between Governance and Development

Development requires leaving behind something of value that is sustainable after aid funding ends. In the context of development assistance, good governance has been defined as the provision of a favorable political, social and economic environment in which sustainable and equitable development can take place. A strong legal framework and strong institutions that promote a government's accountability to its citizens are now recognized as significant components of sustainable development.

In the context of development, good governance and ethical behavior are synonymous with sound management. The key elements of governance (i.e., promoting transparency in the operations of government, and accountability to parliamentarians and other governing bodies) are also elements of sound development management: which include accountability, publicly known rules, availability of appropriate information, and transparency.

The World Bank has pointed out that good governance is central to creating and sustaining an environment that fosters strong, equitable development. It is an essential complement to sound economic policies. Governments play a key role in the provision of public goods. They establish the rules that make markets work ethically and efficiently and, at times, they correct for market failure. To play that role, they need revenues, and agents to collect revenues and produce the goods and services demanded by the public. Doing these things effectively requires systems of accountability, adequate and reliable information, and efficient resource management and delivery of public services.[6] The SAI is an important element of this overall system, as will be discussed in greater detail later.

It is now widely recognized that corruption undermines the credibility of, and public support for, development co-operation and devalues the reputation and efforts of all who work to support sustainable development.[7] The Auditor General of Canada recently conducted an audit of Canada's international development activities. He pointed out that accountability is central to their effectiveness, as is the quality of management employed to deliver development assistance.[8] Where the public sector capacity to manage the economy and deliver public services is weak and where corruption is rampant, the prospects for development are poor. Structural weaknesses in public sector institutions make self-reliant development very difficult. Unless ways are found to strengthen institutional capacity and combat corruption, there is a risk of diminishing returns on any other investment.

The public sector in many developing countries has been characterized by uneven revenue collection; poor expenditure control and management; a civil service that is inflexible, top-heavy and underpaid; a large parastatal sector that provides poor returns on the scarce public funds invested in it; and weaknesses such as unethical practices in the core economic agencies. Those weaknesses hinder the very design and implementation of policies to correct them.[9] In countries where such problems persist, a catalyst is required to speed reform in which case there may be an urgent need to strengthen the role of the SAI.

Need for Strengthening Institutional Capacity

Many development agencies have recognized that there is no certainty that institutional capacity conducive to growth and alleviation of poverty will evolve on its own. If frameworks that help create such capacity are to emerge, incentives and adequate funding are needed to develop and sustain them. Donors and lenders are increasingly involved in helping developing countries build those frameworks and develop the much-needed capacity. The SAI should be identified as an important element of the frameworks. This has not yet happened; the situation warrants attention.

In the area of public sector management, the IFIs such as the World Bank, have broadened their work from assisting with the management of project-related agencies to addressing systemic constraints to sound management. Those constraints include weaknesses in the civil service, in wage structures, and in the central economic agencies responsible for policy formulation and program delivery.

A broader approach is also underway in other areas of governance, such as action to clarify accountability and to strengthen the legal framework where warranted. The role of legislative auditing is rightly being examined in this wider context. Other IFIs, such as the regional development banks, reportedly are moving in the same direction. Those institutions are beginning to realize how crucial the role of audit can be in promoting sustainable development. The need to examine the role of audit as a catalyst to combat corruption may be the next step to take.

Legislative Audit

The Role of Legislative Audit

The currency of accountability is information, but it is transparency that allows accountability to work effectively. In the words of James Madison, a popular government without popular information, or the means of acquiring it, is but a prologue to a farce or a tragedy; or perhaps to both. Auditing is, first and foremost, a function that serves accountability. It can be one of the most cost-effective means of promoting transparency and openness in the way governing bodies operate and improve their performance. The need for objective public reporting on ethics, effectiveness and efficiency is fundamental to good governance.

The concept and establishment of audit is inherent in public financial administration, as the management of public funds represents a trust. Audit is not an end in itself, but an indispensable part of a management system that aims to identify violations of accepted standards of ethics, and deviations from the principles of legality, efficiency, effectiveness and economy in resource management. Audit strives to accomplish this aim early enough so that accountable parties will accept responsibility for their conduct and for their use of public funds, and will take corrective measures to prevent violations from recurring.

The objective of serving accountability is not to assign blame but to discover why something went wrong, what can be done to rectify it, and how its recurrence can be prevented. The behavioral impact of auditing starts well before the audit. Many managers begin to change their actions as much in anticipation of an audit as after its completion. In that sense, a well-performing independent audit function is central to good governance. It is a powerful voice that can speak truth to power.

Audit can also help to combat corruption and act as a potent deterrent to waste and abuse of public funds. For example, audit can help restrain any tendency to divert public resources for private gain. It can help establish a predictable framework of law and government behavior conducive to development. It can reduce arbitrariness in the application of rules and laws, and simplify administrative procedures, particularly where they hinder the smooth functioning of markets. Audit can also expose to the public excessively narrow, or non-transparent, decision making that is clearly not in the public interest.[10]

In its efforts to curb corruption, the Development Assistance Committee (DAC) of the Organization for Economic Co-operation and Development (OECD) has recognized that opportunities may exist for corrupt practices in aid-funded procurement. Together with other efforts to deal with corruption, the DAC has expressed its firm intention to work to eliminate corruption in aid procurement. However, the extent to which SAIs can be expected to play a role in this area has not been defined. There may be an opportunity here for members of the DAC to "walk the talk". They should proactively seek the assistance of the SAI community to promote measures that would minimize the risk and impact of corruption.

Any SAI that provides high-quality audit services clearly has the potential to assist its legislature and other governing bodies in holding the government accountable for its stewardship of public resources.

Evolution of Audit

The aim of audit has evolved beyond an emphasis on minimizing waste, abuse and fraud, and ensuring compliance with authorities. It now aims to improve services to society by promoting value for money in government decision making and enhancing organizational performance.

The earliest references to audit were found in Athens, and in the kingdoms of China and India in the pre-Christian era. Reporting and inspection systems were introduced to ascertain the status of the monarchy's finances, and to safeguard royal property from internal fraud.[11]

Later, the control of money became a contentious issue between royalty and the taxpaying public. Audit tasks were specified and developed over the years to become an integral part of efforts by democratic institutions to put their finances under the vigilant eye of an independent body. A shift took place: the primary client was no longer the Crown but the people's representatives.[12]

As economies grew and institutions strengthened, public expenditures also grew, reflecting the broader scope of public services. A parallel evolution took place in audit. Audit expanded and the traditional emphasis on ensuring legality and regularity was exercised through accountancy audit (detection of accounting errors and fraud), administrative audit (observance of laws and rules), and appropriation audit (ensuring that funds were spent for the purposes intended). New areas of audit have since emerged.[13]

More recently, despite considerable initial controversy and some misgivings, performance or Value For Money considerations have been audited; audit's potential for promoting value for money has been established.[14] Its importance is now undisputed and that aspect of audit is widely practiced in several nations. The purpose is to ensure that funds have been spent well, performance is up to the mark, and taxpayers receive value for money.

Role of the SAIs in Promoting Public Accountability

Audit coverage has increased in recent years to cover the quasi-autonomous organizations attached to government and the whole range of public enterprises. Spending by governments in pursuit of economic and social development, expansion of public enterprises, greater autonomy in local authority and administration, and trends toward privatization in some countries have all steadily increased, yet the character, scope and dimensions of public accountability have not expanded correspondingly.

SAIs believe there is a need to increase awareness about public accountability in all sectors of society. They have become increasingly concerned with the need for proper mandates, systems, controls, checks and balances in government planning, programming, implementing and delivering. These are required in addition to the traditional forms of audit to ensure ethical behavior and value for money in the management of public resources.

At the same time, there is a heightened awareness of the potential impact of information technology on the audit and its environment. Governments are looking for ways to increase efficiency, promote ethical behavior, and to give better service to the public. They are often finding solutions in advanced technologies such as electronic data interchange (EDI). For auditors, using advanced technologies will require a careful re-evaluation and adjustment of the audit approach.

In summary, although different SAIs give different emphasis to the kinds of audits undertaken, they all agree on the need for comprehensive audits linked closely to issues of governance and ethics. The comprehensive audit approach has a variety of components. It is focused on the entity as a whole and, in some countries, the results of audits are reported publicly. In addition, due to increased public interest, issues of equity and environment are being added to the already broad scope of Value For Money audits. For instance, the 1990 Report of the Auditor General of Canada to the House of Commons dealt with the consistency of the level of service provided at Canadian missions abroad.[15] More recent Reports have dealt with questions such as integrity in government, need for public sector reforms, and tax equity. In many countries, the public is increasingly interested in such matters.

The investigative approach is emphasized in some countries. It mainly involves examination of special issues, while ensuring that accounting systems in government agencies and related internal control systems are adequate for their purposes.[16]

The various components of comprehensive auditing are equally important. Each nation must decide the relative prominence that should be given to each.

Characteristics of Effective Supreme Audit Institutions

Independence, objectivity and professionalism are fundamental to the effective functioning of SAIs. With duties often enshrined in the constitution or in legislation, SAIs are legally protected from outside influence since they report to the legislative body, not to the governments they audit.[17] Independence must be real; it must exist both in law and in practice. This is not always easy to achieve.

SAIs are granted full access to information to carry out their functions. They have the right to make the public aware of any situation where access to information or personnel was denied. The heads of these institutions generally have tenure; they are typically appointed for a fixed term. They can be removed only in exceptional circumstances.

SAIs also have the full right to use the funds provided by the legislature as they see fit, within their own framework of responsibility. They determine the scope and nature of their work. The standards they apply are generally based on those of professional associations, not set by law.

Powers. Effective SAIs have full power to investigate the use of money appropriated by the legislature, as well as the collection of revenue and receipts of the government. In some countries, particularly in Latin America, the SAIs can enforce their recommendations. Where fraud is detected, the SAIs may have the power to prosecute. Similarly, in some countries, they provide expert opinions in specified areas dealing with public expenditure.[18]

Key relationships. Effective SAIs work co-operatively with the government. Their audits of the activities, programs, functions, and administrative authorities of government and any other subordinate institutions are carried out in a spirit of mutual respect.[19]

Audit staff. Effective SAIs subscribe to the principle of continuous professional development of their staff. To ensure high-quality work, they employ qualified staff, remunerate them adequately, emphasize continuous improvement, and encourage knowledge of the areas subject to audit. For example, there is an increased need for auditors to improve their skills in fraud detection and information technology through a combination of training, education and experience. Dependence on information systems by all types of organizations continues to increase, thus auditing information systems becomes important and auditors need training and planning for some form of continuing education. The auditing skills and knowledge of today will not be sufficient for auditing in five to eight years. In certain instances where special professional knowledge is required, auditors may call on outside expertise.[20]

Sharing of knowledge and experience. International exchange of ideas, knowledge, and experience is an effective means of raising the quality of audit, harmonizing standards, sharing best practices, and generally helping SAIs to fulfill their mandates. To this end, international congresses, training seminars, regional and inter-regional conferences, and the publication of international journals have all promoted the development of the profession. However, those activities may not be enough. The increasing globalisation of issues such as economic and social development, the environment and migration, the power of technology to transform the way government services are provided, and reported increasing corruption in many parts of the world call for more innovative ways of enhancing SAIs' capacity to deliver audit services.[21]

Increasingly, SAIs liase closely with enforcement officials in other government agencies to ensure that skills and insights are shared and that the office becomes more adept at spotting corruption. Meeting this challenge will require more active participation in the audit process by international development agencies, who have a primary interest in good governance. They may have to invest a large sum of money and assign a higher priority to strengthening legislative audit institutions in developing countries. The IFIs will have to proactivly work with governments around the world and seek their active support to the enhanced role of the SAIs. This calls for a strategy and approach that demands careful deliberation and timely action on the part of all the stakeholders.

Some New Dimensions of Public Sector Audit

Legislative auditors are moving with the times. They are in the business of forming opinions and, more important, are potential opinion makers in the areas of public sector reform, productivity, and innovative societies.

Around the world, the international financial institutions are playing a key role in encouraging structural changes in the public sector to improve governance. In addition, the budgetary situation in many countries, both industrialized and developing, is forcing governments to re-examine the role of the public sector, improve its efficiency, and explore ways to "reinvent" government. Governments are also looking for ways to crack down on bribery and graft.

Many countries have already introduced measures to improve public sector management. The current emphasis is on reducing the size of the public sector, changing the composition and quality of expenditures, and making systemic improvements. Such improvements include a new management philosophy with emphasis on incentives, decentralisation, and detection of fraud and corruption. For example, the United States is emphasizing improved financial management in spending agencies. The performance of public enterprises is under increased scrutiny in India. Accounting and financial reporting have been upgraded in New Zealand. Canada is considering adding ethics routinely to its lines of inquiry.

The power, sophistication, and ease of use of technology are changing at exponential rates. A priority for government is the effective use of information technology to deliver services tailored to the public's changing needs. Information technology offers government the opportunity to deliver more services faster, at the same or lower costs. It also offers significant potential for delivering new services or delivering existing services, in ways that provide added value to the public.

Modern information systems and advanced technologies, such as electronic data interchange (EDI) and client servers, are gaining importance due to the many benefits they provide. These technologies have had, and will continue to have, a major impact on the way business is conducted; their use will require a careful re-evaluation and adjustment of the audit approach. EDI, for example, represents a change in business practices, especially the lack of a paper-based audit trail.[22]

Corruption is reportedly becoming increasingly globalised, particularly in the financial system. Due to the heightened use of more sophisticated technologies in the transfer of funds and information around the world, corruption is also increasingly difficult to combat and control.

It is vital that auditors obtain a knowledge of the client's business. The auditor will need to perform system reviews to gain an understanding of how the client's system operates and to identify and assess the system processes, controls, and risks. Computers can help detect fraud and unethical practices. In a non-EDI environment, much of the auditing is done around the computer. With EDI, one cannot audit around the computer because the paper stream into and out of the computer is replaced by electronic data streams that can be analyzed only by automated means. EDI's strong reliance on computer controls and its lack of paper documentation will make the traditional paper-based audit approach difficult, if not impossible.[23]

The SAI has a potentially major role to play in the effective use of information technology as a tool for combating corruption, and could become recognized as a key instrument for maintaining and enhancing credibility of the "state" in the eyes of the public. It is very probable that this field is likely to grow rapidly in the years ahead.[24]

The Challenges Ahead

There are several challenges ahead. The body of legislative auditors, governments, the international financial institutions and civil society around the world will need to work together to combat corruption. There is a call for innovation. There are no blueprints for action. There is no easy solution. But there is need to experiment and move forward with courage and determination. Clear guidelines on how the role could be played have yet to evolve. It would be timely for the IFIs to give some thought to the next steps needed to make things happen around the world on this important front.

Corruption is essentially a social problem and the decision to combat it has to be ultimately taken by the citizens. In this regard, there is a political dimension. Institutions that can influence political decisions do have a role to play. The IFIs and the SAIs are clearly in this field. The challenge is how to marshall this resource. The strong and widespread support of civil society is a given.

The SAIs of developing countries, in conjunction with the IFIs, could take the lead to develop legislative auditing as the catalyst to enhance good governance and combat corruption. Developing countries have much at stake. Corruption increases poverty and leads to economic stagnation because it diverts resources that otherwise might have been used for a country's social and economic development. The argument is that corruption makes the state less efficient, reducing the effectiveness of its social spending. Moreover, it reduces the faith and trust of the people in their government. This, in turn, has disastrous consequences on the state's ability to raise revenue and borrow capital.

Further Steps

Several steps could be taken to move into the future on the matter of SAIs and the fight against corruption.

First, the SAI should clarify its mandate and mission statement regarding its role as a catalyst for combating corruption and ensure that it is clearly accepted, established, and communicated, as well as endorsed by the legislatures where necessary.

Second, the SAI should proactively pursue more policies and practices that promote good ethical behavior in the public service. The SAIs primary contribution to combating corruption may lie in promoting measures that try to prevent corruption. Some SAIs are already looking at modernising the accountability regime in their respective countries. The need to address questions of ethics is very much on the table for further discussion.

SAIs will need to routinely include questions on "ethics" in addition to "efficiency" and "compliance" in their audit programs and training activities. This will take time to implement. Government auditors could play a clear role in promoting ethical behavior in public life. A clear set of criteria for auditing issues of ethics will be needed to implement this aspect of accountability.

On the issue of 'ethics', questions that auditors can raise could include:
- Are there appropriate standards of public life to govern the behavior of politicians and public servants?
- Is the policy of openness endorsed by governing bodies and those charged with the responsibility to manage the government's affairs? and
- Is transparency an accepted norm for government and business?

The Auditor General of Canada has also proposed a framework for ethics in government decision making. Ethics in decision making means that decisions are made impartially and objectively, and in the public interest. The framework refers to: statement of principles; leadership; public servants; transparent decision making; ethics-related training; a mechanism for discussing and reporting ethical concerns; and a continuous process which makes ethics a conscious and visible part of day-to-day decision making.[25]

Seven principles of public life that can be incorporated into the framework were enunciated by the Nolan Committee in the UK. They were; selflessness, integrity, objectivity, accountability, openness, honesty, and leadership. It was suggested that all public bodies should draw up codes of conduct incorporating these principles. Also, internal systems for maintaining standards should be supported by independent scrutiny. The SAI, as the independent watchdog of the public, can play a major role in the monitoring of the implementation of the principles in public bodies.

An ounce of prevention is better than a pound of cure. SAIs could lead the effort towards providing positive incentives for alternative behavior in order to minimize human, financial, and material resource losses. This task involves establishing clearly defined sanctions for those who break the law and imposing discipline within institutions by implementing sound internal control and reporting procedures. Other areas of interest could include: conflict of interest guidelines, training programs, and ethics counselors, to name but a few.

Third, SAIs should actively promote improvements in the quality of the public service. Public sector reform is on the list of priorities of many SAIs. The need is perhaps greatest in developing countries. It is reported that in one developing country, only a quarter of official development assistance (ODA) was spent in the country - of which about half goes to middlemen in a variety of forms. Improving the terms of employment of public servants and the quality of employees, while reducing their numbers will be the challenge. This too would have to be guided by a well-defined code of ethics. The guiding force here should be the concept of transparency. Perhaps it is time to introduce "sunshine provisions" in legislation. The public and private sectors will need to work in partnership to develop practical approaches in this area.

Fourth, SAIs should strengthen their reporting and communication strategies to benefit the full impact of their audit work in the area of ethics. SAIs work with legislators, bureaucrats and the media to communicate their findings. SAIs would need to focus their efforts towards giving publicity to cases of unethical practices uncovered by audits that are not dealt with swiftly by the appropriate authorities to the satisfaction of the SAI. This step would be particularly relevant in situations where leaders of organizations are found to be at fault. There is a general agreement that the single most important influence on the ethical behavior of employees is the role model provided by an organization's leaders.

Fifth, the SAI can play a role in raising the public's consciousness about ethics and corruption. There is an urgent need to improve the awareness of the costs associated with corrupt practices. One suggestion is the creation of "hot lines" that encourage citizens to denounce cases without having to reveal their identities. Such hotlines can be a valuable source of information on what is happening and why, when, and where. However, there are many that advocate that there are other ways to deal with the problem. There is no consensus on this matter.

Sixth, SAIs should get more directly involved in working with educators to enhance communications in schools and homes on the subject of corruption. This type of action would be new ground for SAIs. This step could lead to very substantive and sustainable change particularly if all the stakeholders involved work together on this front.

Finally, there is a need for the IFIs to use their clout and financing to promote the efforts of developing countries and those of their institutions (such as the SAIs) to show some leadership in combating corruption. Many SAIs may not have the independence and resources to expand their mandates. The IFIs will have to work with the community of SAIs to develop a strategy and approach for proceeding on this front. They will also have to advocate not only the cause of strengthening legislative auditing and promoting greater transparency in the operations of government and commerce on a national and international basis, but also focus on related changes in the international banking sector. The notion of transparency should apply equally to banks and like institutions where the fruits of corruption can often be hidden from the public eye.

Notes

[1] Development Assistance Committee, *Shaping the 21st Century: The Contribution of Development Co-operation* (Paris: OECD, May 1996).
[2] Institute on Governance (IOG), working definition.
[3] World Bank, *Managing Development: The Governance Dimension* (Washington, DC: World Bank, August 29, 1991): i.
[4] Canadian Comprehensive Auditing Foundation, *The Search for More Effective Governance* (update) (Ottawa, Ontario: March 1994): 5.
[5] "The Importance of Measuring Performance in the Public Service: The Official Development Assistance Context," Notes for an Address by L. Denis Desautels, FCA, Auditor General of Canada, May 23, 1996.
[6] World Bank (1991): i-ii.
[7] Recommendation of the Development Assistance Committee (DAC) High Level Meeting, May 6-7, 1996.
[8] Report of the Auditor General of Canada to the House of Commons, 1993. Canadian International Development Agency - Bilateral Economic and Social Development Programs, Chapter 12.
[9] World Bank (1991): 8.
[10] *Ibid*.: 14.
[11] A. Premchand, *Role of Audit Institutions in the Restructuring of the Public Service* (Vienna, Austria: International Monetary Fund, April 25, 1994): 1.
[12] *Ibid*.
[13] *Ibid*.
[14] *Ibid*.

[15] Report of the Auditor General of Canada to the House of Commons, 1990, Immigration - Foreign Delivery, Chapter 13.
[16] Premchand (1994): 2-3.
[17] *Lima Declaration of Guidelines on Auditing Precepts,* The IX Congress of INTOSAI, Lima, Peru (October 17-26, 1977): 8.
[18] *Ibid.:* 10.
[19] *Ibid.:* 9.
[20] *Ibid.:* 11.
[21] *Ibid.:* 12.
[22] "Strengthening Legislative Audit Institutions in Developing Countries: A Catalyst to Enhance Good Governance," IDI (July 1995): 12.
[23] *Ibid.:* 12, 13.
[24] *Ibid.:* 13.
[25] *Ibid.:* 17.

PART V

REGULATION AND INFORMATION

12 Regulation in the Information Age: Indonesian Public Information Program for Environmental Management

Shakeb Afsah, Benoit Laplante and David Wheeler

Introduction

The forces of the "information age" are expected to change our lives, but in ways that are as yet difficult to predict. A salient feature of the new age is the far greater capacity to collect, process and disseminate information. Given that the revolution in information technology (IT) has permeated practically all walks of life everywhere, technological change is effectively disintegrating many geographical, political, and organisational boundaries, creating fertile ground for new forms of human organisation. It has also meant that governments have had to come up with new coping mechanisms on regulation keeping in mind the extensive impact that IT can have on public policy.

In this chapter, the authors argue that regulation should change fundamentally in the new information age. Governments should allocate fewer resources to setting rules that impose standards of behaviour, and more to collecting and disseminating appropriate information. Such information will enable individuals, communities, market agents and regulators to interact in ways which promote socially desirable patterns of production and consumption. This new view of regulation moves well beyond traditional prescriptions, which are based on 'optimal' activity levels or narrowly defined behavioural targets for regulated activity. It puts much more weight on the *process* that leads to efficient levels of consumption and production.

How can this new approach be operationalised? One promising approach is a Public Performance Audit (PPA) System which analyses, rates, and publicly discloses the performance of government agencies, public utilities or private firms. Performance indicators, once publicly disclosed, can provide powerful incentives for reducing negative externalities from private activities. Public scrutiny and review also encourage public managers to improve the performance of their agencies. PPA systems can increase both the transparency and accountability of public institutions, and make it feasible for the public to assess the government's use of their taxes.

A well-designed PPA can increase the efficiency of resource allocation by mobilising the power of reputation to reduce transactions costs and encourage socially-desirable behaviour. It can induce improvements from poor performers which would otherwise require costly litigation. Moreover, public recognition can encourage performance which exceeds legally-required standards.

In this chapter, the authors illustrate the PPA concept with a system recently adopted by Indonesia's Environmental Impact Management Agency (BAPEDAL) for controlling industrial pollution. First, current thinking about appropriate pollution control instruments is discussed. This is followed by a rationale for greater use of public information in regulation, while the subsequent section discusses the Indonesian program and the impact it has had since its introduction in June 1995. In the concluding section, the broader relevance of PPA systems for public sector management is discussed, and their main implications for public policy reform are highlighted.

Traditional Regulation and Its Problems

A significant portion of the literature in environmental economics has focused on the identification of optimal levels of pollution, and the comparative analysis of the various means for reaching given levels of environmental quality or pollution abatement. As shown in Figure 12.1, optimality requires that polluters face standards or prices that are specific to their own characteristics, both in terms of their pollution control costs and the damages from their emissions. *Ceteris paribus*, a polluter whose emissions cause serious damage should face a more stringent standard and/or a higher charge, as shown by the point (S_1, P_1) in Figure 12.1, compared to a less-damaging polluter (S_2, P_2).[1]

While optimal standards and prices are valid concepts for the regulation of pollution, their implementation requires precise knowledge of both pollution control costs and the value of damages at the margin. Since this information is seldom available, regulators often set targets which match the capabilities of currently-available technologies.

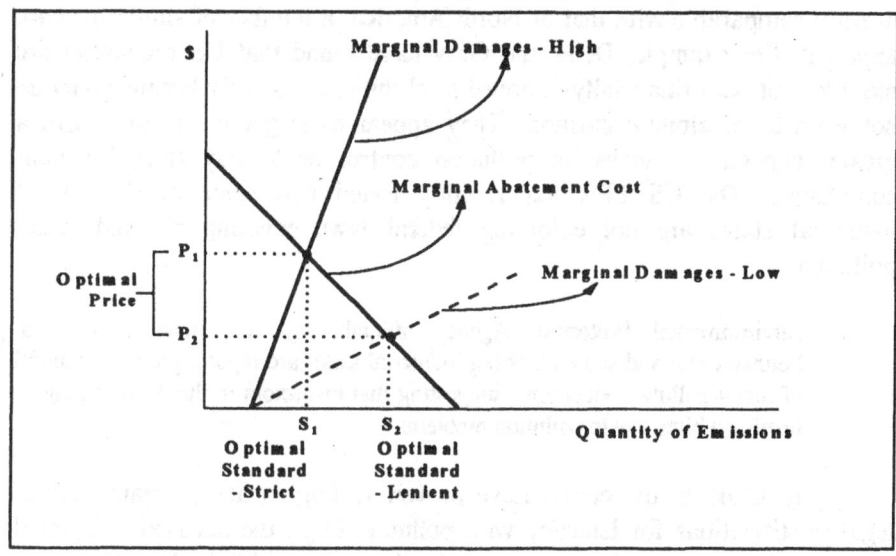

Figure 12.1 Setting Optimal Standards and Prices

The debate over *command-and-control* regulation and *market-based instruments* (such as pollution taxes) concerns the proper instrument to achieve the determined target. While regulators have generally preferred uniform standards for polluters that share certain characteristics,[2] economists have typically advocated instruments which use market forces to induce pollution abatement. Yet both share a common problem of implementation. *Monitoring* the behaviour of polluters and *enforcing* compliance with regulations have proven very difficult in both developed and developing countries.[3] For example, O'Connor cites the experience of East Asia:[4]

> In several of the countries studied here,[5] the monitoring problem is compounded by weak enforcement. In short, when violators of standards are detected, if penalised at all, they often face only weak sanctions. (...) polluters are exempted from fines either on grounds of financial hardship or because the

violators wield undue political influence. Perhaps the most pervasive problem is that, even when fines are levied, they are frequently so low in real terms that they have little if any deterrent value.

While we do not wish to argue that the East Asian experience is directly comparable with that of North America, a number of similarities are apparent. For example, Deily and Gray have found that US regulators are more lenient with financially-strapped steel mills, apparently because they do not want to precipitate closure.[6] They appear to target plants that have a greater capacity to invest in pollution control or to pay fines for non-compliance. The US EPA has recently found that some of the largest industrial states are not enforcing federal laws covering air and water pollution:[7]

> Environmental Protection Agency officials say they have found that Pennsylvania and some other big industrial states are reporting only a handful of major pollution violations, suggesting that inspectors in those states may be turning a blind eye to pollution problems.

In Canada, the courts have proven willing to accept many 'extra-legal' justifications for leniency with polluters (e.g., the accused is a small company; has expressed remorse and the desire to avoid similar offenses in the future; has a strong sense of community pride; or may have to shut down if strict penalties are enforced, with severe financial consequences for local workers). There has also been growing concern that monitoring and enforcement activities performed by the regulator may not have created sufficient incentives for pollution control.[8] Since the early 1990s, regulators have been experimenting with a number of alternative instruments to strengthen those incentives. It is in this context that we perceive a new importance for public information in regulation.

Public Information and Regulation

The US EPA has argued for some time that information provision should be included among its operations:[9]

> EPA's job should grow from primarily the "enforcer" to include greater emphasis on helping citizens make informed choices in their daily lives.

As their access to information becomes easier, both communities and market agents (consumers and investors) naturally generate more powerful incentives for pollution control. For example, recent evidence from Asia, Latin America, and North America suggests that pressure from neighbouring communities can have a powerful influence on polluters' environmental performance.[10] Recent studies from the OECD and developing countries have shown that environmental reputation matters for firms whose expected costs and/or revenues are affected by judgements of environmental performance by customers, stockholders, etc. The reaction of investors to the public release of environmental performance information is the object of increasing interest by researchers.[11] Most of these analyses show a reduction in the market value of poor performers when information on their performance is released.

Hence, for reputationally-sensitive companies, public certification of good or bad performance may translate into large expected gains or losses over time. Knowing this may induce firms to invest in more pollution abatement. For example, Konar and Cohen have recently found that firms with the largest stock price decline on the annual day of release of the Toxics Release Inventory are also those which show the largest reduction in pollution emissions following the publication of the Inventory.[12] Such information leads investors to reassess the long-term profitability of firms, which may respond by investing in pollution control when they had previously failed to do so.[13]

Incentives provided by the impact of disclosure on reputation will in all likelihood generate a different pattern of responses than either pollution charges or command-and-control, and could even generate the greatest overall abatement. Under command-and-control, since polluters in the same regulatory class are all required to meet the same standard regardless of their abatement costs, there is generally convergence to the standard (which may not yield the desired ambient outcome), and great divergence in the marginal cost of abatement across plants. Under pollution charges, or more generally market-based instruments, polluters will tend toward abatement at equivalent marginal cost, but there will be great divergence in abatement practice. In a regime where environmental reputation matters, and is effectively used by the regulator to induce further abatement, polluters will abate to the point where the marginal cost of abatement is equal to the expected marginal gain in reputational value. Where reputation has no value, polluters may choose not to abate at all. However, polluters in sectors, communities or markets where reputation has very high value may choose to abate more than under either command-and-control or market-based instruments. If these polluters are large facilities in pollution-intensive sectors, the result could be overall performance which is also better than under traditional tools of intervention.

The power of public information in regulation depends on the degree to which polluters internalise reputation effects. If these are important, then market agents and communities, *once properly and accurately informed*, can interact with firms to establish jointly-optimal levels of consumption and production. The regulator's role in this system then evolves from pure adoption and policing of rules towards empowerment of other agents through provision of appropriate information. In situations where agents' interactions cannot produce satisfactory environmental results, the regulator must retain its traditional enforcement role.

While information is poised to play a much broader role than might have been expected even a decade ago, its appearance on-stage raises a number of new questions: about the *process* that generates the information used by the regulator to assess environmental performance; the *reliability* of the information that is revealed; and the *nature of the revelation mechanism*. In the next section, we discuss these issues in the context of Indonesia's public disclosure program, which is called PROPER PROKASIH.

Proper Prokasih

The monitoring and enforcement of formal regulation in Indonesia is weak, and the modest size of BAPEDAL's budget suggests that this weakness will persist. However, the manufacturing sector is growing at over 10% annually, and the Government recognises the mounting risk of severe pollution damage. The Environment Ministry has thus decided that a large-scale public disclosure program may induce significant pollution abatement while the formal regulatory system is further developed. BAPEDAL hopes that pressure on factories from public disclosure will provide a low-cost substitute for formal enforcement of the regulations.

Nature of the Revelation Mechanism

Since the purpose of PROPER PROKASIH is to publicly reveal the environmental performance of polluters, the revelation mechanism has been a

primary focus. When the program was developed, certain problems had to be confronted:
- First, the grading system adopted by the Agency had to accommodate polluters with widely different characteristics.
- Second, the grading system had to be simple and easily understood by the public. A few commonly understood categories are easy to process, so it quickly became clear that grading should have a modest number of dimensions. In this context, continuous numerical ratings in many dimensions are generally suboptimal, both because they may not be clearly understood and because their incremental precision does not add value commensurate with the extra costs of providing it. Moreover, categorical ratings (grades) are easily understood because they are omnipresent in public and private evaluation systems. Some grading systems are dichotomous (e.g. pass/fail) while others have several categories (e.g. A, B, C, D, F).
- Third, the grading system had to discriminate between firms in compliance with the regulations and those not.
- Finally, it had to provide incentives for firms to comply with the regulations, but also inducements for them to exceed the regulatory requirements. In late 1993, BAPEDAL settled on the five-colour scheme shown in Table 12.1 in the next page.

The Evaluation Process and the Reliability of Information

Existing environmental regulations in Indonesia cover hazardous wastes as well as air and water pollution. Their compliance requirements vary by type of polluter, generally classified as industrial or non-industrial, stationary or mobile, and point or non-point source. Regulation of hazardous waste and air pollution is very recent, with a Presidential Decree issued in 1994 for hazardous waste and a 1995 Ministerial Decree specifying air emissions standards for stationary sources. Regulation of water pollution has a significantly longer record of development and implementation experience. A 1991 Ministerial Decree (KEP/MEN/03/1991) specifies discharge standards, based on pollution loads for fourteen industries. For the remaining industries, Decree KEP/MEN/03/1991 specifies pollution concentration standards which vary according to water quality objectives in the receiving rivers.

Table 12.1 PROPER PROKASIH's Five Colour Scheme

Compliance Status	Colour Rating	Performance Criteria
Not in Compliance	Black	Polluter makes no effort to control pollution, and causes serious environmental damage.
	Red	Polluter makes some effort to control pollution, but not enough to achieve compliance.
In Compliance	Blue	Polluter applies effort sufficient only to meet the standard.
	Green	Pollution level is significantly lower than the discharge standards. Polluter also ensures proper disposal of sludge; good housekeeping; accurate pollution records; and good maintenance of the waste water treatment system.
	Gold	All requirements of Green, plus similar levels of control for air and hazardous waste. Polluter reaches high international standards by making extensive use of clean technology, waste minimisation pollution prevention, recycling, etc.

Given its relative depth of experience with regulation of water pollution, BAPEDAL decided to focus on compliance with water regulations in the first phase of PROPER. While it had very limited information on air pollution or hazardous waste, the agency had considerable information on industrial water pollution from two sources: its Clean River Program (PROKASIH), which was introduced in 1989, and its regulatory monitoring and enforcement activity (JAGATIRTA) under KEP/MEN/03/1991.

Combined with self-monitoring reports from polluters, these information sources were in most cases judged sufficient for a careful compliance assessment in Phase I of PROPER. As shown in Figure 12.2, existing information on polluters was complemented with a survey questionnaire sent to selected polluters, and with an inspection program by BAPEDAL to verify the validity of the data *on site*.

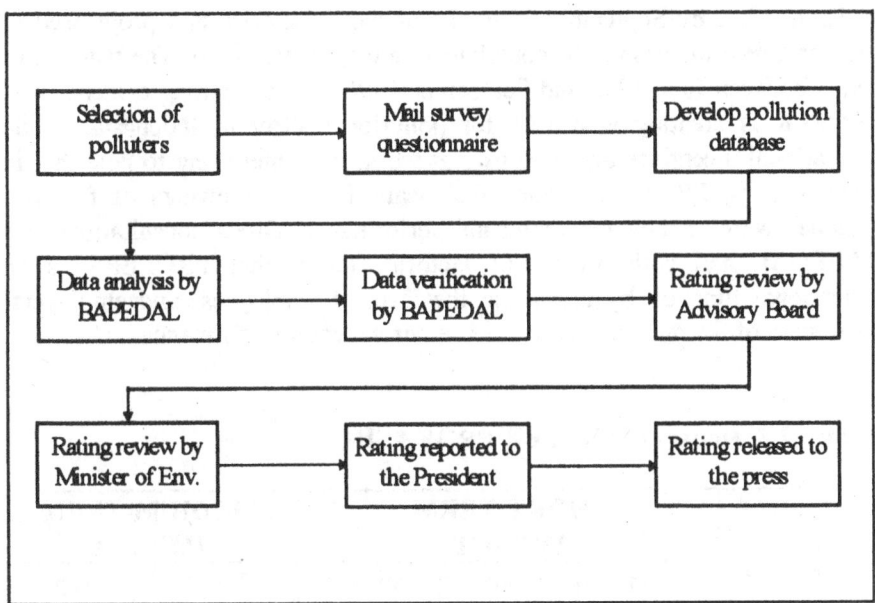

Figure 12.2 Process and Reliability of Information

Impact of PROPER PROKASIH

The program was introduced in June 1995 and was extensively covered in the national as well as the international press. In June 1995, five factories were publicly awarded the Green rating (no factories were rated Gold). Since it was the first time that a program of this nature was implemented in Indonesia, the reaction of neighbouring communities towards those plants rated Black or Red was unknown. It was, therefore, decided in June 1995 that only the distribution of the 182 plants across the colour scheme would be publicly disclosed. Plants rated Black or Red were privately notified of their ratings and were given until December 1995 to improve their performance before their name and rating be publicly disclosed. The threat of disclosure was sufficient to prompt a group of 10 factories to invest in pollution abatement sufficiently to improve their rating to Red or Blue. We believe that the primary driving force behind these improvements are reputational incentives based on the expectations of strong responses from communities and markets.

In December 1995, 120 factories were rated Black or Red. As shown in Table 12.2, by September 1996, 33 of these factories had progressed to Blue or Green increasing the compliance rate by nearly 29%. The reaction of plants between June 1995 and September 1996 provides strong evidence that PROPER is creating incentives for pollution control in Indonesia. While reputational incentives are obviously at work, it is interesting to note that in several cases, PROPER became the means by which owners of factories became aware of their environmental performance. Direct consultations that BAPEDAL had with owners of factories reveal that PROPER has an educational function by increasing the level of employees' and employers' awareness of the regulations and their environmental performance.

Table 12.2 Impact of PROPER PROKASIH

RATINGS	SHORT-TERM IMPACT			MEDIUM-TERM IMPACT	
	Jun 1995	Dec 1995	Percent Change	Dec 1995	Sep 1996
Gold	--	--	--	--	--
Green	5	4	- 20%	--	1
Blue	61	72	+18%	--	33
Red	115	108	- 6%	115	80
Black	6	3	-50%	5	6

It is also very interesting to note that the number of factories that volunteered their participation in PROPER increased from 11 in June 1995 to 23 by December 1995. As would be expected, we find that volunteers have on average a superior environmental performance than non-volunteers. Clearly, these factories saw some positive values from their environmental performance being publicly disclosed. Finally, we have anecdotal evidence that financial markets may create incentives for pollution control. In mid-1995, a factory wanted its shares to be traded on the stock market but was deeply concerned with the impact of its poor rating on the value of its shares. Within a period of 3 months, the firm invested in pollution control equipment, achieved a Blue rating, and then went public.

PROPER also has an important impact on BAPEDAL itself. In particular, the need for accuracy in the ratings has compelled BAPEDAL to increase the number of inspections it is conducting, and improve the quality and reliability of the data it is collecting. Moreover, the database provided through PROPER is currently used to identify priorities of action. The information collected through PROPER also provides BAPEDAL with solid evidence of a factory's compliance status and can support stronger enforcement actions if desired.

Conclusions

A new approach to regulation in Indonesia is showing that local communities and market forces can be powerful allies in the struggle against excessive industrial pollution. PROPER's ratings are designed to reward good performance and call public attention to polluters who are not in compliance with the regulations. Armed with this information, local communities can negotiate better environmental arrangements with neighbouring factories; firms with good performance can advertise their status and earn market rewards from their performance; investors can accurately assess environmental liabilities; and regulators can focus their limited resources on the worst performers. Moreover, transparency is increased because the environmental agency itself is opened to public scrutiny. By committing itself to a public disclosure strategy, it chooses to reveal its own ability to process information reliably and enforce the existing regulations.

During its first two years of operation, PROPER has proven quite effective in moving poor performers toward compliance, and motivating some firms to pursue higher ratings by abating beyond the requirements and investing in pollution prevention. Undeniably, public information is having an important impact on industrial pollution control in Indonesia. Inspired by this example of public information in action, the governments of Philippines,

Colombia, Mexico, and Brazil are now moving rapidly toward developing their own public disclosure programs.

To conclude, we must rethink the regulator's role in pollution management once we recognise that local communities, consumers, and investors may all provide incentives for pollution control if empowered to do so. In the information age, the regulator's role is no longer confined to producing and policing rules and standards. Instead, the regulator can gain important leverage through programs such as public disclosure, which harness the power of communities and markets. A broader implication is that one size no longer "fits all" for regulatory policy design. Optimal combinations of regulatory tools, including new information strategies, will depend on country-specific social, economic, and institutional conditions.

Notes

[1] Similarly, other things being equal, a polluter with lower costs of pollution control should be facing a more stringent standard and/or a lower price than a polluter with high control costs.

[2] For example, pollution standards are typically defined for a group of plants belonging to the same industrial sector.

[3] We define *monitoring* as the set of activities aimed at verifying the regulatory compliance of a specific polluter. Among others, these activities include inspections of a polluter's facilities and effluent sampling for a description of the various types of inspections undertaken by the US Environmental Protection Agency). We define *enforcement* as the set of actions which penalise non-compliance with regulations. Monitoring and enforcement together determine a polluter's expected penalty for non-compliance. A profit-maximising firm will compare this expected penalty with the expected cost of abating pollution to determine the most profitable level of pollution control. See W. A. Magat and W. K. Viscusi, "Effectiveness of the EPA's Regulatory Enforcement: The Case of Industrial Effluent Standards," *Journal of Law and Economics* 33, 2 (October 1990): 331-360.

[4] D. O'Conner, *Managing the Environment with Rapid Industrialisation: Lessons from the East Asian Experience* (Paris: OECD, 1994): 94.

[5] The countries studied are Japan, Korea, Taiwan, Thailand, and Indonesia.

[6] M. E. Deily and W. B. Gray, "Enforcement of Pollution Regulations in a Declining Industry," *Journal of Environmental Economics and Management* 21, 3 (November 1991): 260-274.

[7] *New York Times*, December 15, 1996.
[8] Russell writes: "Efforts to monitor regulated behaviour appear to have been inadequate to the task - a very difficult task in many instances - and *typical enforcement practices appear to have been insufficiently rigorous*," see C. Russell, "Monitoring and Enforcement," in P. R. Portney (ed), *Public Policies for Environmental Protection* (Washington, DC: Resources for the Future, 1990): 243; italics ours.
[9] Environment Protection Agency, "Environmental Education," *EPA Journal* 17: 4.
[10] For evidence from Asia and North America, see S. Pragal and D. Wheeler, "Informal Regulation in Developing Countries: Evidence from Indonesia," *Journal of Political Economy* 104, 6 (December 1996): 1314-1327, and M. Hettige, S. Pragal, M. Singh, and D. Wheeler, *Formal and Informal Regulation of Industrial Pollution: Comparative Evidence from Indonesia and the US* (Washington, DC: World Bank, Policy Research Department, 1996). Evidence from Brazil and Mexico can be found in D. Wheeler and D. Witzel, *Development, Regulation and the Fate of Sepetiba Bay* (Washington, DC: World Bank, Policy Research Department, 1996), and M. Hettige and D. Witzel, *Pollution Control Priorities for Mexico* (Washington, DC: World Bank, Policy Research Department, 1996).
[11] See M. Muoghalu, et al, "Hazardous Waste Lawsuits, Stockholder Returns, and Deterrence," *Southern Economic Journal* 57, 2 (October 1990): 357-370; P. Lanoie and B. Laplante, "The Market Response to Environmental Incidents in Canada: A Theoretical and Empirical Analysis," *Southern Economic Journal* 60, 3 (January 1994): 657-672; and J. T. Hamilton, "Pollution as News: Media and Stock Market Reactions to the Toxic Release Inventory Data," *Journal of Environmental Economics and Management* 28, 1 (January 1995): 98-113. For a survey of this literature, see P. Lanoie, B. Laplante, and M. Roy, *Can Capital Markets Create Incentives for Pollution Control?* (Washington, DC: World Bank, Policy Research Department, 1997).
[12] S. Konar and M. A. Cohen, "Information as Regulation: The Effect of Community Right to Know Laws on Toxic Emissions," *Journal of Environmental Economics and Management* 32, 1 (January 1997): 109-124. In 1986, the US EPA introduced the Toxics Release Inventory (TRI), a program which covers every manufacturing facility with 10 or more employees which emits at least one of 300 specified toxic substances above a given quantity. In TRI, these plants must report their annual releases of all 300 substances. The US EPA provides this information to the public through an easily-accessible database.
[13] While this paper focuses on the role of public information in pollution regulation, the growing ease of access to information is also stimulating many other applications. For example, the medical license board of Massachusetts now gives the public access to the disciplinary records and malpractice history of physicians in the state. Recently, consumer advocacy groups have argued that the airlines

should give the public access to their safety records: number of crashes, safety violations, etc. The Government of Philippines is currently developing a Public Performance Audit System to disclose the performance of private concessionaires providing water to the various areas of Manila.

13 Building Information "City Streets": The Internet as a Tool for Effective Governance

Bhavya Lal

As a great social leveller, information technology ranks second only to death. It can raze cultural barriers, overwhelm economic inequalities, even compensate for intellectual disparities. High technology can put unequal human beings on an equal footing, and that makes it the most potent democratising tool ever devised.

Sam Pitroda
Harvard Business Review
1993

Imagine a world where the only communication tools are paper and pens. In the society there are only three actors. They are the business-media, the government, and the citizens.

There is plenty of paper to go around. However, only the business-media and the government have pens and the ability to distribute written words. It only takes one a moment to realise who has real power and a voice in agenda setting in this world.

Citizen-based electronic democracy is about getting pens to the people.

Steven Clift
Founder of the Minnesota E-Democracy Project
1996

Background

Created to support military research and communication in the United States, the Internet expanded greatly when the US National Science Foundation (NSF) created five supercomputer centres around the country, and developed regional networks to link researchers and scientists in educational institutions and industry to the supercomputers. The networks supported e-mail, FTP, and listservs. Use of the Internet gradually expanded throughout the academic research world to faculty, staff, and students on many college campuses.

Today, the usefulness of the Internet has been demonstrated by users far from college campuses. Organisations and businesses use e-mail and mailing lists to alert their workers in far-off locations of new policies, prices, and procedures, or to communicate with their suppliers and customers. As local area networks are developed for federal, state, and local government agencies, connections to the Internet are being established and use of the Internet by public officials is becoming a reality.[1] In North Carolina in the United States, the Office of the State Controller's Information Resources Management Commission has issued the "Principles for Statewide Information Resource Management," which recommends that the state encourage agencies to "promote sharing of resources, including data and information, and to support direct access and interaction by citizens" and that "once captured, information will be stored and exchanged using electronic means." Similar declarations are being made by democratic governments all over the world.

In this chapter, the author discusses how local governments can use the Internet as a tool for achieving policy goals. These goals could include but are not limited to: improving communications among government officials and citizens and within the government itself, to provide government information and services to citizens, to promote economic development, and to encourage citizen participation in public affairs.

Effective Governance at the Local Level

First of all, why should local governments, more than any others, care about using the Internet? One reason is that local government is the level of government closest to the citizen, its task being "to consult, discuss, and make decisions on behalf of the local community; to provide specific services; to protect citizens and their environment; and to monitor and protect the community from disease and pollution".[2] In conducting these tasks, the responsibilities and tasks of local government sometimes overlap with other levels of government and other local or regional organisations, in addition to local citizens. Local governments, therefore, must forge partnerships with citizens, the private sector, non-governmental organisations, and community-based organisations. Such a mandate demands a high level of communication and co-ordination on the part of the government.

As will be shown in this chapter, the Internet provides a handy way to improve such communication and co-ordination efforts - by expediting citizen access to adequate and reliable government information, and thereby enhancing government transparency and accountability; by promoting equitable and affordable citizen participation in government decision-making; and by supporting a multitude of local government obligations.

Uniqueness of the Internet

What makes the Internet such a miraculous tool for local governments? Simply put, Internet-based communication reduces the costs of communication and co-ordination among individuals and organisational units because of its speed and low cost, its asynchronous nature, its ability to connect multiple people simultaneously, and its capacity for automation and intelligent applications:[3]

- *Speed* and *low cost*. Measured by the cost of transmitting a single character, Internet-mediated communication is cheaper than the telephone or written letter. For example, a 10-minute phone call from the Netherlands[4] to Ghana costs $34. The same information (2000 words) transmitted via fax machine costs $7, and via an E-mail message - using a 14.4kb modem - $0.40.
- *Asynchronous communication*. Asynchronous media like the Internet allow the receiver to receive a message at any point after it was sent (unlike a telephone, where the receiver must generally be present to receive information). The capacity for asynchronous communication reduces transaction costs associated with co-ordination as senders can transmit electronic mail messages or post computer files to be retrieved at the receivers' convenience.
- *Connect multiple people simultaneously*. Unlike "one-to-one" (such as telephones) and "one-to-many" (such as newspapers) media, a "many-to-

many" communication medium such as the Internet combines the personal and interactive quality of one-to-one media with the broadcast capabilities of one-to-many media. Many-to-many communication makes co-ordination and information dissemination efficient. Individuals are able to post "does anybody know?" questions that tap into the collective informal wisdom of the on-line community.

- *Automation.* Unlike telephones, computers are "smart" communications devices because they can manipulate the information being transmitted. Tasks that would ordinarily require hiring people can be automated and delegated to computers, saving time and expense. For instance, mail filters can sort incoming messages by sender, subject matter, or recipient. Mailbots can automatically respond to simple E-mail requests. Survey systems can send forms to citizens or other recipients, process their responses and format the results without the need for human oversight or intervention.

Specific Uses of the Internet for Local Governments

Two particular tools of the Internet - the World Wide Web and Electronic Mail - are especially useful in furthering local government's communication and co-ordination goals:

- expediting citizen access to adequate and reliable government information;
- promoting equitable and affordable citizen participation in government decision-making; and
- supporting local government obligations such as promoting economic growth.

Expediting Citizen Access to Information

A local government Web site can provide local citizens access to administrative information such as directories of government officials, tax rates, crime reports, demographic information, voter registration, and local election information, planning documents, city council minutes and agendas, and budgets and spending. If the government chooses to, it can also enable citizen access to political candidates' campaign financing, or provide description of public projects, including E-mail addresses or contact information of the officials responsible. Needless to say, information such as this makes government operations transparent and its officials accountable.

> In the US, the VOICE (Voter Online Information and Communication Exchange) Project, begun by the League of Women Voters, the Public Information Exchange, and Project Vote Smart, was a four-city pilot program to provide information on local, state, and national candidates via a Web page. Project terminals were located in public libraries, and the Web page was available to anyone with a computer and modem. Citizens could find candidate profiles for local, state, and national campaigns in addition to polling place information, voting information, candidate voting records, campaign contributions, and third-party ratings of candidates.

Experience in the US and Europe has shown that providing government information electronically is easier, less expensive, and less time-consuming to produce and keep up-to-date than paper files. Enabling searches of government documents and databases enhances the value of the material for the public since it is not always clear to citizens which agencies provide which services. For example, the US-based *Minnesota Datanet* provides on-line access to state-wide statistical, demographic, and geographic data. In Massachusetts, the city of Cambridge has begun to provide municipal documents via the Internet. The city of Boston has begun to offer information through its own computer bulletin board.

By making information and resources accessible twenty-four hours a day, officials can use Web sites as another highly convenient way to serve other government agencies and local residents. Providing access to the most heavily requested local documents and answers to the most frequently asked questions may reduce phone inquiries and staffing requirements as well as allowing more time for more complex information requests. ATM-like machines can provide 24-hour service to citizens, both at the town hall and at convenient locations around town. In California, for instance, InfoCal kiosks provide access to government services in malls and other public places. In Massachusetts, the city of Newton is planning a similar system.

In addition to providing government-related information, there are several other services a local government Web site can provide its citizens, such as links to regional colleges and universities, museums, social and political organisations, state or national parks, or other attractions, regional resources, state and federal legislative information, educational resources for students, local job listings, volunteer opportunities, or a listing of hospitals and community organisations that serve the area.

Promoting Citizen Participation

Local governments can encourage public participation in government by enabling citizens to communicate with each other and with the government electronically. By providing electronic mail directly from the Web site, local governments offer citizens another vehicle for interacting with government. Officials can ask for input on specific issues and options or let citizens communicate what they are interested in and what they like or don't like about government services.

> In the Fall of 1994, the US-based Minnesota E-Democracy Project created an electronic meeting space where State candidates could answer public questions and critique their opponents - and where citizens could find detailed information on politics, comment on the candidates, and discuss the democratic process. The goal was not merely cost-benefits and public accessibility, but "to increase citizen participation in elections and public discourse through on-line civic forums and collection of information."
>
> The dynamics that were created as a result challenged the traditional relationship between candidates, media, and citizens. For example, instead of reading a reporter's account of a speech, a voter could retrieve the entire speech.

Web sites can provide online feedback forms or surveys that citizens can simply fill out and transmit without needing to use a separate e-mail program or know an Internet address. Online forms also make it easy for citizens to request additional information about a program or service.

Using sites on the World Wide Web, citizens can also participate in interactive on-line debates with political candidates, or participate in local decision-making via e-mail and electronic *Newsgroups*. Governments can conduct rapid turn-around E-mail- or Web-based surveys to assess citizen satisfaction with public services, or solicit citizen opinion on controversial issues as the Internet permits the compilation, processing, and formatting of the data within hours.

> Advantage West, formerly known as the Western North Carolina Regional Economic Development Commission, created a Web site to provide information for prospective visitors and to promote business and investment opportunities. The site displays information about existing businesses, industry, including agribusiness, arts and crafts, and tourist attractions. A calendar of events in the region is also available, updated daily, listing activities in the twenty-two-county Western North Carolina region.

Promoting Economic Growth

Some cities and counties set up Web sites to promote tourism and to encourage local and regional business and industrial development. Marketing the community via the Internet is an inexpensive way to rapidly disseminate interesting, current information about economic, cultural and recreational opportunities. A local government Web site could include a guide to investments, museums, parks, etc. This form of advertising has the possibility of attracting the attention of a worldwide audience of potential tourists and new residents, both individuals and corporations.

Services for local businesses might include information about enterprise zones, incentive and assistance programs, permits, and loan programs. Local governments can pull together economic development and statistical information from a variety of local, state, and federal sources already on the Internet and provide it on the Web site in an easy-to-read format for both local and outside entrepreneurs. Web sites developed by other local organisations and neighbouring jurisdictions can be linked to the local governments Web site, making it an integrated information resource for the region. A number of federal agencies in the US routinely distribute tenders electronically; and the federal government is about to initiate a government-wide program to support electronic commerce.

The box on the next page provides a summary of the variety of ways a government can improve governance by using the World Wide Web.

Comparative Advantages of the Internet

Needless to say, the Internet is neither necessary nor sufficient to address governance goals such as those described above. The advantage Internet offers is that it can dramatically lower the cost of such efforts, even after accounting for the initial capital investment. Briefly, Internet-based communication can be:

Government Services that Can be Provided via a Web Site

Provide the public with easy and *timely* access to information about:
    health services
    government services and procurement
    education resources
    official documents
    welfare information
    elections and voter registration
    local affairs and meetings
    job opportunities

Support disenfranchised groups:
    small businesses
    minorities and women

Promote tourism

Encourage outside investment in community

Provide an alternative means to solicit citizen input especially on government spending/ public projects

Network with other governments and government agencies

Provide an electronic forum for citizens to network with each other

Provide online services:
    find and apply for jobs online
    pay taxes and fines online
    apply for permits, etc., online

Enable/promote telecommuting

More Timely. Marketing to the community via the Internet is a way to rapidly disseminate critical information.

Cheaper. Providing government information online is often less expensive and less time-consuming to produce and update than paper files, especially information that changes frequently. In many cases, an ongoing presence on the Internet can cost less than a single full-page ad in a major newspaper or periodical and could reach many more people than any single publication could.

Larger Reach. This form of advertising has at least the possibility of attracting the attention of a worldwide audience of potential tourists and new residents, both individuals and corporations. Moreover, with the use of tools such as telecenters, it allows the government to reach citizens in rural or inaccessible areas.

Efficient use of Government Resources. Providing access to the most heavily requested local documents and answers to the most frequently asked questions may reduce phone inquiries, allowing more time for more complex information requests. Similarly, providing online guidance on, say, how to register to vote may save staff time for other more pressing tasks.

Conclusions and Caveats

Governments around the world have recognised the benefits of addressing policy goals using information technology. The technology is only now trickling down to the local government level and interest in the field is high. The Internet is seen as a panacea for many governance ills and many of its drawbacks are ignored. For example, although the Internet reduces some transaction costs for governments, it also introduces new costs arising from the use of computers and networks – individuals and organisations must have computers, must know how to use them, and must pay network connection charges. Lack of Internet access to the less affluent also exacerbates existing distortions in the political system - citizens with a higher socio-economic status, already over-represented in the political process, can build an even stronger lobby in the government. Furthermore, those well-versed in technology and computers can have an advantage over those who are not.

Finally, there are problems such as lack of citizen interest and, paradoxically, local governments' unwillingness to share control of information, regulation, and decision-making. In the design of an Internet strategy, all these challenges must be taken into account.

Notes

[1] In the US, a federal law (the Paperwork Reduction Act of 1995) passed in May 1995 mandates that federal agencies reduce paperwork and encourage the dissemination of public information by federal agencies via the Internet.

[2] As defined on the Public Technology, Inc. Web site, http://world.localgov.org.

[3] M. Boncheck, *Cyberspace: Using Computer Networks to Facilitate Political Participation*, 1995.

[4] M. Hegener, *Telecommunications in Africa*, 1996.

PART VI

CAPACITY BUILDING AND LOCAL GOVERNANCE

PART VI

CAPACITY BUILDING AND LOCAL GOVERNMENT

14 Decentralised Governance: Empowerment Without Capacity Enhancement is Meaningless

Gambhir Bhatta

There has been in evidence in the Nineties a new paradigm of government intervention in the economy: that of a partnership between government and private sector such that there is a decline in the public sector's role in producing and providing services. This new role of government - as enabler rather than provider - is encapsulated in the term "governance". The literature on governance has tended to show a preponderance of emphasis on ways and means to best promote good governance more or less confined to the macro level (i.e., upstream in the policy formulation and implementation continuum and at the central level). What does not seem to be emphasised is what governance means at the local level (or, more appropriately, if the meaning of governance at the local level is different from that normally used), and what specific steps can be taken to enhance good governance at the local level. The term local level as used here includes downstream (i.e., at the policy implementation end of the continuum) and entities such as villages, communities, and districts.

Governance, as construed at the macro or central level, incorporates two key elements: civil service reform, and policy-making and institutional capacity building. It is important, however, to translate these to be applicable and relevant at the local level in concrete and operationalisable terms or else there is a danger that the idea of governance will be extremely remote to the general citizenry.

This chapter focuses on the issue of governance at the local level arguing that the conceptual framework used to study governance at the national (or macro) level is not necessarily entirely useful to view the same at the local (or micro) level. It also argues that empowerment - that is, decentralising authority and powers to the local level - is meaningless unless the capacity of selected leaders, managers, and key participants of civic society is enhanced. Finally, the paper discusses how that capacity can be enhanced.

Governance at the Macro and Micro Levels

Among the many useful definitions of governance, the following suffices for our purposes here: "governance stands for the practical exercise of power and authority by governments in the management of their affairs in general and of economic development in particular..."[1] Governance, in general, is said to consist of the following core elements: accountability, transparency, openness, and rule of law.[2] Any governance system that has as its fundamental characteristics these elements is thus considered to be "good".

Accountability is simply about being able to hold public officials responsible for their actions, and it is central to good governance. Three types of accountability can be identified:[3] political, financial, and legal. The latter refers to citizens being able to hold public agencies legally responsible for their actions. Political accountability is most commonly ensured by popular elections,[4] and bilateral donors have tended to focus attention on multiparty elections as a key indicator of a government's readiness to be politically accountable.[5]

Transparency refers to the fact that the methods of governments (from central to local) are clear to the public and they can see for themselves how the policies are being formulated and implemented. It requires that governments do things in a manner that is open to scrutiny. Included in the analysis of how transparency is determined are variables such as existence, and application, of sunshine and sunset laws, etc.

Openness, on the other hand, refers to the availability of opportunities to the public to critique any actions they perceive as not being transparent. Openness and transparency both presuppose that all the information needed to make assessments is readily available to the public. In less-developed countries (LDCs), for example, bid and tender procedures are often not transparent and since relevant information is rarely made public, the common citizen has no recourse to bring up the matter for public debate. Two types of openness are usually identified:[6] economic and political. While economic openness refers to competitive economies with limited restrictions and a liberal trade regime, political openness refers to competitiveness and tolerance for diversity in policy making.[7]

The final core element of governance is rule of law (or predictability). Predictability is characterised by "policies and regulations developed and implemented according to a regular, institutionalised process with opportunities for review".[8] The public needs to be assured that there is a process of conflict resolution, and that there are known procedures for amending the rules. This is important to mention here because the private sector is now increasingly being involved in national and international economies, and there is, therefore, the need for a legal framework that protects property rights and ensures respect for contracts.

Governance at the Local Level

Local governance is defined as "the process by which communities address their own needs, problems, and priorities through more responsive and accountable local governments."[9] The link between governance as understood at the macro level and at the local (or micro) level is that even at the local level, there has tended to be use of the same conceptual framework - that is, the insistence on government-private sector partnership within the context of an accountable, open, transparent and predictable local government. But this paper asserts that this is not necessarily the best way to view governance at the local level. While the core concepts of governance provide a useful backdrop to understanding the term as applied at the local level, it is more important to understand that given the exigencies of varied community needs, a different approach is necessary.

For one, it is not very realistic to assume that accountability as practised at the central level can be replicated at the local level through decentralisation laws without first some preconditions being met. Otherwise, all the countries that have experimented with decentralisation programmes would have by now found a solution to their governance problem.

The concept of rule of law also has to await a base at the central level which brings about a uniform code of legal conduct (something that LDCs have but recently tried). A complete legal framework needs to be in place at the central level before the rule of law can be effective at the local level.[10] And since the concepts of openness and transparency depend to a large extent on the legal framework, it is difficult - although not impossible - to have in place an environment at the local level where local governments have completely transparent procedures and there is an open environment to put the local governments to task.

It is the contention of this paper that by far the most pressing - and possible - task at the local level is to enhance opportunities for the communities to participate in development projects. While in some countries (such as the Philippines through its Local Development Code, 1991), participation by NGOs and private organisations is mandated by law, in many others, the practice has been pre-empted by various development partners (including international organisations, bilateral donor agencies, etc.). This enhancement of participation opportunities is the first step in effectuating good governance at the local level.

Enhancement of Governance at the Local Level

There are various methods of enhancing governance at the local level. First and foremost, policy makers need to do what can be termed a comprehensive downstream diagnostic work.[11] All too often, we have seen governance programmes that have been top-down in orientation and have, in essence, been contextualised in the oft-touted decentralisation programmes as if this in itself would lead to an enhancement of good governance at the local level. Such a diagnostic work would have to take into account not only such rather-evident features as local capacity, physical resource base, pattern of socio-cultural behaviours, etc., but also more important, leadership patterns. This last component is crucial as that would determine the extent to which the local leadership can be co-opted into being involved in effectuating good governance. Unless such a baseline situation is available and known to central leaders, it is inconceivable that governance programmes can be successful.[12]

The second thing to note here is that concurrent with - and it could even be argued, prior to - any governance programme being implemented, it is necessary to first begin to alter the attitudes of the public towards what they have all along perceived as their role in governance. In developed and newly-industrialised countries, this alteration has to a large extent already been effectuated and so governance takes on a deeper meaning there; but in countless LDCs, the same cannot be said to hold. It is one thing for the people to realise that they should have the right to express themselves, or be free to associate with like-minded people, but it is entirely a different matter to say that the people should know what their responsibilities are too. In many countries, decentralisation programmes have failed because central and local level officials - as well as the general populace - continue to possess old-fashioned ideas about their role in governance.[13]

Probably the most widely used tool to enhance governance at the local level has been decentralisation programmes. In many countries (such as Nepal, Ghana, Botswana, Uganda, etc.), the decentralisation programme has come to be viewed as a linchpin in the government's governance programme. After all, "decentralisation is an ideological principle, associated with objectives of self-reliance, democratic decision-making, popular participation in government, and accountability of public officials to citizens..."[14] These are all implied characteristics of good governance.

In most countries, however, decentralisation programmes have tended to falter for various reasons. Some of these include: (1) lack of capacity to plan, mobilise and utilise financial and other resources; (2) lack of political commitment at the centre to see through the decentralisation programme (for fears that it would completely erode central level control); (3) lack of popular involvement at the local level in development activities; and (4) the fact that all decentralisation programmes are imposed from top-down and are often oblivious to inherent socio-economic-political characteristics of the local communities (i.e., one introduced without the consensus of the population).

The jury is still out on the efficacy of the decentralisation programme in promoting good governance. In general, it can be safely said that with a few notable exceptions,[15] decentralisation programmes have not yet contributed in any measurable way to truly enhancing good governance.

One of the issues raised above as to why decentralisation programmes have not tended to be very successful is the lack of capacity at the local level to plan, and to mobilise and utilise resources. Thus increasing local capacity (or capacity building - CB) has turned out to be the most important facet of making decentralisation programmes successful which, in turn, would have positive impacts on making governance programmes successful. How exactly capacity can be enhanced at the local level is discussed in the final section of this paper; the purpose here is to highlight the importance of CB in governance at the local level.

The fact that CB is crucial to a successful decentralisation programme has been made amply clear in the development literature.[16] It is thus evident that one of the main conditions seen as necessary for successfully promoting decentralisation is "adequate human and economic capacity and sufficient financial resources, either already in place or to be built up".[17] It is also felt necessary to "introduce capacity-building and management development programmes to support the delegation of power".[18]

To date, countless LDCs (such as Benin, Guinea, Uganda, etc.) - with the assistance of organisations such as the Harare-based African Capacity Building Foundation (ACBF) - have embarked on rather ambitious CB exercises at the central level (primarily to bolster analytical capacities of national assemblies, parliaments, and central government ministries, all in the name of institutional development); however, not much is heard about similar exercises at the local level. And even if such programmes do exist, they tend to focus on regional or central level institutions that have a presence at the local level rather than target the local-level institutions in the first place.

Going hand in hand with the need to build capacity at the local level is the need to ensure that community participation is encouraged in development activities. After all, participation is key in the governance concept. As Kalin suggests: "a strong desire by the population at the grassroots level to turn to local self-government is a prerequisite for successful decentralisation ... this can be achieved only through people's participation".[19] It has also been well-documented that there is "a strong correlation between participation in the design and implementation of development projects and the sustainability of project benefits".[20] After all, "projects prepared through wide participatory processes have a greater chance of success, in terms of intended impact, than projects prepared by traditional methods".[21]

The final manner by which to enhance governance at the local level is to empower local leaders and use traditional organisations and leadership structures to co-opt them to support the governance programme. After all, it is quite evident that with the decrease in the role of government at the local level, the vacuum is initially likely to be filled not by NGOs but by local leadership structures. (As is often the case though, these NGOs are products of the machinations of the local leaders themselves).

The need to bring in traditional leaders and indigenous organisations in the development process has been realised for quite some time now,[22] primarily since this makes the communities want to join knowing that their traditional leaders have agreed, and - at a minimum, given tacit support - to the developmental activity and its process.

One of the key issues in this regard has been whether local organisations - or organisations based elsewhere but with a field presence in that particular area - should be used to mobilise the people and implement development activities. There are apparent benefits to both but it is evident that even those organisations that bring facilitators and animateurs from outside, still rely heavily on the support of local organisations to mobilise people and resources. The United Nations' Volunteer Programme is one such case where its Field Worker volunteers work extensively with local counterparts.

Areas for Capacity Enhancement at the Local Level

Enhancement of good governance can only be done when the existing capacity of the local authorities and other development partners is augmented. The areas in which such capacity needs to be enhanced have to be identified by a capacity assessment exercise, but in general the following are key:[23]

(1) <u>Capacity on financial accounting and auditing</u> - one of the key weaknesses of local governments has been found to be in this area. In order that accountability may be ensured, it is important that local officials be trained in financial accounting and auditing. Since, in general, about four-fifths of local government expenditure in LDCs is met from national government funding, local governments should be accountable for public spending and thus capacity enhancement in this area is important.[24] Examples of this type of training include the World Bank's assistance on strengthening accounting and auditing for Burundi and Uganda in 1993, and for Tanzania in 1992.

(2) <u>Financial mobilisation and management</u> - the former (i.e., financial mobilisation) is important since local governments continue to face funding problems despite a larger and larger share of the central resources, and the latter (i.e., financial management) reflects their inability to utilise and manipulate the resources once they are received. One thing to note here is that the ability to collect taxes is also a key task in financial mobilisation capacity.[25]

(3) <u>Development investment prioritisation</u> - too often, we see local governments come up with a "wish list" of what they would like to see happen inasmuch as investments in their areas is concerned. These are unrealistic and only serve to make the planning exercise futile. What is needed is capacity to prioritise their needs (based upon the funding situation, and other variables) and to follow up on that by linking it up with their development plans for that area.

(4) <u>Environmental planning and management</u> - of late, one of the key areas of capacity enhancement has been in environmental planning and management. All too often, development activities neglect this area of concern and

irreparable damage is done by resorting to measures that do not support the environment. In many countries now it has been mandatory to prepare an Environmental Impact Assessment (EIA) for every project; there is thus need for capacity for local officials to be able to prepare such EIAs and to incorporate environment-friendly techniques in their plans. Africa 2000, for its part, is a very good example of an organisation that actively incorporates this theme in all its project support.

(5) Legal matters and human rights - another key area where capacity training is considered to be of vital importance is in legal matters and human rights. As has been mentioned elsewhere in this paper, it is important that a legal framework for participation in economic and developmental activities be established at the central level first. Once that is done, local level officials then need to be trained to first understand, and then uphold, those legal provisions. Only then will a conducive environment for participation in the economy and polity by the public become possible.[26]

(6) Participation methods - finally, there is also need to enhance the capacity of local officials to encourage participation among the masses (particularly the women,[27] and disadvantaged). As has been mentioned, participation is a key element of governance as understood at the local level, and thus there is need to train people to mobilise others to participate in development activities. To a large extent, this already exists in many LDCs where training in such participation methods as Rapid Rural Appraisal (RRA), Methods of Active Participation (MAP), etc. is being provided by bilateral and multilateral donors. This contributes to good governance because increasing participation at the local level in development projects is also "an important means for ensuring accountability",[28] and accountability, as has been pointed out, is a core element of good governance.

Key Players

There are various key players in the local scene that need to be trained in the six areas mentioned above:

(1) The first group includes the mayors and other local level political leaders in areas such as entrepreneurship and also in what is called co-operative leadership meaning "leadership in action, one more participatory in nature".[29] Experiences of countries that have practised good governance (such as

Singapore) show that the key variable in economic development is the quality of leadership.[30] In transitional societies where leading by example continues to be an effective method of fundamentally altering the attitudes of the people toward their roles in ensuring development, this kind of training for leaders takes on great significance.

(2) The second group constitutes of local NGOs and community-based organisations (CBOs). NGOs and CBOs have continued to play a key role in local development in LDCs and it makes sense to impart training to them so that they can, in turn, transmit the knowledge to their members and other affiliates. It has been mentioned, however, that in the economic and political arenas, there tend to be tensions between the governments on the one hand, and NGOs and CBOs, on the other, primarily because "small community groups have shown a surprising ability to raise substantial amounts of money on their own..."[31] In the political arena too, the ability of some NGOs to organise people - especially the poor - around long-neglected social issues has caused some concern in some governments.[32] That notwithstanding, however, it would defeat the purpose of enhancing good governance if the peoples' organisations were not given capacity-building training.

(3) Training should also be given to local level civil servants. These refer to the officials that are either field-based from the centre or those locally recruited. Their role in implementing the policies necessitates that they too be identified for the training. Furthermore, to the extent possible, these civil servants should be trained together with people from the non-government sector. This enables a sharing of experiences and perceptions that can only enlarge the policy-making sphere and enable a diversity of views to be incorporated in the development process. As an example, training on local level capacity building provided by the UN Volunteer Programme throughout many countries of the world has as its key feature the participation of local level government officials together with community activists and members of local NGOs and CBOs.

(4) Local opinion leaders: these are people who belong to groups that have historically been at the forefront of how indigenous communities internalised external interventions (i.e., reacted to development policies imposed from outside). In local communities throughout the LDCs, such opinion leaders include religious figures, the landed elite, business people, clan leaders, etc. It is inconceivable to think that governance programmes of any kind could be

successful without the involvement of these groups of people - hence the need to train and sensitise them.

(5) Community workers: finally, it serves the purposes of awareness enhancement of governance to have intensive "train the trainers" programmes so as to make as many people as possible aware of, and trained in, mass mobilisation strategies, participation techniques, etc. This is best done by bringing in community workers to work with outsiders in the initial stages. Most bilateral donor agencies (including those that have volunteer programmes associated with them, such as the Peace Corps, etc.)[33] emphasise this arrangement.

Two more issues deserve mention here:

(1) If "animateurs" (variously termed facilitators, catalysts, change agents, etc.) need to be brought from outside to be involved in this type of training and community involvement, then it serves no purpose to have animateurs who are consultants and experts and hence cause considerable resources to be spent on them. Even organisations such as the World Bank and UNDP are now realising this and increasingly national consultants, and external experts as volunteers, are utilised whenever possible. This is a trend that needs to be strongly encouraged.

(2) Secondly, it has to be noted that overarching all the issues of inclusion of key players and areas for capacity enhancement is the gender perspective. Good governance presupposes effective participation from all sectors of civil society, and to not emphasise the role of women groups in local level development would be a grave mistake. All donor agencies and national governments have more or less completely internalised this truism by now.

Conclusion

The emphasis that is currently evident on "good governance" is likely to continue for quite some time. In that context, it has become important to begin to shift focus from governance at the macro or central level to the micro or local level. This is because no initiative is going to survive if the impetus for change comes only from the top (the rejection of the various top-down models of development testify to that). It is thus that this paper asserts that it is time for us to put the microscope on the local level and study how best to enhance governance there rather than concentrate largely on the centre. The considerable focus of such organisations as UNDP, World Bank, etc., on civil service reforms in numerous LDCs attests to this preponderance of emphasis on the centre. Obviously, a basic framework needs to be established at the centre, but once that is done, the focus needs to shift. More important, the two can go hand in hand since resource needs are not that high for the type of local level interventions that are recommended here.

This chapter also asserts that local institutions and leaders need to be co-opted into the development process if these efforts are to succeed. Their support to the development process is crucial in order that governance programmes be effective. One particular way of co-opting them is to provide sensitisation training to local opinion leaders.

The final point that needs to be highlighted here is the fact that training on capacity building at the local level needs to be action-based, and focused on planning, mobilisation and utilisation of resources. Without such capacity enhancement, "empowerment" - as a prelude to fostering good governance at the local level - will be rendered meaningless.

Notes

[1] R. F. Pinto with assistance from A. J. Mrope, *Projectising the Governance Approach to Civil Service Reform: An Institutional Environment Assessment for Preparing a Sectoral Adjustment Loan in The Gambia*, Discussion Paper Number 252, Africa Technical Department Series (Washington, DC: World Bank, 1994): 8.

[2] L. Adamolekun and C. Bryant, *Governance Progress Report: The Africa Region Experience*, Capacity Building and Implementation Division Study Paper (Washington, DC: World Bank, 1994): Annex 3. The authors have added two more variables: public management competence, and human rights. But it is felt that while the latter could certainly be incorporated within the rubric of governance, the former is more a symptom of good governance than constituting one of its core elements. Yet others have broadened the meaning of the term governance. UNDP, for example, incorporates the following elements as constituting governance: (1) form of political regime; (2) legal and institutional framework; (3) pursuit of economic production in markets in the private sector; (4) availability of information, knowledge and technology; (5) provision of services for the common well-being of the people; (6) management and development of natural resources, environment, infrastructure, and built-up habitat; and (7) maintenance of public peace and security. Its own definition of governance is contained in its new development paradigm of Sustainable Human Development (SHD). See UNDP, "A

UNDP Policy Paper: Strategy on Governance," draft paper (New York: United Nations, 1995) for a fuller discussion of this.

[3] See, for example, D. Brautigam, *Governance and Economy: A Review*, Policy Research Working Papers (Washington, DC: World Bank, 1991): 13.

[4] It is, however, argued by some that elections do not necessarily enforce political accountability (see, for example, H. Root, *Small Countries, Big Lessons: Governance and the Rise of East Asia* (New York: Oxford University Press, 1996)). It is more the fulfilment of policy objectives that should determine its true extent. Root's exposition of this with respect to the East Asian economies is compelling reading.

[5] Various governments, for their part, have accepted this in good faith - countries such as Uganda, for example, turned to the UNDP and other bilateral and multilateral donor agencies for official requests for technical assistance in response to key events relating to political transition (including elections for a Constituent Assembly in 1994).

[6] Brautigam (1991): 21.

[7] As the literature on the East Asian miracle economies attests (see, for example, J. E. Campos and H. Root, *The Key to the Asian Miracle: Making Shared Growth Credible* (Washington, DC: Brookings Institution, 1996)), it is not necessarily true that political and economic openness are positively correlated and the two have to be analysed quite distinctly.

[8] Adamolekun and Bryant (1994): 11.

[9] USAID, *Governance and Local Democracy (GOLD) Project*, project paper (Manila: USAID, 1994): 6.

[10] This is not to suggest that while we await such a framework to take hold at the central level, the local level will have a highly unpredictable legal environment. But it is indeed hard to conceive of a predictable legal environment at the local level without a similar one being in place at the central level.

[11] This term is adapted from Pinto (1994) who talks of an upstream diagnostic work "to reach a thorough understanding of the institutional environment and the contextual idiosyncrasies of each country..." (p. 1).

[12] Samute (1996), for example, mentions that one of the primary causes as to why the decentralisation effort in Malawi has been counter-productive is precisely because it was "operationalised without prior assessment of the capacities of the local level". W. Samute, "Decentralisation in Malawi: Status and Trends," paper presented at the First International Conference on Decentralisation in Southeast Asia, Manila (January 1996): 29.

[13] In this vein, Kalin (1993) mentions: "it is necessary to build a political culture of decentralised government. This means that values, traditions and attitudes of politicians, officials, and people must be supportive of the decentralised government". W. Kalin, "Legal Aspects of Decentralisation," in UNDP, *Management Development Programme (MDP) Workshop on the Decentralisation Process*, volume 1, Report of the Workshop, Bern, Switzerland (April 1993): 11.

[14] D. Rondinelli, et al, *Decentralisation in Developing Countries: A Review of Recent Experience*, Staff Working Paper No. 581 (Washington, DC: World Bank, 1983): 8-9.

[15] New Zealand appears to be one such exception; see P. McDermott, "How Has Local Government Reform in New Zealand Served the Public Interest?" paper presented at the First International Conference on Decentralisation in Southeast Asia, Manila (January 1996).

[16] For a discussion of this issue in relation to the ESCAP region, see UN, *Fiscal Decentralisation and the Mobilisation and Use of National Resources for Development: Issues, Experience, and Policies in the ESCAP Region*, Development Papers No. 11, Bangkok (ESCAP, 1991); in relation to Uganda, see F. Lubanga, "Decentralisation in Uganda," paper presented at the First International Conference on Decentralisation in Southeast Asia, Manila (January 1996); and in relation to the Philippines, see A. Brillantes, "Empowering Local Institutions Through Devolution: The Local Government Code of 1991," paper presented at the First International Conference on Decentralisation in Southeast Asia, Manila (January 1996).

[17] UNDP (1993): 2.

[18] *Ibid.*: 3.

[19] Kalin (1993): 11.

[20] Brautigam (1991): 33.

[21] Pinto (1994): 24.

[22] See, for example, M. Esman and N. T. Uphoff, *Local Organisations: Intermediaries in Rural Development* (Ithaca, NY: Cornell University Press, 1984).

[23] See also USAID (1994): ii.

[24] See, for example, J. S. Edralin, "Summary of Issues," summary of papers presented during a session of the First International Conference on Decentralisation in Southeast Asia, Manila (January 1996): 2.

[25] See UN (1991), p. 22.

[26] In Uganda, as an example, UNDP is supporting training for national NGOs, district level officials, and those in sub-districts, on how to recognise and respect the rights of people to participate in the affairs of the communities they serve, and for local judicial bodies on following proper legal procedures when taking action against law-breakers. Such training is the foundation of good governance at the local level.

[27] In many countries now (such as Mali, Mozambique, Burkina Faso, Uganda, etc.), there is a legal component of "women in development" which seeks to provide a legal basis for the means of active participation of women in development activities.

[28] Adamolekun and Bryant (1994): 8.

[29] Edralin (1996): 2.

[30] See, for example, Campos and Root (1996).

[31] A. Williams, "A Growing Role for NGOs in Development," *Finance and Development* 27, 4 (December 1990): 32.

[32] *Ibid.*

[33] Some bilateral donors, such as USAID, have also, of late, taken to including Governance Advisors/Experts in the projects and programmes they fund. Their task is to provide technical advice on all matters pertaining to governance as it relates to that individual project/programme.

15 Capacity Building and Administrative Innovations in the Philippines: The Integrated Capability Building Program[1]

Alex B. Brillantes, Jr.

Introduction

This chapter describes the approaches to capability building/training for local officials in the Philippines after the enactment of the Local Government Code in 1991. The Code drastically transformed the nature of power relationships between and among the various levels of government in the Philippines, especially between the national and local government units (LGUs). Substantive powers were devolved to the LGUs making them primarily responsible for the delivery of basic services, i.e., agriculture, health, social services and natural resources, that formerly belonged to the national government. Not a few sectors raised doubts about the absorptive capacities and administrative capabilities of local governments to ably perform the new roles expected of them as defined in the Code. Where before, for decades, local structures, institutions, processes, behaviour, attitudes and mindsets were oriented towards dependency upon the central government "imperial Manila," now LGUs were thrust to play the principal role in local governance.

The task, therefore, of assisting LGUs in absorbing the new responsibilities under the transformed system is enormous. Traditional approaches to training and capability building have to be reviewed and recast in order to enable them to catch up with the very quick changes and increasing demands in local governance. This is particularly true for nationally-based training institutions such as the Local Government Academy (LGA) of the Department of Interior and Local Government (DILG). It is imperative to continuously re-examine its role in the environment of local governance in general, and of capability building in particular.

This chapter first locates the context of capability building for LGUs by providing a brief overview of the Philippine government system. The basic features of Local Government Code of 1991 are then discussed. This is followed by a discussion of the Integrated Capability Building Program (ICBP) of the DILG in whose implementation the LGA plays a principal role. In fact, the ICBP is identified as one of the "flagship" programs of the Department primarily as a result of the enactment of the Code. Approaches to training and capability building of the LGA under the ICBP are also described. Finally, issues and concerns in local capacity building and administrative innovations in the Philippines are raised.

The Philippine Local Government System: An Overview

There are four levels of local governments in the Philippines: provinces, cities, municipalities and *barangays*. Provinces and municipalities are classified from first to sixth class depending on annual revenue or income. Cities are classified as component, highly urbanised, independent component, or special city. The Philippines has 77 provinces, 65 cities, 1,542 municipalities, and 41,926 *barangays*.

The province, headed by the governor, is composed of municipalities and component cities. A political and corporate unit of government, it serves as a dynamic mechanism for developmental processes and effective governance within its jurisdiction. The city, headed by the City Mayor, consists of *barangays*. It serves as the general purpose government for the co-ordination and delivery of basic, regular, and direct services, and for effective governance within its jurisdiction.

The municipality is headed by the Municipal Mayor and, like the city, consists of a group of *barangays*. It also serves as a general purpose for the co-ordination and delivery of basic, general, and direct services and for effective governance within its jurisdiction.

The *barangay* is the basic political unit that serves as the primary planning and implementing unit of the government at the community level. It also serves as a forum where the people's ideas and concerns are expressed and crystallised and where disputes can be amicably settled. It is headed by the Punong *Barangay*.

Local governments are geographically clustered into one autonomous and fourteen administrative regions.

The Local Government Code of 1991: Features of the Code

In 1991, the Local Government Code (RA 7160) was passed. It drastically shifted powers from the central government to the local governments. Philippine local governments have for long been stunted by over-centralisation stultifying creativeness, imagination, and flexibility at the local level. Well-entrenched and accepted traditional national and local bureaucratic administrative structures and processes have served as obstacles to growth. It was within the above context that the Local Government Code was enacted with the general goal of unleashing the potentials at the local level. Former Senator, Aquilino Pimentel, principal author of the Code, aptly described the Code as the "key to national development".

The Local Government Code has five major characteristics. First, it devolves to the local government units the responsibility for the delivery of various aspects of basic services that earlier were the responsibility of the national government. These basic services include the following:

- health (field health and hospital services and other tertiary services);
- social services (including social welfare services);
- environment (community based forestry projects);
- agriculture (agricultural extension and on-site research);
- public works (funded by local funds);
- education (school building program); and
- tourism (facilities, promotion and development).

The devolution of such responsibilities meant the transfer of appropriate personnel, programs and projects, records, and equipment of the concerned national agency to the LGUs. Among those most affected by the devolution process, primarily because of the transfer of personnel to the LGUs, were the Departments of Health, Agriculture, Social Services, and Environment and Natural Resources. Such a transfer has the potential of shaking the local bureaucracies to the core. And that is exactly what has been happening in many LGUs. Viewed from a different perspective, an opening for fundamental public administration reform has been made because of devolution.

Second, it devolved to local governments the responsibility for the enforcement of certain regulatory powers, such as:[2]

- the reclassification of agricultural lands;
- enforcement of environmental laws;
- inspection of food products and quarantine;
- operation of tricycles;
- enforcement of national building code;
- processing and approval of subdivision plans; and
- establishment of cockpits and holding of cockfights.

Third, the Code lays the legal infrastructure for the participation of non-governmental organisations (NGOs) and people's organisations (POs) in the process of governance. They are mandated to be members in local special bodies. These special bodies include the local development council, health board, and school board. Because of their ability to organise and mobilise the people, one door wide open for NGO and PO participation in governance is in the area of promoting local accountability and answerability, specifically through the recall and people's initiative provisions.

Fourth, the Code increases the financial resources available to local government units by: (1) broadening their taxing powers; (2) providing them with a specific share from the national wealth exploited in their area, e.g., mining, fishery, and forestry charges; and (3) increasing their share from the national taxes, i.e., internal revenue allotments (IRA), from a previously low of 11% to as much as 40%. Where some *barangays*' budget did not exceed 500 Philippine Pesos, now *barangays* under the present formulations can have as much as 150,000 Philippine Pesos! That certainly is a respectable figure. The same goes true for municipalities, cities, and provinces whose annual IRA have all increased as a result of the Local Government Code. The transfer of increased financial resources to local governments, and the devolution of additional powers to generate revenue, provides excellent opportunities for local governments to be creative and innovative, not only in the generation of additional financial resources, but also in their allocation. These, likewise, provide opportunities for teaming up and entering into joint ventures with other LGUs, the national government, and the private sector itself. Local governments are actually encouraged to become entrepreneurial governments, and to go beyond the borders of the Philippines. The Code also increases the elbow room of local governments to generate revenues from local fees and charges.

Finally, the Code enhanced the governmental and corporate powers of LGUs by granting them full autonomy in the exercise of proprietary rights, enter into loans with other LGUs, enter into build-operate-transfer (B-O-T) arrangements, joint ventures with the private sector, and even float bonds.

Local Government Academy (LGA)

As the training arm of DILG, LGA's vision is to be a national training resource for local governments and a centre for excellence that seeks to develop a corps of competent and dedicated local government executives and functionaries in support of the aims of decentralisation and local autonomy. Given that among the major reforms to approaches in capability building is the de-emphasis of direct training of local government officials, the role of a national training institution, such as the LGA, is to build training capacities of locally based front-line academic and training institutions who may be more realistically positioned to respond to the training needs of the LGUs in their localities.

To date, the Academy's efforts have been centred on two major thrusts: (1) that of continuously seeking better ways of doing things, e.g., by building upon hard-earned gains of the past and exploring innovations; and (2) of maximising available resources in the Department, other government agencies, and the non-government organisations. Recently, the LGA has also been active in providing training to LGUs to enhance their capacity to be involved in economic development. Among the approaches to local capacity building adopted by the LGA within this framework are the following:

- deploying multi-disciplinary mobile teams (MDMT) of specialists throughout the country who serve as consultants and coaches to the LGUs;
- setting up of locally-based institutes of local governance that would respond to the capability building needs of the LGUs they are directly in contact with in accordance to the "town and gown" principle;
- recognising outstanding innovations/best practices in local governance, and facilitating cross visits and exchanges among LGUs in order to encourage local officials to observe and witness first-hand how other LGUs "did it;" and
- establishing innovations laboratories from the pool of winners in the best practices program that would host cross visits and exchanges among LGUs.

ICBP: LGA's Modest Contribution Towards Building Local Capacities

On October 25, 1993, the President of the Philippines issued Proclamation No. 284 adopting the Integrated Capability Building Program (ICBP) with the Local Government Academy taking the lead. This is to be implemented in close co-ordination and partnership with the other bureaus and field operating units in the Department, and local partner institutions referred to as the Institute for Local Government Administration (ILGA). The ICBP provides the general framework for all training and capability building activities being implemented in all the local government units (LGUs) in the country.

Under the ICBP, local officials learn rudiments of local governance through the Multi-Disciplinary Mobile Teams ((MDMTs) of the DILG. The MDMT is a pool of departmental specialists in the various areas of local governance and deployed in all the provinces of the country. They are supported by a Research and Evaluation Team which assesses the program implementation at different states. At the LGU level, a Quality Improvement Team composed of local officials and functionaries has been organised to serve as the counterpart of the MDMT. The objective is to effect the transfer of technology from the MDMT to the Quality Improvement Team. The Team, as the prime mover of the LGU, aims to install a leadership philosophy and work culture that advocates excellence by voluntary creative involvement of everybody in the organisation to continuously improve LGU work processes and service delivery.

Another major program delivery mechanism of the ICBP is the Institute for Local Government Administration (ILGA) within the context of the "town and gown" philosophy. This means that the institution becomes more relevant in its area of operation if it is directly involved in developing its own community. The LGA's vision is to have at least one ILGA per province. The local ILGA will respond to the basic capability-building needs of the LGUs in the area and LGA will simply provide staff support and other resources it may be able to offer as a national training resource for local governments. The LGA has, therefore, concentrated its efforts in developing new modules that will be made available to ILGAs and other interested training institutions. Examples of modules developed by LGA include disaster management, environmental management, feeling the public pulse, human rights in local government, and global competitiveness and sustainable development.

The institutionalisation of ILGAs forges a partnership among the local government, LGA and DILG regional offices, and the locally-based learning institutions. The program is generally founded on the academic expertise of the faculty of the institutions vis-à-vis actual practice or experienced-centred knowledge and skills of the DILG specialists. This is specially exemplified in terms of resource speakers since they will both come from the academic institutions concerned and DILG specialists or accredited resource speakers. The LGA, likewise, makes available to the ILGAs training courses and modules that have been developed. To a certain extent, this is where a national government institution might be able to maximise its own potential and contribution among the network of training institutions out there by developing, and even making referrals to, appropriate training modules to institutions that might need them.

Finally, the LGA offers the ILGA a financial assistance of up to 100,000 Pesos as seed money to start off the ILGA. This money is then leveraged by the local institution to generate counterpart resources at the local level, say from the provincial government, or from the local participants themselves who pay fees to join the program. There have even been cases where the local institutions offered to have participation in the training program credited for some units towards a masters degree after, of course, having satisfied the necessary academic requirements. To a certain extent, this has led to some kind of a win-win situation: for the LGUs who have undergone the training program and even earned some units, and for the local school whose enrolees have increased.

The LGA has, so far, entered into memoranda of agreement with sixty-three ILGAs in most of the regions. Among the ILGAs are the University of Northern Philippines, the Benguet State University, Central Luzon State University, Bicol University, University of San Carlos (Cebu), University of Eastern Philippines (Northern Samar), and Mindanao State University. Parenthetically, there might be a need to mention here that the implementation of the ICBP, with the active involvement of local academic institutions, has been noted by a number of international agencies and partners who are interested in supporting local ILGAs within the framework of the ICBP and Proclamation No. 284. This is, after all, a form of decentralising training and capability building.

Recognising its role in the Philippine Administrative System as the primary training arm for local governments of the DILG, the LGA has embarked on an extensive networking and linking program with other local government training institutions that include the academe, other national government agencies, private consulting firms, and even NGOs. It has organised an inter-agency unit that serves as a forum for exchange of information and sharing of training technologies among themselves. The LGA has similarly been involved in an inter-agency/inter-institution research forum. Such a forum has served as a venue for sharing the results of policy studies and analyses, and for reaching policy-makers.

Taking cognisance of the very innovative provision of the Code encouraging direct participation of NGOs and POs in local governance, the LGA has played a supportive role in the organisation and conduct of partnership workshops and conferences participated in by NGOs and POs at the national and regional levels. The general objective is for both sectors to come up with specific action plans to operationalise the nascent partnership at the appropriate level of local government.

Innovations in Increasing Local Capacities

The Galing Pook Awards Program: Documenting Best Practices at the Local Level

Towards the general objective of encouraging creativeness and dynamism among local governments, the LGA - together with the Asian Institute of Management - has conducted the Galing Pook Awards Program. Given the opportunities and environment provided to local government units under the Code, it is anticipated that LGUs will be able to use their newly acquired responsibilities and powers very creatively and innovatively as they navigate previously untried and uncharted waters. The general objective is to highlight innovations and excellence at the local level which could be replicated in similar settings in other LGUs.

While the Code has been operational for the past four years now, there are those who suggest that it has not effectively empowered local communities in general and local governments in particular. This chapter, however, argues otherwise. There are a number of "success stories" at the local level that prove that devolution is working. A number of these have been nationally recognised in the Galing Pook Awards Program jointly conducted by the Asian Institute of Management and the Local Government Academy. Now in its third year, close to 1,200 nominations have been received. The winners are selected by a broad-based National Selection Committee based on the following criteria:

- effectiveness of service delivery (the extent to which the program made good its promise);

- positive socio-economic and/or environmental impact (the improvement the program made on life in the community, and how much the community cared for the environment);
- promotion of people empowerment (how many in the community were encouraged to participate in activities meant for the common good); and
- transferability (the likelihood of the program inspiring other communities to successfully adopt it).

The program aims to recognise local initiatives, or best practices, as it were, that would inspire other similarly situated local governments. Sixty winners have been recognised so far. The winning programs have initially been classified thus:

- health services;
- environmental management;
- public finance;
- peace initiatives;
- integrated approach to development;
- socio-cultural development;
- employment generation/livelihood; and
- productivity improvement.

It has been very inspiring to see success stories in local governance. We have seen how LGUs have addressed critical environmental problems. Creativeness in the delivery of basic services to the populace has also been documented. Dynamism among LGUs in generating local revenues has been observed. All these because of the increased powers devolved to LGUs under the Local Government Code.

The Galing Pook Program has brought about a number of downstream activities in the implementation of capability building programs for local governments. For one, the methodology and approach to "training" for local governments has been shifted away from lectures and classroom instruction to experiential learning by the participant local officials. In accordance with the general philosophy that "example is the best teacher", we have encouraged the winners themselves to tell their stories to their fellow local officials during training programs, with the national government agency, such as the LGA, simply providing the framework. In partnership with the league of local officials themselves, we have organised study visits for local officials (*lakbay aral*) to the winning programs of other local officials to observe the innovations themselves and encourage appropriate replication and adaptation. We are currently organising "innovations laboratories" to support the efforts of the winners to showcase their stories and ensure their wider dissemination.

Cross Visits: Lakbay Aral Program

Aimed at developing and upgrading the administrative and technical capabilities of local officials, and promoting social, cultural, economic, and political exchange, a *Lakbay Aral* Program has been implemented in collaboration with the League of Municipalities. This is an exchange among LGUs in order to encourage local officials to observe and witness first-hand how other LGUs "did it". The participating LGUs are expected to identify and adopt new technologies on local governance suited to their areas of jurisdiction and which they have learned from the *Lakbay Aral* Program.

The key role played by the Leagues of Local Governments (especially the League of Municipalities, in this regard) is a major factor for the modest success of *Lakbal Aral*.

Establishment of LGU Innovations Laboratories

Towards transforming successful LGUs into innovations laboratories, and serve as replication models for the LGUs, the LGA, with funding support from the Ford Foundation, embarked on a joint project called *Establishment of LGU Innovations and Laboratories*. The program, whose implementation duration is three years, is actually a follow-up to the Gantimpalang Paglingkod Pook Awards which gave public recognition to innovative LGUs. The LGU innovations laboratories come from the 1994, 1995, and 1996 Galing Pook winners, and are handled by the National Selection Committee of the Galing Pook Awards.

The establishment of the Innovations Laboratories is also programmed to promote Galing Pook Awards by showcasing the previous winners and encouraging the replication of the strategies and projects proven to be successful in promoting local self-governance.

To date, numerous study visits of local officials and other organisations to these innovations laboratories have already been initiated.

Radio Program/Barangay School-On-the-Air Program (BSOAP)

Aimed to equip *barangay* officials with the necessary knowledge on *barangay* governance through the radio, supplemented by print-based materials, the program is a two-hour interactive structured approach to enhance the knowledge of *barangay* officials on the aspects of local government. It has the following features: (1) sessions on the air as the primary means of information and technology transfer; (2) curriculum and materials are structured in short self-contained modules; (3) off-classroom, self-paced study, using learning guides and resources; (4) feedback strategies such as self-assessment activities, and written examinations after each session to support learning process; and (5) tutorial support, when necessary, throughout the learning process.

The School-on-the-Air Program shall initially focus on the module *Barangay* Administration. This module has been selected as a primary consideration to *barangay* officials who must perform their duties and functions effectively and in accordance with the provisions of the Local Government Code of 1991.

The Inter-Agency Committee on Capability Building

The LGA played a key role in the organisation of an Inter-Agency Committee (IAC) on Capability Building that aims to bring together various institutions and organisations involved in capability building for local governments. Membership in the IAC synergises and adds value to each other's work.

Conclusion

Capability building for local governance in the Philippines has become a priority after the enactment of the Local Government Code of 1991. Together with the devolution of powers to LGUs came the challenge to assist them in improving their local absorptive and administrative capacities. The Local Government Academy has played a modest role towards the attainment of this objective.

Capability building for local governance has also become a very exciting field in contemporary local governance. Innovations in implementing training strategies have to be made in order to cope with the enormous demands for capability building "out there". Hence, the shift in training approaches from rowing to steering (using the paradigm of Reinventing Government) has been tried by the LGA. So far it seems to be working. Only time will tell though if such a program will be very effective. But based on initial response, it is working.

Notes

[1] This chapter is based on earlier papers presented in various local and international conferences by the author. The assistance of Ms. Thelma Tercino and Winnie Clare Odssey is gratefully acknowledged.

[2] Looking at the list, one wonders why it took so long for these regulatory functions to be devolved to local governments. For instance, why has the regulation of tricycles - a local frontline and basic service - always belonged to the national government? The same goes true for cockpits. One explanation would, of course, be "because that's the way it's always been done before!" This is one case where the core values of tradition and stability have served the cause of underdevelopment of local organisations.

16 Choice of Community Forestry by Voice of Local Participation in Northeastern Villages of Thailand

Tipaporn Phimphisut

Over the past three decades, the process of modernisation has taken its toll on Thailand's natural resources and environment. The forests coverage area, for example, has decreased from approximately 385,000 square kilometers in 1938 to a little over 98,000 square kilometers at present. The government survey in 1992 reported that the remaining forest area was only about 18 percent of the total area of the country.

In the past, the northeastern region of Thailand was rich with open deciduous forests on large plateaus which has subsequently became a major source of logging since 1968. The business of logging, the conversion of forests to economic farms, rampant clearing of forests in forest concessions, and the slash-and-burn farming methods have all contributed to the deterioration of forests in this region. The extensive land clearance reached 4,333 square kilometers within four years between 1973 and 1976 and up to 5,333 square kilometers in three years between 1976 and 1978.

Deforestation in the northeastern region was extended into Tha Wang Sai and Bung Phra villages in Nakhon Ratchasima province. Learning from their experiences, Tha Wang Sai villagers have turned the deteriorating lands into a dense and green community forest. By contrast, Bung Phra community forest has proven to be a failure of management under state support. The successful case of Tha Wang Sai brings to fore the question of how the villagers have become conscious of the conservation of natural resources and how they have participated in the management of community forest. What factors have contributed to the success of this case? And why is it not the case with the Bung Phra community forest?

The Bung Phra Community Forestry

This case has focused attention on the failure of community forestry management under the umbrella of state support. This study has found that there are both internal and external factors contributing to the failure of this case.

Community in the Wave of Socio-economic Change

Approximately four square kilometers of Bung Phra community forestry is located at Choakchai district in the Nakhon Ratchasima province. As the country became modernized, the community of Bung Phra gradually adjusted to the wave of rapid socio-economic change so that simple traditional values were swept by values of materialism. Migration of the younger generation from the rural to urban areas, including Bung Phra village, became evident. Under such circumstances, only the elderly people in the community were left behind to conserve the community forestry. New migrants into Bung Phra village had no incentive to conserve the forests.

The cleavages between the newcomers and the indigenous population meant that community based conservation programmes were not developed. Villagers were driven more by self-interests than the greater social good like the care of the community forest. As such, self-interest always tended to prevail as villagers took individual profit over the community forest.

Management Strategy of Bung Phra Community Forestry

With support from government, community forestry projects have been implemented throughout this region by local forestry officials for purposes of reforestation in degraded lands. After launching the project in Bung Phra, the villagers selected a community forestry committee to take responsibility for incorporating with the state. Twenty-three committee members representing the people of four villages in adjacent areas set up regulations to ensure that there would be a sustainable forest. These villagers would participate in meetings with the committee twice a year to consider all relevant matters regarding the community forest. Those who violated the regulations would be fined at least 500 baht (US$ 20) and those who cut trees would be arrested and handed over to the police. The community forest area was divided into several zones for each village to look after.

Environmental Conditions

The forest areas surrounding the community have been destroyed and converted to seasonal economic farms. The continuously shrinking of the forest areas has been cited as evidence of management failures of the Royal Forestry Department. These have been accompanied by drought and other detrimental effects. Certainly, a community with as little community spirit would not be able to restore the forest.

Awareness of Community Forestry

The local villagers always ask what benefits they would receive from the community forest but rarely asked what they could contribute to it. They are unaware of the forest ecosystem and unconscious of the conservation of natural resources. Individual interests overrode considerations of public interest as evidenced by the felling of these trees for individual profit with little regard for the regulations and benefits for the community. Yet there is the awareness about protecting the forest from poachers as there is fear of losing the material benefits of these natural resources to outsiders.

Community Leadership

The study has found that the management failure of the community forest in Bung Phra village resulted from weak local official leaders who did not pay much attention to the conservation of natural resources. Only a strong unofficial leader - a monk in the village - has played an active role in trying to protect and preserve the forest. Without any incentives, local villagers are not willing to cooperate with officials and project implementors.

Changes in Traditions and Customs of the Community

Elderly people tend to uphold the traditional value of living in harmony with nature. However, the newcomers and the younger generation in the village have ignored traditions and do not subscribe to the traditional community ways of life. The virtue of materialism rather than spiritism has tended to prevail. The idea of preserving forests is no longer of importance to them. In this way, local traditions have been declining in importance in binding the villagers to nature.

Local Participation

The villagers have shown little interest in participating in the community meetings. Instead, government officials have played a major role in the decision-making process of community forest management. To confirm this, as seen in Table 16.1, our study found that 63.2 percent of the nineteen respondents said the community forests were effectively managed by the state as government officials were deemed to be knowledgeable about the forests and had full authority to make decisions and get financial support. Only 26.3 percent of the respondents disagreed with that believing that the government could not manage the project effectively and efficiently. However, this group believed that the local community had potential to manage its natural resources more effectively than other agencies.

Yet a majority agreed with the community forestry policy formulated by the state. As seen in Table 16.2, 68.4 percent of respondents agreed on the formulation of the policy by the state and only 26.3 percent disagreed.

In short, various internal and external factors of the community such as a lack of an appreciation of the intrinsic value of the community forest, weak leadership, infusion of new migrants and outflow of the younger generation of villagers, changes in customs and norms of the community, low level of local participation, and weak capacity of government agency have all contributed to the failure of the efforts to restore and maintain Bung Phra community forestry in spite of state support.

Suggestions

The villagers of Bung Phra suggested that the policy of natural resource management should have clearer objectives and provide effective means of management. The locals should be made to understand better the concept of community forestry, and to pay more attention to the management of the forest by actively participating in the decision-making and management processes. Those with such views felt that local initiative and participation should be promoted by the state instead of allowing all actions to be centrally managed by the state. This idea is supported by the attitudes of the respondents in the survey in Table 16.1 which explains that 68.4 percent of respondents agreed that community forests initiated by the local villagers would be much more effective than by other agencies and only 10.5 percent of them said ineffective. Possible reasons could be the indigenous knowledge and the willingness of the villagers in those communities to cooperate and participate in the management process.

Table 16.1 Attitudes of Villagers toward the Effectiveness of Community Forestry Management in Bung Phra Village

Implementing agencies	Ineffective	Effective	No answer
1. Government	26.3	63.2	10.5
2. NGOs	26.3	52.6	15.8
3. Community	10.5	68.4	15.8
4. Cooperation between the public and private enterprises	10.5	21.1	63.2

Note: The figures are in percentages; N=19.

Table 16.2 Attitudes of Villagers toward the Formulation of Community Forestry Policy by the State in Bung Phra Village

Formulating agency	Agree	Disagree
Policy formulation of community forestry by the state	68.4	26.3

Note: The figures are in percentages; N=19.

Tha Wang Sai Community Forestry

The Tha Wang Sai villagers have successfully turned the deteriorating land in the village into an astonishingly green community forest. It is the success of this case that is the focus of this study.

The Tha Wang Sai community forest covering 0.5 square kilometers, and initiated by the local community, is located at Wang Nam Khieo district in Nakhon Ratchasima province. The local villagers have been well aware that their ecological forest stands as an oasis surrounded by devastated lands. This dense and green forest has been a rich natural resource for their basic needs such as food, medicine, and materials to build houses with. As such, the villagers have found sufficient incentive to conserve the forest.

Characteristics of Tha Wang Sai Community

This tightly-knit community has been conscious of the need to conserve natural resources ever since the community members agreed on the importance of such a move to the community. Compared to other villages, they are proud of their forest and have graciously taken care of it with a high level of cooperation evident among themselves. Once again, a monk has been a hub of the community network in the village and has become an important leader in forest conservation.

Management Strategy of Tha Wang Sai Community Forestry

The community forest of Tha Wang Sai has been managed by a committee comprising twenty-seven members working jointly with the local people and led by a respected monk of the community. At the beginning, according to the villagers, they received a great deal of support from NGOs and the government until the local committee was capable of taking over the work on its own.

The members of committee selected by the villagers have cooperated with the local residents by meeting with them twice a year, or whenever there was a need to. The committee members themselves meet once a month. At least two volunteers are responsible for guarding against any activity that would damage the forest. Strict rules and regulations of the community have been established and enforced by the committee. Cutting trees in the community forest, for example, is prohibited, and it is only in the case of fires and natural disasters damaging the properties of the residents of the villagers that they are allowed to utilize natural resources from the community. The punishment for cutting trees is a fine of at least 5,000 baht (US $200) for a small tree and up to 10,000 baht (US $400) for a big one. The committee can use its authority to expel those who severely violate the rules and regulations.

In the case of illegal poaching, the committee asks the government to enforce the law instead of applying community regulations.

Environmental Conditions

By harnessing the potential of the community, the villagers have turned degraded land into a dense and green forest in the midst of seasonal economic farms. More importantly, the local villagers have helped to protect and preserve the forest from the destructive activities based on the idea of management that respects community rights.

Awareness of Community Forestry

The villagers are knowledgeable about the natural ecosystem that provides them a diversity of vegetation, clean air, moist soil, and streams. Therefore, they are always conscious of the need for conservation of the forest. As mentioned above, a monk has been the community leader in the conservation of the community forest. His strong leadership is highly respected by the villagers which accounts for the success of the community forest. The encroachment of the forest by poachers, and the government's own projects of planting eucalyptus trees in the exhausted areas for reforestation, have been strongly opposed by the community.

On the other hand, the villagers have had the negative experience of prolonged seasonal droughts in the region which tends to take its toll on the vegetation and upset the natural balance. This has highlighted to them the effects of neglecting the forest or allowing it to suffer degradation thus motivating their conservation efforts further.

Community Leadership

The monk has played a fundamental role as a spiritual center of the community and successfully promoted local cooperation in the conservation of community resources. His strong leadership has also strengthened the potential of local organisations.

Traditions and Customs of the Community

Conforming to the rules, regulations, and norms of the community, Tha Wang Sai villagers have lived happily in harmony with nature. They apply the traditional belief systems in protecting their natural resources, for instance, by placing a statute of Buddha in the community forest, knowing that all the villagers will respect it and not engage in behaviour such as cutting trees or damaging the ecosystem of the forest. They share the forest products for sustainable livelihoods and also share their responsibility of preserving and protecting it.

Local Participation

The villagers have continued to play active roles in the management of their natural resources as they believe that the local community does indeed manage the community forestry more effectively than any other agency. As is evident in Table 16.3, the figures show that 81 percent of respondents in a survey said that community forests initiated by the community and supported by NGOs were more effective than those initiated by other agencies.

Table 16.3 Attitudes of Villagers toward the Effectiveness of Community Forestry Management in Tha Wang Sai

Implementing agencies	Ineffective	Effective	No answer
1. Government	57.1	23.8	9.5
2. NGOs	4.8	81.0	14.3
3. Community	9.5	81.0	4.8
4. Public & private enterprises cooperation	0.0	42.9	57.1

Note: The figures are in percentages; N=21.

In Table 16.4, 52.4 percent of the twenty-one respondents disagreed with any centralized action in the management of community natural resources because they believe that the government officials will not understand the problems the community is experiencing. Also, project implementation always tends to be delayed by the state. The villagers are more knowledgeable about their community than the government officials and thus more capable of initiating appropriate policies responding to their own felt needs. Only 38.1 percent agreed with the central role of the government since it could provide support to the community to help implement the project more effectively.

Problems of Management

The problems of management in the case of Tha Wang Sai suggested by the villagers are on the issues of leadership, cooperation, and community rights. The problems of weak official leaders such as village headmen, irresponsibility of government officials, and lack of cooperation between the state and the villagers could translate into failure of the community forest management in the future. More importantly, in order to forestall such failures, it is felt that the community rights on natural resources should be legally recognized by the state.

Table 16.4 Attitudes of Villagers toward the Formulation of Community Forestry Policy by the State in Tha Wang Sai

Policy formulation	Agree	Disagree
Policy formulation of the community forestry by the state	38.1	52.4

Note: The figures are in percentages; N=21.

Suggestions

As suggested by the villagers, government could provide financial support and knowledge for the villagers to enable them to initiate their community resource policy and to develop their skills in resource management. Also, the communication between government officials and the villagers could be improved for purposes of successfully managing the policy.

Summary

A matrix of the relationship between the strength of internal and external factors and the success of natural resource management is shown in Table 16.5. It explains that strong internal factors, as in the case of Tha Wang Sai, lay a firm foundation for the success of community forestry management. It has been proven that even without external support, the local organization is capable of managing its resources by depending on its cache of indigenous knowledge and the strength of its internal cohesion. With state involvement, as in the case of Bung Phra, it is possible that a weak official agency, jointly working with a weak local organization, will bring the programme to ruin.

Table 16.5 Strength of Internal and External Factors and Effectiveness of Community Forestry Management

	Internal	External
Success	Tha Wang Sai (strong)	
Failure		Bung Phra (weak)

Thus, the best model of community forestry management is based on the local community itself. The strategy of management depends mainly on the strength and cooperation among members of the community to ensure the sustainable development of natural resources. In addition, success depends upon the state of the environment which can be re-established and on the potential of human resources that are capable of initiating and participating in the processes of policy-making and management. Such external factors as government agency may support the community to some degree (depending on the capability of those enterprises), but with such strong internal factors as those evident in Tha Wang Sai, the community itself is capable of managing its natural resources.

PART VII

CONCLUSIONS

17 Moving Beyond 20th Century Myths to an Appreciation of State-Society Synergy

Peter Evans

The purpose of this chapter is, first, to look at two prior sets of myths about governance and development that I think need to be transcended, and second, to try to characterise the general theoretical perspective that has been offered here over the course of the last two days, adding a couple of examples of my own as I do so. Let me begin by presenting what I consider to be two unhelpful sets of myths that have prevailed in the recent past.

20th Century Myths

From the days of kings and peasants, myths have played a powerful role in defining the relationship between nation states and their citizens. The 20th century is no exception. Myths are not fantasies. They always capture part of the complex realities of state-society relations. If they didn't, they would have no power. They are credible because they do reflect a facet of reality. They gain further power because, by taking part of the reality and turning it into the whole, they can offer simple relief from complicated decisions. This makes them dangerous. Simple formulas make it easy to take action, but they also obscure solutions that don't fit their "one-eyed" vision of the world and lead to wrong-headed action. In order for policy and social action to move forward, myths must eventually be transcended.

At the end of World War II, the dominant myths of state-society relations exaggerated the positive potential of the state as a developmental actor. In the advanced industrial countries of Europe and North America, the apparent success of Keynesian policies in alleviating the great depression legitimated economic activism and the success of wartime mobilisation during the Second World War further enhanced the belief that modern states could tackle any problem. In the Third World, national liberation movements were convinced that once the reins of state power were wrested from the old colonial powers, newly independent states would become powerful agents of development.

Optimistic expectations of what central state bureaucracies could accomplish implied in turn a negative evaluation of what local communities could accomplish for themselves. States were seen as modern, staffed by technically sophisticated experts. Local communities were "traditional," burdened with outmoded beliefs and practices that would inhibit development. Development required overcoming the resistance of local communities and imposing "modern and efficient" ways of doing things devised by central government decision-makers.

The "myths" embodied in this perspective were not, of course, entirely wrong. Effective central governments must be a crucial component of national development. Technical expertise is important and development does involve changing certain local attitudes and practices. Indeed, in a substantial part of the Third World, Latin America, for example, efforts to implement this perspective during the 1950s and 1960s were associated with quite impressive rates of economic growth. Nonetheless, by the 1970s, it was clear that this mid-20th century perspective was deeply flawed.

Most Third World central governments floundered in the face of the ever wider range of tasks that they had optimistically taken on. Worse yet, too many of them became "predatory states," extracting resources from society, providing little besides repression in return and subverting any possibility of development. Local communities looked more like obstacles to development than victims. In the 1970s and 1980s, as growth slackened throughout the Third World and turned negative in most of Africa, mid-20th century myths were replaced with a new vision of development.

In this new vision, states became the primary obstacle to development rather than its primary agent. Where mid-20th century myths had enthroned central government bureaucrats, late-20th century myths now enthroned markets. Markets were the "magic bullet" of the 1980s. In the advanced industrial countries, Margaret Thatcher and Ronald Reagan preached against the evils of big government. In the Third World, "liberalisation" became development orthodoxy.

In this new "market as magic bullet" vision, the traditional beliefs and practices of local communities were no longer a problem, but not because they were suddenly seen as making a contribution to development. It was assumed that insofar as they were incompatible with economic growth, the expansion of the market would dissolve them.

Once again the myths captured an important part of the reality. Exposing previously protected producers to more competition did help reduce entrenched inefficiencies. Allowing local producers to take advantage of market prices did increase their incentives to produce. The fiscal distress of central governments made the necessity of cutting back the scope of their activities more than obvious. Nonetheless, the one-sidedness of late-20th century myths soon became apparent.

For most Third World countries, the market was not a magic bullet. Despite increased reliance on markets, growth rates in the 1980s lagged behind those of the 1950s and 1960s. As efforts to expand the sway of markets increased, the logical relation between capable states and effective markets became more obvious: without the underpinning of an effective state apparatus it is extremely difficult, if not impossible, to get markets to work the way that they are supposed to. Regional contrasts made the point. On the one hand, there was the apparent inability of liberalisation to stimulate new entrepreneurial initiatives in Africa and most parts of Latin America. On the other hand, the region where growth was most impressive - East Asia - was also the region in which governments were most actively involved in promoting industrialisation.

As the economic efficacy of late-20th century myths was drawn into question, other doubts began to surface as well. They still left no role for local communities in defining developmental trajectories. Local ties and community norms were still treated as economically irrelevant. The new vision still required that members of local communities relate to each other in ways that conformed to an externally constructed vision that was developmentally efficient. Not only did "market as a magic bullet" models leave communities out of the process of shaping development, but the economic gains these models produced tended to be very unevenly distributed. Communities not initially endowed with competitive resources fell further behind even when overall national income increased.

There were also less tangible but equally serious problems with the social and political environments associated with these models. One Latin American commentator, Guillermo O'Donnell, has spoken of the "browning of Latin America." Well-intentioned but overzealous efforts to curtail the government's economic involvements, O'Donnell argued, contributed to the destruction of "the state as law" in many parts of Latin America which led in turn to an "angry atomisation of society" in which neither state nor communities are able to check predatory private practices.[1]

Uneasiness with the social consequences of "market as magic bullet" models is equally salient in advanced industrial countries. The United States is perhaps the society most thoroughly penetrated by market relations. Its popular culture and beliefs are most thoroughly dominated by market-based assumptions. Yet the thorough-going triumph of market rationality in America is combined with an equally thorough-going apprehensiveness over the evaporation of civility and civic engagement and the proliferation of socially-destructive behaviour by individuals disconnected from any sense of community.

All of this gets us to the themes of this conference which I would argue represent an effort to transcend both earlier sets of 20th century myths and bring us to a more adequate understanding of how states, markets, and communities fit together in the process of development. The idea of "governance" focuses attention on the organisation and operation of public institutions. As such, it moves beyond late-20th century myths in which the formula for dealing with any public agency is "shrink it or get rid of it." Yet the approach to governance that is being put forward here is clearly not a return to mid-20th century myths in which developmental solutions came in the form of plans imposed by omniscient experts from the central government.

Not only does the conference start from the premise that states must embrace the flexibility and incentives that markets offer but it also opens up space for a set of resources largely ignored by both mid- and late-20th century myths: the resources that inhere in communities themselves. In the vision proposed here, communities are important participants in the process of defining developmental trajectories, but they are more than that. Communities are also being seen as the source of a special set of economically valuable resources.

Social Capital

Everyone has always known that social relationships can be an asset that makes people more productive, just as money or technology are assets that can make people more productive. Shared norms and social networks can lower the cost of economic transactions, and make it easier for people to co-ordinate their efforts and compensate for the lack of other, more tangible, resources. As a way of capturing conceptually the economic value of shared norms and networks, people have begun to talk about "social capital".

Recently, there has been a burst of interest in the concept of "social capital" that extends from the halls of the World Bank to small communities in the rural United States to activists in the Third World. Robert Putnam helped start the ball rolling a few years ago in a historical study of regional developmental differences in Italy.[2] Putnam noticed that higher rates of economic growth, and more effective governments, in Northern Italy were built on a long history of people getting together in simple organisations like singing groups and football clubs. He saw this kind of social practice as creating the foundations for things like the co-operative relationships among small businesses that make cities like Modena economically successful in the contemporary global economy.

Putnam's vision of the historical process underlines one of the things that makes social capital a potentially important asset. Unlike machines or farmland, which gradually wear out as they are used, social relationships become stronger and more valuable as they are used. Building social capital is a "virtuous circle" kind of mutually reinforcing process. Co-operative interaction helps generate trust. Trust makes more co-operative interaction possible, and associating in simple ways builds foundations for more complicated forms of collective action. Any group - from owners of big corporations to poor farmers - can take advantage of this mutually reinforcing process, but it is obviously especially important for those that lack other kinds of assets.

Following Putnam's lead, Deepa Narayan and a group of collaborators in Tanzania, decided to see if social capital could make a difference to poor people in contemporary Third World countries.[3] In order to make sure that their evidence would convince sceptics, they gathered systematic quantitative data from a range of villages. The results were startling. The incomes of households living in communities where people were more likely to belong to inclusive voluntary groups and associations were compared to households in villages with less associational life. The effect of associational life in the village as a whole on the incomes of individual household was stronger than either higher levels of education among household members or increasing amounts of non-farm assets.

While these results are startling in their strength, they make sense, even in terms of conventional economic theory. Economists have talked for a long time about co-ordination problems, risk aversion as an obstacle to innovation, the value of information flows, and the importance of lowering transaction costs. Once you think about it, it is obvious that social capital can help with all these problems.

The mounting combination of theoretical arguments, historical evidence, and statistical data has helped theorists and policy makers see local community as potential developmental assets instead of dismissing them as impediments to development as mid-20th century myths did, or as assumed essentially irrelevant in late-20th century "market as magic bullet" models.

Recognising the value of communities and informal social ties is a step forward, but we have to be careful not to go overboard. "Social capital" is not a magic bullet either. An exaggerated vision in which trust, solidarity, and shared norms are all that it takes to achieve developmental goals would be just as much of a disservice to communities as older visions in which they were considered reactionary or irrelevant. If old visions that saw the state as omnipotent were misleading, a vision that sees communities as omnipotent would be even more misleading. In the contemporary world, even the most solitary, well-organised community needs supportive connections with a formal network of public institutions.

This brings us to what I consider to be the heart of this conference: building an understanding of how communities (or "civil society" more generally) and the formal bureaucratic organisations of the state can work together to achieve developmental goals. In earlier work, I have called this "state-society synergy".

State-Society Synergy

The idea of state-society synergy is very simple. Communities and state agencies need each other. Having strong, sophisticated government bureaucracies is an advantage from the point of view of communities, while having organised communities with high levels of social capital is an advantage for government bureaucracies.

If these seem like simple and self-evident propositions to you, I should remind you that they run directly counter to both mid- and late-20th century developmental myths. They also run counter to conventional wisdom which posits a zero-sum relationship between the power of communities and the power of government. This conventional wisdom assumes that the more capable government agencies become, the more intrusive and domineering they will be, which gives communities an interest in having the weakest possible set of government agencies.

Obviously, government agencies can indeed be intrusive and domineering. When they are, communities need to organise to rein them in. The problem is that focusing only on the potential for conflict distracts attention from the gains that can be achieved through state-society synergy. As the many examples that have been raised here at this conference indicate, these gains are considerable.

Let me add a couple of examples in order to make it clear what I mean by state-society synergy. Both examples are probably familiar to most of you. Both have to do with water. First I would like to look at irrigation systems, then at sewer systems.

Irrigation Systems

Irrigation systems are a great example of the potential gains from state-society synergy. On the one hand, it is clear that local communities cannot finance or build massive main canals to bring water from other areas. The large scale public works, and the general task of allocating water among different areas of the country, have to be done by a government agency. Yet, experience has shown that without active participation of local communities in the maintenance and operation of small canals and ditches that run between the main canals and the farmers' fields, irrigation systems tend to be wasteful and inefficient. Government agencies simply cannot do the job by themselves. They need communities as "co-producers".[4]

The necessity of relying on local communities is obvious once you think about it. Intimate, detailed knowledge of local terrain, local crops, local agricultural techniques, and the local farmers themselves, is the first prerequisite of efficient local water allocation. Members of local communities have this knowledge in abundance. Convincing local farmers that allocation is fair and preventing "cheating," would be an extremely time consuming and costly job if performed by government officials. "Water guards", selected by the community because they are held in respect by other villagers, have the power of local norms (social capital) behind their allocational decisions and enforcement efforts. Maintenance of local ditches and small canals becomes much more economical if local farmers organise it themselves.

In short, efficient irrigation requires a complementary division of labour between local communities and government agencies. Local communities need a government agency to integrate local needs into a broader plan of allocation and make sure that the promised water is delivered according to the plan. Government agencies need the active participation, local expertise, and "social capital" of local communities to ensure that getting the irrigation system to work after the water leaves the main canals is not prohibitively expensive.

Not surprisingly, irrigation systems with reputations for exceptional efficiency are organised along precisely these lines. Taiwan's irrigation associations are a prime example.[5] Taiwan's irrigation system combines reliance on "grassroots" participation with a very tightly structured government bureaucracy. On the one hand, the government agencies in charge of irrigation in Taiwan are highly organised bureaucracies with intricate internal hierarchies, even at the local level. On the other hand, the directors of these irrigation associations are elected by local farmers. The operation of the system within villages is very clearly in the hands of voluntary "irrigation groups" and respected older farmers who serve as "water guards." Local irrigation officials depend on the water guards and irrigation groups to construct a plan for how much water the village needs and when they will need it. Villagers depend on the bureaucratic efficiency of the agency to ensure that the water is in fact delivered as promised.

This combination of grassroots participation and bureaucratic efficiency doesn't fit the conventional wisdom in which community-agency relations are zero-sum struggles over power, but they make sense. Oddly enough, having robust, sophisticated bureaucracies on the government side makes it easier for the irrigation agencies to develop tight connections with the communities they serve. Carefully constructed systems of controls within the government agency create the confidence that local officials won't be "captured" by locals. Thus, instead of trying to insulate the agency by proscribing ties to the local community, local officials can be encouraged to develop close ties with the communities they serve. Thus according to one analyst, "irrigation agency staff are so much part of local society that they can neither escape uncomfortable censure if they are seen to be conspicuously performing poorly, nor ignore representations made to them by members".[6]

Just to make this point more firmly, it is worth contrasting the Taiwanese case with a couple of other irrigation systems, less well known for their efficiency. In Nepal, irrigation officials are less well paid, careers are less well developed and the bureaucracy as a whole is much less sophisticated. Consequently, the irrigation bureaucracy lacks the capacity to develop the kind of decentralised relations with communities that characterise Taiwan's irrigation associations.[7] Because the agency lacks the organisational capacity to institutionalise a system of career incentives at the local level, no competent official wants to get "trapped" in the countryside. Lacking the bureaucratic capacity necessary to engage locals as "co-producers," the irrigation agency fails to take advantage of the energy and expertise of local communities. Worse still, the agency gets in the way of farmer's efforts to self-manage at the local level.

India offers another contrasting case. The Indian irrigation bureaucracy is more organisationally sophisticated than its Nepalese counterpart, but still fails take advantage of the potential for state-society synergy. Instead of focusing on building ties with local communities, the organisers of the Indian irrigation system focus their energy on insulating bureaucrats from farmers. Officials are transferred frequently to make sure that they won't get too involved with local communities. Ironically, as Robert Wade has pointed out, the transfer system itself becomes a focus for corruption.[8]

These quick comparisons underline two central points:

- "Weak" bureaucracies are not more likely to create opportunities for community involvement. On the contrary, it takes a robust, sophisticated bureaucracy to successfully institute the kind of division of labour that is necessary for state-society synergy. Less well-organised bureaucracies are more likely to fall back on simplistic centralised rules.
- Trying to circumvent engagement with communities being served is a counter-productive strategy for avoiding corruption.

Sewer Systems

My second example also involves networks that carry water, but of a very different kind. Sewer systems are almost as important to urban dwellers as irrigation systems are to farmers. Even more clearly than in the case of irrigation systems, sewer systems are not something that communities can provide on their own. Yet, fiscally pressed government agencies are often unable to provide sewer systems to poor urban dwellers, especially those that live in densely populated shanty towns. Consequently, these neighbourhoods send their waste into pit latrines that rapidly fill-up and contaminate the ground water, or into gullies or footpaths, creating problems for public health as well as for the quality of the environment.

One of the many countries where urban sewers are glaringly under-supplied is Brazil,[9] but Brazil is also the source of an important innovation in the provision of sewers for poor people. At the beginning of the 1980s, a young sanitation engineer by the name of Jose Carlos de Melo, working in one of the cities of the poor northeast region, came up with a new idea for sewers which he called "condominial sewers".[10] From an engineering point of view, de Melo's idea involved a creative technical innovation.

Conventional sewers are laid deep below streets with separate feeder lines going from the trunk to each individual house using relatively high quality but costly materials. They can only be maintained by specialised professionals. Why not, de Melo reasoned, lay shallow lines through people's yards where they would not have to bear the weight of traffic and be easier to maintain? These shallow lines could go directly from house to house rather than having individual feeder connections to a trunk line and use less durable and less expensive materials. They would be of lower quality than conventional sewers but far better than no sewers at all which is what these neighbourhoods would get if they had to wait until cities had the money to bring them conventional sewers.

As it turns out, de Melo was right. Condominial sewers could be constructed and maintained for as little as one-third to one-fourth of the cost of conventional sewers. Not only were the materials cheaper, but the simple, shallow design meant that local people could construct their own feeder systems themselves. Given the high rates of unemployment in these communities, people were giving up very little when they did the work themselves. Condominial systems soon became so popular that they spread to other cities. By now, condominial systems represent "a sixth of all sewerage construction in Brazil and the majority of all new sewerage in squatter and low income neighbourhoods."[11]

Condominial systems were successful not just because they offered a way of supplying improved sanitation and public health despite the fiscal crisis being experienced by Brazilian municipalities (and indeed the entire Brazilian state). Their success is also reflected in the private benefits experienced by home owners in terms of sharp increases in housing values. Moreover, they had a positive spillover effect on private investments by individual homeowners in household sanitation equipment like new floor drains, sinks, and toilets.

From the point of view of our concerns here today, however, the fact that condominial sewers represent an economically successful civil engineering innovation is not what makes them interesting. What makes them interesting is that they are an excellent example of how recognising the possibility of "state-society" synergy can open up new solutions to otherwise intractable problems.

The engineering design problems that had to be solved in order to make condominial sewers successful were relatively trivial compared to the institutional problems. When they build conventional sewers, state agencies don't need to interact with the communities the sewers serve. This makes things much simpler, but it also has disadvantages. One of the disadvantages is that often the connection rate to trunk lines is low, especially in poor neighbourhoods when people are expected to pay their share of the costs. Much as people want sewers, they would rather not be hooked up than make payments beyond their means. Low connection rates make conventional systems inefficient as well as expensive in poor neighbourhoods.

The shift to condominial systems requires a new relationship between the state agency and the sewer users. The agency cannot work from the street; it has to move through people's yards. More important, the cost savings depends in good part on the contribution of people's labour to the construction of the feeder systems. Plus, the cost savings on maintenance depends in good part on residents understanding the system well enough to repair feeder lines and being motivated to do so. Instead of being passive consumers of sewers, residents must become active "co-producers" of sewers. In short, reaping the potential advantages of the technical differences between condominial and conventional sewers depends entirely on being able to create some state-society synergy which, in turn, depends on transforming the normal character of the state agencies involved.

In order to turn clients into co-producers, it was necessary to invest considerable energy in building ties with the neighbourhoods in which systems were being installed. In the pioneering case, De Melo and his co-workers spent two years working intensively with residents in order to figure out how to make condominial sewers work. Even after the process was more fully understood, successful implementation of condominial sewers required a four to six month mobilisation process in each neighbourhood. First of all, levels of service had to be negotiated. Neighbourhoods must understand that they have (in principle) the option of high cost conventional sewers, less expensive condominial sewers, which will require their involvement in both installation and maintenance, or no sewers at all. The options were explained first in neighbourhood meetings, then in block by block meetings in which attendance by at least 50% of all the residents on the block was required. Residents had to be actively involved in the design of the system. Explanations had to be repeated many times, and even then it was only when residents became actively involved in the construction of the system that they really began to appreciate the technical aspects of how the system worked.

Obviously, the standard training received by sanitation engineers (to say nothing of that received by the managers of private construction companies) does little to inculcate expertise in mobilising neighbourhoods and negotiating with them. The original Natal experiment was made possible in part because of an unusual cadre of young engineers who had been involved in the student movement, literacy campaigns, and health campaigns before joining the state water service company. Subsequent cases required the formation of multi-disciplinary teams including both social workers and engineers. In short, state-society synergy requires a transformation not just in the way those state agencies think about their relation with society but also in the ways in which state agencies themselves are organised.

State-society synergy also implies changes on the side of society. Earlier I argued that some level of social capital or community organisation is a prerequisite for state-society synergy and I think that this is true, but it is also the case that taking a state-society synergy approach can also provoke changes at the level of community organisation. The impact of condominal sewer systems went beyond public health improvements and increased housing values. Active neighbourhood involvement in the production and maintenance of sewers provoked both increases in collective action to keep sewers maintained and an increase in the level of demands made on the state. According to the World Bank report on condominial sewers, getting residents actively engaged in project implementation "fosters an active, vocal constituency that puts in motion the accountability mechanisms that are necessary for good agency performance." Condominial customers were more likely to define maintenance problems as a collective problem. Their demands "activated dormant neighbourhood associations" which either organised collective "community-wide line clearing" or tried to build their legitimacy by being more aggressive in demanding solutions from state agencies.[12]

Two points are important here. First, state-society synergy not only depends on initial endowments of social capital, but also tends to increase those endowments. Second, state-society synergy not only depends on an initial willingness of state agencies to treat the people they serve as partners rather than passive clients, it also tends to intensify demands for responsiveness and accountability. In both cases, it can be argued that state-society synergy helps put in motion a self-reinforcing "virtuous circle" of reciprocal causation.

Caveats in State-Society Synergy

Let me make it clear here that I am not arguing that a state-society synergy perspective offers a formula for assured success. Let me use condominial sewers one more time to underline this point. Condominial systems were by no means successful in all the cities they were tried. Resistance from sanitation engineers who are trained in constructing and maintaining conventional systems is one potent source of opposition. In a number of cities, state water companies engaged in a form of passive sabotage by neglecting maintenance. In the largest city, the state water company refused to cooperate in the maintenance of the 80% of the systems that it considered "non-standard" leading to the breakdown of many of these systems. Once again, it must be emphasised that competent, sophisticated state bureaucracies are a necessary starting point, but continual transformation of these agencies is necessary if strategies based on state-society synergy are to succeed.

Overzealous politicians generated problems for opposite reasons. Finding that condominial sewers generated political support, mayors made quick installation of new lines a pre-election priority. Neglecting to allow sufficient time for community education and mobilisation led to low connection rates, residents unprepared to take care of maintenance problems, and refusals to pay connection fees.

As you would expect, the social capital side of the equation is not something that can be taken for granted either. For example, the very success of condominial systems in raising real estate values encouraged poor residents to reap their share of the returns by selling their homes. The new owners, not having been part of the process of mobilisation and education, lacked both the knowledge and the appreciation of their responsibilities that were necessary for them to play their role in the operation of the system. Even without turnover, it was often difficult to get residents to work together to maintain feeder lines. Some even closed off their yards to other members of the community and made it impossible to clear blockages.

The point is obvious: it would be a terrible mistake to try to replace previous myths with an early-21st century myth which elevated state-society synergy to magic bullet status. Adopting a stance that emphasises state-society synergy does allow you to exploit social and institutional resources that are neglected by other approaches and, therefore, opens up a chance of success where other approaches have failed. But, realising the potential gains from state-society synergy is anything but easy. Success depends on the usual combination of imagination, hard work, and luck, and failure is always a likely outcome.

Conclusion

Let me close by reiterating what I consider to be three basic propositions that underlie the state-society synergy idea:

- <u>State agencies need communities.</u> Most state agencies can't accomplish their jobs unless they are able to take advantage of the information, expertise, and energy of local communities. They need "co-producers" not passive clients.
- <u>Communities need state bureaucracies.</u> In the modern world, relatively few services can be organised effectively at a purely local level, nor can any community hope to encapsulate the full range of expertise and abilities required to satisfy its needs. A decentralised division of labour with communities as "co-producers" requires higher levels of bureaucratic capacity than centralised imposition of simple rules.
- <u>When state-society synergy works it creates a "virtuous circle" of institutional change.</u> Active engagement in "coproducing" state services helps build social capital, and engaged communities make more demands which push state agencies toward greater accountability, responsiveness, and organisational innovations.

These three propositions are not a formula for success. As I hope I have made clear, success in particular cases depends on a combination of hard work and imagination. What these three propositions should do, however, is to encourage people who have the imagination, and are willing to invest some hard work, to make the most of under-utilised institutional resources both within governments and outside them. To my mind, generating that sort of encouragement is what this conference is about.

Notes

[1] Guillermo O'Donnell, "On the State, Democratisation and Some Conceptual Problems: A Latin American View with Glances at Some Postcommunist Countries," *World Development* 21, 8 (August 1993): 1355-1369.

[2] Robert Putnam, *Making Democracy Work: Civic Traditions in Modern Italy* (Princeton: Princeton University Press, 1993).

[3] See Deepa Narayan and Lant Pritchett, "Cents and Sociability: Household Income and Social Capital in Rural Tanzania" (Washington, DC: World Bank, August 1996), unpublished manuscript.

[4] On this point see, Elinor Ostrom, "Crossing the Great Divide: Coproduction, Synergy, and Development" *World Development* 24, 6 (June 1996): 1073-1088.

[5] For analysis of Taiwan's irrigation associations, see W. F. Lam, "Institutional Design of Public Agencies and Coproduction: A Study of Irrigation Associations in

Taiwan" *World Development* 22, 6 (June 1994): 1039-1054. See also Michael P Moore, "The Fruits and Fallacies of Neo-liberalism: The Case of Irrigation," *World Development* 17, 11 (November 1989): 1733-50.

[6] Moore (1989): 1742.

[7] See Wai Fung Lam, "Institutions, Engineering Infrastructure, and Performance in the Governance and Management of Irrigation Systems: The Case of Nepal," unpublished Ph.D. dissertation (School of Public and Environmental Affairs and Department of Political Science, Indiana University, Bloomington, Indiana, 1994).

[8] Robert Wade, "The Market for Public Office: Why the Indian State is not Better at Development," *World Development* 13, 4 (April 1985): 467-97.

[9] In 1980, 80% of Brazil's urban population lacked sewerage services according to the Brazilian Society of Sanitation Engineers (ABES). In 1990, the figure was still under 40%.

[10] Gabrielle Watson, *Good Sewers Cheap: Agency Customer Interactions in Low-Cost Urban Sanitation in Brazil* (Washington, DC: World Bank, Water and Sanitation Division, 1995), see also Gehan Sinnatamby, "Low Cost Sanitation," in Jorge E. Hardoy, Sandy Cairncross, and David Satterthwaite (eds), *The Poor Die Young: Housing and Health in Third World Cities* (London: Earthscan Publications, Ltd, 1990).

[11] *Ibid.*: 51.

[12] Watson (1995): 49, 36-39.

18 The Future of Governance in the Asia-Pacific and Areas for Further Research

Joaquin L. Gonzalez III and Gambhir Bhatta

All the chapters in this book emphasise that good governance is critical to effective social and economic development especially in the Asia-Pacific region. They also expose a number of areas that could be the focus of further research and experimentation. It needs to be noted that care must also be taken with regards to replicating some of the lessons highlighted here. The cross-country cases illustrate that cultural and demographic factors need to be examined with care and sensitivity. Additionally, governance innovations need to go beyond mere public sector reforms and more importantly take on board new ideas about how to enhance citizen-business-government (CBG) partnerships and to begin to rethink traditional norms and understanding of public accountability.

The CBG relationships are often characterised by mistrust and misunderstanding. How can this be overcome? Can these three key actors identify a mutuality of benefits and create synergies in pursuing common goals? Or are these necessarily competitive actors in which case, allowing each to thrive is a question of opening-up enough 'space' and creating a clear division of labour and work to achieve optimal results in development? Political will and bureaucratic inertia have also been cited as essential factors to consider in reform implementation.

Furthermore, there appears to be evident in the literature a greater concentration on national-level reforms and macro orientation of governance as opposed to community-level innovations or micro aspects. There is thus a need to look seriously into the key issues raised regarding local level leadership, local capacity building, and stakeholder participation in the development process at the grassroots level.

Scepticism about Continued Growth in the Asia-Pacific

Let us begin by revisiting the issue of East Asian growth and what that means for studying further the issue of replicability of governance innovations. While the World Bank's *East Asian Miracle: Public Policy and Economic Growth*,[1] and many others, predicted continuation of economic growth,[2] some are now beginning to raise questions about whether East Asia's growth is on the decline.[3]

On the face of it, the High-Performing Asian Economies (HPAEs) are indeed being increasingly characterised by infrastructure bottlenecks, breakdowns in traditional economic bases and benefits (such as lifelong employment in Japan and S. Korea), shortage in skills and expertise, etc. In mid-1997, for example, Thailand and Malaysia had to make serious adjustments in their currencies to stabilise their growth. These events have begun to recast the entire *problematique* of the East Asian Growth model - if ever there was one.

This has been best brought out by eminent scholars like Paul Krugman, Dani Rodrik, Lawrence Lau, Alwyn Young, and others, who talk about the myth of Asia's miracle and assert that since growth did not necessarily raise the Total Factor Productivity in some of these miracle countries (e.g., Hong Kong, Singapore, South Korea, and Taiwan), the boom would eventually fizzle out as factors of production, e.g., labour and capital, dwindled. This has not been quite so evident in the HPAEs at the moment, but could indeed be a portent of things to come in the near future.

Some Critical Issues as Areas for Further Research

From the macro (i.e., upstream) concern regarding continued growth in the region, interestingly, the focus of recent critiques on matters related to governance has tended to be more downstream, i.e., as related to local governance, and to other issues previously considered to be peripheral and/or marginal in the whole formulation of the governance concept. Apart from local governance, these include the political dimension, culture and values, database and measurement, and participatory approaches. As good governance sustains good policies, strategic fine-tuning in these areas is a must.

Local Governance

Incisive as the various authors have been in their analysis of the realm within which this miraculous development in the Asia-Pacific region has occurred, there is very little written on the downstream aspects of governance. Local governance as an issue is not seem to be given its due weight. There exists a sizeable gap in the area of local governance even given the many books about this popular development emphasis. J. Gonzalez, for instance, brings this issue out rather forcefully when he talks about the need to reach out to the real stakeholders of development (i.e., those at the grassroots).[4] Moreover, while HPAEs do very well with socio-economic indicators according to the *World Competitiveness Report* (1989-1995), when it comes to the index showing the degree by which local authorities are able to make independent decisions free from central government control (referring here to decentralisation), the HPAEs rank well below most developed countries, and even some developing ones. Ironically, many social scientists working for international development agencies have been pushing for decentralisation in East Asia and other parts of the world for the last two decades.[5] Local governance, as a field of study, is not something new but the application of the growth philosophies of East Asia in the context of local governance is sorely missing. One key issue that merits further scrutiny is the role being played by community-level non-governmental organisations (NGOs) in national development in the various countries of the region (notably Japan, South Korea, Hong Kong, Malaysia, Indonesia, and Thailand).

Prescribing increased government in development endeavours at the local-community level is not new. This idea has its roots in the decentralisation movement. As advocated by development experts of the 1980s, decentralisation is the institutionalisation of more participatory modifications on the traditionally non-participatory processes perpetuated by the governmental bureaucracies. Development experts believed that a solution to the dysfunctions associated with planned development through a highly centralised governance system was to decentralise the functions of bureaucracy. The problem of implementing plans through a centralised development approach led to a call for a more decentralised administrative approach. In one of their studies, Cheema and Rondinelli, for example, summarised numerous arguments for a more decentralised approach to governing local areas, some of which we reproduce here because obviously they are central to the study of governance:[6]

- By *decentralising functions and reassigning central government officials to local levels*, these officials' knowledge of and sensitivity to local problems and needs can be increased;

- decentralisation could also allow *better political and administrative "penetration"* of national government policies into areas remote from the national capital, where central government plans are often unknown and ignored by the rural people or are undermined by local elites, and where support for national development plans is often weak;

- decentralisation might allow *greater representation for various political, religious, ethnic, and tribal groups in development decision making* that could lead to greater equity in the allocation of government resources and investments;

- decentralisation could lead to the development of *greater administrative capability* among local governments and private institutions in the regions and provinces, thus expanding their capacities to take over functions that are not usually performed well by central ministries; and

- a decentralised governmental structure is needed to *institutionalise the participation* of citizens in development planning and management.

In order to increase the likelihood of implementation, development experts need to concentrate their governance efforts at prescribing ways and means aimed at devolving the power and authority of the central governmental bureaucracy as prescribed by Cheema and Rondinelli.

Political Dimension

Two major political challenges that social scientists will face in prescribing good governance reforms to developing countries are: (1) how to define governance within the context of the country's political culture? and (2) how to implement changes that are not going to touch sensitive political nerves? As stated in the introductory chapter, governance as generally envisioned is the power, influence, and relationship between government and citizens in countries that is utilised to implement social and economic programs. To reiterate, the World Bank and many international institutions subscribe to the philosophy that the dimensions to governance are the form of political regime, the process by which authority and control are exercised, and the capacity to design, formulate, and implement policies and discharge functions. Given these parameters, therefore, any serious reform initiatives by a country should take into consideration all three dimensions. However, a major limitation of a social scientist working for one of these development agencies is that the focus of any of their governance prescriptions can only be directed at the last two since reforms pertaining to the political regime of a certain developing country are beyond the World Bank's and other international aid agencies' socio-economic development mandate.

Thus, viewing governance as only the public bureaucracy's organisational process and institutional capacity is definitely a major challenge to reform initiatives since all three facets are intertwined. For instance, the ADB's proposed good governance prescriptions on accountability, transparency, predictability, civil service reform, public enterprise reform, and legal and regulatory reform have political spill-overs and side-effects inherent in their implementation, depending on the developing country's political culture. Even though it seems that clear lines of distinctions can be drawn in a well-prepared Board Paper, the actual application of the reforms could be a totally different story. Root, one of the main authors of the ADB's governance board paper, justifying the prescription of good governance reforms, argued correctly in *The Asian Wall Street Journal* that "bureaucratic reform is economic reform."[7]

Economists and public policy specialists will certainly agree with this point since good governance does have an economic base and an economic impact. For example, a public bureaucracy that chooses to streamline its operations will definitely be contributing to savings in the national budget. Additionally, more transparency and increased accountability in government operations will indeed create a better business environment that breeds less corruption and greater responsibility. However, political leaders, public bureaucrats, and even regional scholars especially from the high-performing Asian economies, will surely argue with Root and remind him that any good governance reform is not simply an economic reform but also a political one. This is also one of the lessons from the East Asian miracle. The actual practice in most of the region, especially among the tiger economies, is such that leadership, both executive and legislative, in tandem with high-level civil servants, takes an active political role in successfully formulating, implementing, and monitoring growth-sustaining public policies and socio-economic projects. As a matter of fact, many political scientists and public management specialists would argue that the working relationship between politicians and bureaucrats is an integral and an inseparable feature of a country's governance system. This is probably the major reason why representatives from China and Malaysia raised strong objections to any "governance projects" by the Asian Development Bank in the 1996 annual meeting.

Culture and Values

Various non-economic factors such as environment and human rights will certainly dominate world headlines and will continue to be crucial issues in the 21st century as international actors (such as the World Trade Organisation) - with prodding from the West - begin to zero in on these themes. Obviously, they will need to be analysed rigorously. Other things that still need to be analysed include: the cultural dimension of development (specifically, the so-called Confucian tradition - and by extension, "Asian Values" - that all the authors allude to even though Root has sought to debunk this as the Confucian Cliche); China's spectacular and sustained growth rates for the past decade or so and the impact its own development philosophy has on others (including the possibility that it debunks some of the policy prescriptions being put so aggressively by various authors); and pursuant to this China factor, the impact of a particular type of political system on the economic growth rate.

Using the concept of governance as an analytical tool, it is quite evident that some of the HPAEs are interpreting good governance from their own politico-administrative culture. To consider one characteristic of good governance (transparency), in Malaysia, for example, the Bakun Dam controversy has shown that the public had very little information of what was going on behind the planning and proposed development of the project. And in Indonesia, in February 1996, the Suharto Government offered tax breaks and special privileges to a joint venture firm involving the President's son for a national car project. Such blatant favouritism can hardly serve to foster public confidence in the government (one of the hallmarks of the East Asian miracle). In South Korea, the long-cozy relationship between big business and the military has begun to generate some heat. In August 1996, for example, Asiaweek reported that a scandal was tainting four major arms suppliers who bribed military officials to buy weapons at inflated prices. Prosecutors also focused attention on corruption involving civil servants and business leaders. And in late 1996, two ex-Presidents and several prominent *chaebol* leaders were tried and sentenced in court, one of the former - and all of the latter - on charges of corruption.

It is also interesting to see the issue of governance within the context of recent developments in this region. In Indonesia, for example, while too much was probably made of the July 1996 riots in Jakarta, they do highlight the fact that strong economic performance has not had its consequent - and anticipated - effects; not yet anyway. It may have been this that prompted Suharto to call attention to the existing chasm between the "haves" and the "have-nots" and the need to do something about it on an urgent basis. In South Korea, the national psyche is beginning to undergo a subtle change keeping in mind that several *chaebol* bosses have now been tried for briberies and given punishments, and a new crop of younger politicians and business leaders are coming up who were not even born when the Korean War broke out in 1950. In Japan, the once-vaunted Ministry of Finance and Ministry of Trade and Industry (MITI) are now facing increasingly critical public scrutiny, and even Hashimoto himself has unveiled plans to reduce the number of ministries and to give civil servants less control over the crucial tasks of deciding the national budget.

Database and Measurement

Bolongaita, in Chapter Five, alludes to the use of surveys conducted at the local government level which could be the key to creating a more cohesive database and measurement system. But there is a general lack of governance databases, and hard measures that could be used for policy research pertaining to governance - and in various stages of a governance project from planning and implementation to monitoring and evaluation - are clearly missing from the most of the chapters in this volume. Elsewhere, attempts have been made to use governance indicators at the national-level from information sources such as the *World Competitiveness Report* (WCR), *Political and Economic Risk Consultancy* (PERC), *Business Environment Risk Intelligence* (BERI), *International Country Risk Guide* (ICRG), and *Transparency International* (TI), but these are not applicable to governance at the local community or village level since they concentrate on aggregated data on corruption, accountability, bureaucracy, and political system which are all macro-oriented.[8] In Thailand and the Philippines, Minimum Basic Needs (MBN) indexes and databases, which are indirect forms of governance measurement, are being utilised as proxies to determine effective governance at both the urban and rural settings. The results and reactions regarding

MBN's utility are mixed. While the MBN has been hailed by numerous academics, development experts, and NGOS, there are certain rigidities inherent in the MBN that have disillusioned local leaders and social researchers who complain that it is not an accurate measure of their performance.[9]

Recently, though, Dr. James Mayfield, Professor of Political Science at the University of Utah, and Chairman of CHOICE (Centre for Humanitarian Outreach and Inter-Cultural Exchange), developed a framework for measurement which could be used as a critical starting point for a more governance-oriented evaluation and monitoring tool especially at the village-community level.[10] It also leads to the establishment of local-level data on governance and socio-economic development. Through CHOICE, Dr. Mayfield has established the Twenty Points of Progress Program which has been field-tested in Bolivia, Mexico, Kenya, and Egypt. The purpose of the program is to provide a very simple technology for measuring and assessing the impact of village development programs being implemented throughout the world. While billions of dollars have been allocated for village development programming over the past fifty years, there is no central database available by which such efforts might be evaluated and assessed. CHOICE seeks to work with all NGOs, government agencies, and other donor organisations that are presently implementing village development programs and to participate in this data collection activity. Each organisation participating would be encouraged to use the CHOICE Twenty Points of Progress Worksheet, first inviting the villagers themselves to participate in a general meeting to determine what they think their score for each of the indicators might be, and then to send the results to the CHOICE office. CHOICE will prepare an annual report, summarising the data collected, noting any areas where great success has been achieved, and what specific strategies or programs have proven to be especially successful, and then sharing a summary of this information with all participating organisations.

The purpose of this Twenty Points of Progress Program is first to develop some base-line indicators that will help determine the status of villages throughout the world, and then to allow monitoring in a more systematic way. While there have been other efforts to create a system of monitoring, many have been so complex, and have required data collection on so many indicators, that few organisations have been able to afford, or have shown the commitment, to collect such data over a long period of time. The CHOICE Twenty Points of Progress Program is a simple technology, utilising a limited number of indicators that any community could use, but which gives a fairly diverse set of program options that suggest areas of emphasis and prioritisation for communities desiring to take more responsibility for their own development.

Participatory Approaches

The CHOICE program alludes to a critical area which is stakeholder participation in development, and on this, there appears to be a never-ending search for ways and means around obstacles that hinder project and program success in developing countries.[11] One of the "miracle cures" that have been prescribed since the mid-1970s is the use of participatory development techniques. In broad terms, participatory development implies increasing stakeholder or client involvement in almost all aspects of a project cycle - from the planning and design to the actual implementation and monitoring phases. With the help of academics and NGOs, participatory development, like the current concern for governance in the 1990s, was made out to be a virtual panacea in the 1980s. Consequently, bilateral and multilateral development agencies, like the ADB, World Bank, USAID, etc., which traditionally emphasised the economic, financial, and technical aspects of development projects, slowly began to place more serious emphasis on the social and civic dimensions primarily to increase the likelihood of development sustainability--the continuation of the benefits and activities of a development project beyond donor funding or supervision.[12]

As a result, concern for community participation intensified in both development research and practice in Asia and the rest of the developing regions in the world. It became imperative for development projects in the 1980s to have a community participation component to ensure sustainability.[13] Overwhelming empirical support for this method poured in from both researchers and practitioners of social development. The latest international conferences to throw in endorsements have been the 1994 World Bank Workshop on Participatory Development in Washington, DC, and the 1995 Social Development Summit in Copenhagen. These conferences have merely added to the appeal of the participatory approaches in furthering local development.

In the developing countries, at the local government level, increased stakeholder participation was encouraged to empower communities to take responsibility for maintaining a project's output(s) with less - or even no - central government support. However, governance experts nowadays have tended to be careful about prescribing participatory development in all scenarios they encounter since, contrary to widespread expectations, there have also been misgivings about the "miraculous abilities" of this panacea. Various studies on development projects from Asia, Sub-Saharan Africa, and Latin America claim that this view is an exaggeration. They seem to portray the affirmative perspective of participation (i.e., community participation is the much-needed factor for success), as a myth.[14]

Growth Triangles and Governance

Another potential area of research relating to governance is the issue of bureaucratic and institutional structures and administrative support bases needed to sustain the activities of the established as well as emerging subregional growth areas in the Asia-Pacific region such as the Singapore-Johor-Riau (SIJORI) Growth Triangle, the East ASEAN Growth Area (Southern Philippines, Indonesia, Malaysia, and Brunei), the Northern ASEAN Growth Triangle (comprising the northern states of Malaysia, Sumatra, and southern Thailand), and broad areas of co-operation in the Mekong Basin.[15] Governance aspects, in general, have normally been assumed, and have not, therefore, been analysed with any great degree of rigour. However, this dimension of the growth area phenomenon has been highlighted by senior officials from the southern growth triangle, and they have pledged that their governments will continue to play the role of facilitators of co-operation and investment by working to remove obstacles and administrative impediments.[16]

The private sector generally feels that inadequate governance infrastructures - along with bureaucratic red-tape and bottlenecks - impede investment, co-operation, and development. Towards this end, Indonesia, for example, has expressed a commitment to cutting red-tape and removing other impediments in support of development of growth areas. There now seems to be growing realisation in both the public and private sectors about the need for governance arrangements, or some rules of the game, that should be institutionalised. Possible arrangements could include deliberation councils similar to the Singapore National Wages Council (NWC),[17] Malaysia Business Council (MBC), Saskatchewan Consultative Committee on Educational Policy (SCCEP), as well the consultative councils attached to Japan's Ministry of International Trade and Investment (MITI). These deliberation councils have successfully facilitated the development of effective social and economic policies in these countries.[18]

However, there first needs to be an identification of the obstacles, bottlenecks, and impediments to governance, institutional development, and sustainability in the growth areas as perceived by all the stakeholders concerned. In addition, the following questions need to be answered: How have the regional governments dealt with these impediments so far, and how do they intend to do so henceforth? What exact roles can ASEAN's nine dialogue partners - in particular international organisations such as the UNDP and the European Union - play, if at all, in helping remove obstacles to sustainability? How much capacity do local governments have in order to successfully implement economic policies, and does anything need to be done about the issue of capacity-building? Answers to these and other pertinent questions will act as a basis for understanding the realm of policy scope available to regional governments to push for - and participate in - different forms of cross-border developments.

Replicating Governance Lessons: A Caveat

Finally, the chapters in this volume, and the actual discussions in the 1996 International Conference on Governance Innovations (Manila), highlight the fact that there are many limitations to replicating governance lessons. Many of the countries in the Asia-Pacific region have unique historical, cultural, economic, political, and social experiences. The Southeast Asian currency crisis illustrated that even with efficient public institutions one cannot always respond effectively to every issue area especially those that are at the international systems level. Hence, development experts who seek to proceed further and extract lessons from the successful governance experiences of other countries must be cognisant of the following five degrees of transferability identified by Richard Rose at the nation-state level:[19]

- Copying: adoption, in a more or less intact form, of a programme already in effect in another jurisdiction;
- Emulation: adoption, with adjustment for different circumstances, of a programme already in effect in another jurisdiction;
- Hybridisation: combination of elements of programmes from two different places.
- Synthesis: combination of familiar elements from programmes in effect in three or more different places; and
- Inspiration: programmes elsewhere used as intellectual stimulus for developing a novel programme without an analogue elsewhere.

Keeping in mind these varying degrees and the contextual constraints mentioned earlier will increase the chances of effectively replicating some general lessons from the successful governance innovation experiences in the Asia-Pacific enumerated in this book.

Notes

[1] World Bank, *The East Asian Miracle: Economic Growth and Public Policy* (Oxford: Oxford University Press, 1993).

[2] See, among others, M. Prowse, "Miracles Beyond the Free Market," *Financial Times*, April 26, 1993; S. Sankaran, "IBRD Sees Model in Asia's Government-Industry Link Councils," *Economic Times* (New Delhi), June 10, 1993; M. Tira-Andrei, "Sustaining East's Economic Growth," *Business World*, June 23, 1993; Y. Kim (ed), *The Southeast Asian Economic Miracle* (New Brunswick, NJ: Transaction Publishers, 1995); M. C. Fong, "Developing Nations Can Copy Singapore Miracle," *The Straits Times* (Singapore), July 20, 1996; and M. G. Quibria, "Productivity Will Come With Time," *Far Eastern Economic Review*, August 22, 1996.

[3] See, for example, J. Wanundi, "Is East Asian Growth on the Decline?" *The Straits Times* (Singapore), January 29, 1997.

[4] J. L. Gonzalez, "The Problem with the ADB and Their Proposed Good Governance Reforms," *The Straits Times* (Singapore), May 16, 1996.

[5] See D. Rondinelli, *Development Projects as Policy Experiments: An Adaptive Approach to Development Administration* (London and New York: Methuen, 1981); G. S. Cheema and D. Rondinelli (eds), *Decentralisation and Development: Policy Implementation in Developing Countries* (Beverly Hills, CA: Sage Publications, 1983); D. Rondinelli, et al, *Decentralisation in Developing Countries: A Review of Recent Experience* (Washington, DC: World Bank, 1984); and J. Silverman, *Public Sector Decentralisation: Economic Policy Reform and Sector Investment Programs* (Washington, DC: World Bank, 1992).

[6] G. S. Cheema and D. Rondinelli (eds), *Decentralisation and Development: Policy Implementation in Developing Countries* (Beverly Hills, California: Sage Publications, 1983): 14-15.

[7] H. Root, "Transparency and China's Aspirations," *Asian Wall Street Journal*, January 13, 1997.

[8] See J. L. Gonzalez, "Governance, Socio-Economic Development, and the East Asian Miracle: Some Lessons for the Philippines," *Asian Journal of Political Science* 4, 1 (June 1996): 36-63; J. E. Campos and H. Root, *The Key to the Asian Miracle: Making the Principle of Shared Growth Credible* (Washington, DC: Brookings Institution, 1996); and H. Root, *Small Countries, Big Lessons: Governance and the Rise of East Asia* (New York: Oxford University Press, 1996).

[9] Based on interviews with a few local leaders who attended some of the MBN seminars conducted by the Philippine Department of Interior and Local Government (DILG), Local Government Academy, University of the Philippines-College of Public Administration (UP-CPA), and Asian Institute of Management (AIM), Manila.

[10] J. B. Mayfield, "The Egyptian Basic Village Service Program: A New Strategy for Local Government Capacity Building," in J. C. Garcia-Zamor (ed), *Public Participation in Development Planning and Management: Cases from Africa and Asia* (Boulder, Colorado: Westview Press, 1985); J. B. Mayfield, *Go to the People: Releasing the Rural Poor Through the People's School System* (Hartford, Connecticut: Kumarian Press, 1985); and J. B. Mayfield, *Local Government in Egypt* (Cairo, Egypt: American University of Cairo Press, 1996). For those interested in reviewing various strategies, interventions, and approaches that have been successful in helping rural villages to improve their quality of life in the Twenty Points of Progress in the areas of health, education, income generation, environment, and local culture enhancement, J. B. Mayfield's new book *One Can Make a Difference: The Role of Rural Development Facilitators (RDFs) in the Process of Rural Development* (New York: University Press of America, Inc., 1997) is recommended reading.

[11] See, for example, J. Gonzalez, *Development Sustainability Through Community Participation: Mixed Results from the Philippine Health Sector* (Aldershot, UK: Ashgate, forthcoming 1998); J. Gonzalez and J. B. Mayfield, "Conceptualising the Process of Community Participation in Development Projects: An Assessment of Sectoral and Regional Trends," *PRAXIS: Journal of Political Studies* 7, 1 (April 1995): 13-45; and J. Gonzalez and R. Buendia, "Is Community Participation Really Essential to Program Effectiveness - Negative Answers from Three Philippine Cases," *International Journal of Sociology and Social Policy* (forthcoming 1997).

[12] See, for instance, United Nations Development Programme, *Human Development Report* (Oxford: Oxford University Press, 1993); and *The World Bank and Participation* (Washington, DC: World Bank, Operations Policy Department, 1995).

[13] See M. Bamberger, *Readings in Community Participation: Community Participation Experience in Multi-sectoral Programs and in Population Health, and Water Supply* (Washington, DC: World Bank, 1986); J. Briscoe and D. de Ferranti, *Water for Rural Communities: Helping People Help Themselves* (Washington, DC: World Bank, 1988); and B. Bhatnagar and A. Williams (eds), *Participatory Development and the World Bank: Potential Directions for Change* (Washington, DC: World Bank, 1992).

[14] For the arguments of these authors, see, for example, J. Gonzalez (forthcoming 1998).

[15] See T. Y. Lee, *Growth Triangles: The Johore-Singapore-Riau Experience* (Singapore: Institute of Southeast Asian Studies, 1991); S. Y. Chia and T. Y. Lee, "Sub-regional Economic Zones: A New Motive Force in the Asia-Pacific Region," Paper presented at the 20th Pacific Trade and Development Conference, Washington, DC, September 10-12, 1992; M. H. Toh and L. Low (eds), *Regional Cooperation and Growth Triangles in ASEAN* (Singapore: Times Academic Press, 1993); and M. Tang and M. Thant, "Growth Triangles: Conceptual and

Operational Considerations," in M. Thant, et al (eds), *Growth Triangles in Asia* (Hong Kong: Oxford University Press, 1994).

[16] See P. Handley, "Seeds of Friendship: Four Neighbors Forge Tentative Partnership," *Far Eastern Economic Review*, September 7, 1993; and M. Than, "Striking it Rich in the Golden Quadrangle," Trends in *Business Times*, November 27, 1993.

[17] See C. Y. Lim, "The NWC as I See It," in S. Jayakumar, *Our Heritage and Beyond* (Singapore: National Trades Union Congress, 1982); National Wages Council, *National Wages Council (1972-1992)* (Singapore: Singapore National Printers, 1992); and Singapore Institute of Labour Studies, *Wage Negotiations in a Maturing Economy* (Singapore: SILS, 1993).

[18] See J. Campos, "Improving Business-Government Relations: The Deliberation Council," *Outreach 9* (Washington, DC: World Bank, 1993); Campos and Root, 1996; and Campos and Gonzalez, "Deliberation Councils and Effective Policy Making: Experiences From Malaysia, Singapore, and Canada," in J. Campos and S. Taschereau, *Governance Innovations: Lessons from Experience* (Canada: Institute on Governance, 1997).

[19] Quoted from J. S. T. Quah, "Singapore's Model of Development: Is It Transferable," Working Paper No. 13, Department of Political Science, National University of Singapore (1997): 31. R. Rose's original piece is found in "What is Lesson Drawing?" *Journal of Public Policy* 11, 1 (January-March 1991): 3-30.

Index

References from Notes indicated by 'n' after page reference

access creation 13, 144, 147-49, 152
accountability 5, 9, 10, 11, 12, 13, 14, 15, 16, 18, 25, 55, 70, 137, 147, 183, 185, 186, 187, 188, 189, 190, 191, 192, 193, 194, 199, 232, 233, 235, 238, 248, 280, 282, 285, 289, 291
  corruption and enforcement 9
Adamolekun, L. 241n, 243n
adaptability 76, 78
adaptation, modes of 78-80
ADB 4, 5, 7, 19n, 289, 290, 293
  and good governance 289
administrative accountability 77
Advantage West 225
African Capacity Building Foundation 236
Afsah, S. 15, 205
animateurs 236, 240
ASEAN 8, 13, 21n, 120, 124, 131, 140, 294, 297n
Asia Foundation 4, 12, 13, 19n, 121, 144, 158
Asian Institute of Management 12, 105, 106, 111n, 112n, 252, 296n
Asian Values 290
Asia-Pacific Region 3, 8, 285, 286, 287, 294, 295, 297n

barangay 107, 108, 246, 248, 255
Basic Law 82, 83, 84, 85, 88
Bhatta, G. 3, 16, 231, 285
Binder, L. 96, 99n
Bolivia 39, 41, 42, 292
Bolongaita, E. 12, 103, 111n, 112n, 291
Brautigam, D. 19n, 242n
Brazil 39, 40, 42, 216, 277, 278, 283n
Brillantes, A. 17, 243n, 245
Britain 163, 164, 167, 168
Bryant, C. 19n, 241n, 243n
Bung Phra village 257, 258-61, 266
bureaucracy and leadership 9, 10-11
bureaucratic efficiency 44n, 276
bureaucratic elite 49, 50, 51, 54
bureaucratic rationality 49, 51, 52, 55
Burns, J. 14, 183

CAGIN 21n
Campos, J. 7, 21n, 242n, 243n, 296n, 297n, 298n
Canada 4, 5, 21n, 185, 188, 189, 190, 194, 197, 199, 201n, 208, 297n
capacity building 9, 13, 16-17, 18, 231, 232, 235, 239, 245-56, 285, 295, 297n
  and local governance 16-17, 255
  approaches to local 246, 249
  at local level 9, 17, 18, 126, 235, 236, 237, 252-55
capacity enhancement 231, 240
  areas for 237-38
chaebol 290, 291
Cheema, G. 287, 288, 296n
China 11, 75, 77, 83, 84, 85, 88, 90, 91, 94, 97, 129, 193, 290

CHOICE 292, 293
Chulalongkorn University 14, 146, 148, 153n, 157, 160
CIDA 4, 5, 8, 10, 19n
citizen accountability 14
citizen participation 17, 77, 220, 221, 222, 224-225
citizen-business-government linkages 9, 10, 11-13, 127, 184, 285
citizen-technocrat 63
citizens and customers 104-05
    insensitive to 104-05
civic virtues 65, 70
civil service 4, 61, 80, 89, 96, 231, 289
Civil Service College 50, 61, 62, 69, 71, 73n
civil society 3, 15, 18, 116, 120, 124, 143, 198, 232, 274
    market and community 3, 9
    state, citizens and business 3
clientelism 167
co-producers 275, 276, 279, 282
Cohen, M. 209, 217n
Cole, W. 12, 113
community empowerment 62
community forestry 17, 257-58, 260, 261, 263, 266
community participation 236, 293, 294, 297n
community leadership 17, 259, 263
Confucian Cliché 290
constituency and coalition building 13, 144-47, 150, 152
convergence 11, 82, 84
cooperative leadership 238
corruption 9, 10, 13-15, 25, 40, 44n, 105, 143, 145, 146, 147, 155-62, 163-82, 183-202, 277, 289, 291
    and public awareness 200
    consequences of 161, 180-81, 198, 200
    counter programs in 143, 144, 145, 146, 147, 149, 151, 152
    four strategies of 144, 149, 152
    in Thailand 145, 146, 148, 155-62
    strategies against 161, 174-79
    training programmes against 163-81
        content 166-69
        objectives 163-65
        outcomes 171
        participants 165-66
        products 170-71
cult of rationality 56

decentralisation 17, 19n, 161, 196, 233, 234, 235, 242n, 249, 287, 288, 296n
decentralised governance 231-44
Deily, M. 208, 216n
Deliberation Councils 8, 294, 297n, 298n
de Melo, J. 277-79
democracy 11, 19n, 82, 83
Deutsch, K. 76, 98n
Developmental(ist) State 7, 49, 51, 53, 54, 70

E-Democracy Project 219, 224
East Asia(n) 3, 6, 7, 8, 23, 37, 53, 71n, 208, 242n, 271, 286, 287
    Growth Model 8, 286
    replicability of 8
    Miracle 7, 19n, 44n, 242n, 286, 289, 290, 296n
Easton, D. 75, 76, 98n
empowerment 107, 231, 232, 236, 241, 253, 293
emulation 295
Evans, P. 18, 53, 62, 72n, 269
Evans and Rueschemeyer thesis 53
export contest 36-42
ex post rate of return 34, 45n

Ford Foundation 4, 111n, 254
Freedom House Indicator 35, 36, 45n

Gaebler, T. 20n, 105, 173
Galing Pook Awards Program 105, 111n, 252-54
generic management 11, 51
Goh Chok Tong 50, 56, 57
Gonzalez, J. 3, 19n, 285, 287, 296n, 297n
good governance 3, 4, 8, 9, 13, 14, 18, 19n, 20n, 114, 116, 144, 183, 184, 186, 189, 191, 192, 199, 231, 232, 234, 235, 237, 238, 240, 285, 288, 289, 290
    characteristics of 235
    definition of 186, 189
    dimensions of 25
    fund to promote 20n
    principles of 187
governance
    accountable 144
    advisors/experts 244n
    and civil society 18
    and development 13, 19n, 20n, 189-90, 292
    and economic performance 7
    and ethics 198-200
    and growth 25-32
    and HPAEs 6-8, 23, 286, 290
    and Small Business Policy reform 113-17
    as a conceptual tool 3, 8
    as an analytical tool 3, 290
    at macro and micro levels 231, 233
    at the local level 16, 220-21, 229, 233-37, 241, 243n, 291
    citizen-customer 105-06
    context of 3-21
    corporate 6
    database 291
    definition of 24, 186-87, 231, 232, 241n
    dimensions of 5, 18
    downstream aspects 287
    effective 5, 11, 17
    future of 285-98
    growth triangles and 294
    how to measure 24-25
    in Singapore 11
    innovations 8, 13, 17, 18, 20n, 21n
    key elements of 9, 189-90, 231, 232, 241n
    link with accountability and SAIs 187-89
    meaning and origins 3-6
    political dimension 288-90
    reinventing 6
    replicating lessons 6, 12, 20n, 21n, 295
    resurgence of interest in 4
"grassroots" participation 276
Gray, W. 208, 216n

Hanke, S. 143, 153n
Hashimoto 291
Hong Kong 6, 7, 11, 75-99n, 168, 286, 287
    civil servants 75, 76, 77
        behavioural tendencies of 76
        political adaptation of 75, 78-80, 85-94, 96, 97
    public service 11, 85
        bureaucratic values of 76
        leadership 75
        dilemmas of 78
Hood, C. 78, 81, 98n
Human Development Report 44n
hybridisation 295

imitation 11, 79, 97
India 39, 105, 106, 193, 197, 277
Indonesia 7, 12, 15, 28, 117, 118,

119, 120, 121, 123, 124, 126, 206, 207-18, 277, 287, 290, 291, 294
Environmental Impact Management Agency 15, 206
Small Business Law 121, 122
information 5, 9, 15, 16, 145, 147, 148, 149, 153n, 188, 189, 190, 191, 194, 195, 197, 205, 209, 210, 211, 213, 215, 216, 217n, 219-28, 292
citizen access to 149, 221, 222-24
institutional capability/capacity 10, 27, 28, 29, 31, 32, 191, 289
institutional capability index 26, 27, 28, 29, 31
Integrated Capacity Building Program 17, 245, 246, 250-52
International Conference on Governance 8, 20n, 295
internet 16, 219-28
comparative advantages of 225-27
uniqueness of 221-22
IOG 4, 5, 8, 10, 19n, 20n, 186, 201n, 298n
Iran 28
Italy 273

Japan 4, 6, 7, 20n, 286, 287, 291, 294

Kalin, W. 236, 242n, 243n
Kant, I. 56
Kenya 39, 41, 42, 292
Klein, J. 13, 143
Klitgaard, R. 166, 172, 173, 181n
Koh, G. 11, 49
Konar, S. 209, 217n

Lakbay Aral Program 254
Lal, B. 16, 219

Lam, J. 11, 75, 99n
Laos 13, 127
administrative reforms 132-36
assessment of 137
future of 137-39
development priorities 131-32
governance innovations 127-29
transition to market economy 129-32
Laplante, B. 15, 205
late development 71n
Lau, S. 98n
leadership 7, 9, 10, 11, 15, 17, 18, 20n, 21n, 75, 107, 115, 116, 139, 149, 199, 234, 238-9, 250, 259, 263, 265, 285
legislative audit 191-93, 198
Legislative Council 75, 76, 77, 83, 86, 87, 89, 90, 91, 92, 93, 95, 96, 98n
LGU Innovation Laboratories 17, 254
local governance 16-17, 233, 245, 249, 250, 252, 253, 255, 286, 287-88
local governments 12, 220, 221, 222, 225, 227, 228, 233, 237, 246, 247, 248, 250, 252, 254, 255, 291, 295, 297n
local opinion leaders 239, 241
local participation 257, 260, 264

Malaysia 7, 19n, 168, 286, 287, 290, 294, 297n
Managerialist Revolution 51, 52, 54
"market as magic bullet" 270, 271, 272, 274, 281
Mauro, P. 25, 43n, 44n
Mayfield, J. 292, 297n
MBN (minimum basic needs) 291, 292, 296n
Methods of Active Participation 238
Mintzberg, H. 55, 56, 72n, 103, 111n

Narayan, D. 273, 282n
Nepal 235, 276, 283n
New Zealand 197, 243n
NGOs 4, 118, 123, 124, 158, 159, 165, 221, 234, 236, 239, 243n, 244n, 248, 251, 252, 261, 262, 264, 287, 292, 293
  and community-based organisations 239
normative-control model of governance 56, 71

ODA 4, 5, 181n
O'Donnell, G. 271, 282n
OECD 5, 23, 181n, 192, 209
Offe, C. 52, 56
openness 191, 232, 233
organisational rationality 52
Osborne, David 20n, 105, 111n, 173
Osborne, Denis 14, 163, 173, 181n

Pack, H. 38, 43n, 45n
Page, J. 10, 23, 38, 45n
PAP (People's Action Party) 60, 70, 72n
Parker, S. 12, 113
Parkin, F. 51, 56, 63, 65, 72n, 73n
participation 25, 121, 234, 236, 238, 240, 248, 251, 260, 275, 285, 294
  and performance 32-36
    halo effects 33
    measures 33
    methods 238
patrimonialism 167
Patten, C. 83, 85, 86, 89, 91, 95
Paul, S. 105, 106, 111n
peoples' organisations 248, 252
peoples' participation 17, 236
performance-control model of governance 71
Peters, G. 20n, 55, 56
Philippine Local Government Code 17, 106, 234, 243n, 245, 246, 247-49, 253, 255
  characteristics of 247-49
Philippines 8, 12, 16, 17, 19n, 20n, 21n, 105, 215, 218n, 234, 245-56, 291, 297n
  Local Government Academy 245, 246, 249, 252, 255, 296n
  local government system 17, 246
Phimphisut, T. 17, 257
Phongpaichit, P. 14, 153n, 155
phronesis 63, 73n
piecemeal adjustments 79, 91, 97
policy fundamentals 24
political accountability 77, 86, 232, 242n
political economic approach 116
political sensitivity 56, 65
political will 12, 18, 114, 115, 120-21, 122, 125, 126, 144, 146, 147, 148, 150, 152
predatory states 270
predictability 233, 289
project success 35
Proper Prokasih 210-15
  five colour scheme 212
  impact of 213-15
prototyping 11, 79, 97
PS21 50, 63
public bureaucracies 4
  characteristics of effective 7
Public Performance Audit System 15, 205, 206, 218n
pungutan 118
Putnam, R. 273, 282n

Rapid Rural Appraisal 238
recombination 11, 79, 97
regulation and information 9, 10, 15-16, 205-18
  command-and-control regulation 207, 209, 210

market-based instruments 207, 209, 210
reinvention exercises 6
Rodrik, D. 39, 40, 45n, 46n, 286
Rondinelli, D. 243n, 287, 288, 289, 296n
Root, H. 7, 8, 21n, 242n, 243n, 289, 296n
Rose, R. 295, 297n
rule of law, 232, 233 *see also* predictability

Sahgal, V. 14, 183
Savoie, D. 20n, 55
scenario-based planning 73n
shared growth 7, 21n
Singapore 6, 7, 11, 49, 51, 54, 56, 57, 60, 65, 70, 72n, 239, 286, 296n
   administrative elite 52
   "next lap" of development 57, 59, 64
   public sector leadership 57-70
   Public Service 50, 57, 63, 65, 69, 70, 71, 72n, 73n
sin nam jai 145, 156, 158
social capital 9, 18, 272-74, 275, 280
South Korea 6, 7, 21n, 38, 39, 41, 42, 286, 287, 290, 291
state-society synergy 269-83
   basic propositions 281-82
   caveats in 280-81
structural reform 13, 144, 149-51, 152, 153
substantive rationality 56
Suharto 290, 291
supreme audit institutions 14, 183-202
   characteristics of effective 195-96
   role of 193-96
Sustainable Human Development 241n

systems reform 150, 152, 153
system strengthening 13, 144, 153
systemic rationality 52, 54

TAF Program 121, 122, 123, 126
   key elements of 122-23
Taiwan 6, 7, 8, 276, 282n, 286
Tanzania 170, 237, 273, 282n
technocratic rationality 56
Tha Wang Sai village 257, 261-65, 266
Thailand 7, 14, 17, 28, 129, 145, 146, 148, 153n, 155-62, 257, 286, 287, 291, 294
   illegal economy 157, 158
   money politics 157, 162
Total Factor Productivity 30, 31, 32, 38, 286
'town and gown' principle 249, 250
TQG 12, 103, 106, 107, 108, 109, 110, 111n, 112n
TQM 12, 103, 106
transparency 5, 15, 16, 137, 183, 185, 186, 189, 191, 200, 201, 215, 232, 233, 289, 290, 296n
   and accountability 188
Turkey 39, 40, 41

Uganda 235, 236, 237, 242n, 243n
UN Volunteer Programme 236, 239
UNDP 4, 8, 20n, 33, 44n, 135, 136, 240, 241, 241n, 243n, 295, 297n
United States 4, 5, 6, 71n, 122, 123, 125, 197, 220, 223, 225, 272, 273
USAID 4, 19n, 33, 114, 115, 121, 125, 153n, 242n, 244n, 293

Value For Money 177, 193, 194
virtuous circle 273, 280, 282
VOICE 223
Vorachith, S. 13, 127

Wade, R. 277, 283n

Wheeler, D. 15, 205, 217n
World Bank 4, 5, 7, 8, 10, 19n, 20n, 21n, 23, 33, 34, 134, 186, 190, 191, 237, 240, 241n, 273, 280, 288, 289, 293, 296n, 297n
World Competitiveness Report 287, 291
World Development Report 24, 115, 122